THE WAY OF LAO TZU

The Library of Liberal Arts
OSKAR PIEST, FOUNDER

THE WAY
OF LAO TZU

(*Tao-te ching*)

Translated, with introductory essays,
comments, and notes, by
WING-TSIT CHAN

● ●

The Library of Liberal Arts
published by

Prentice Hall, Upper Saddle River, New Jersey 07458

Library of Congress Catalog Card Number: 62-21266

ADAPTED FROM CHAPTER SEVEN, "THE NATURAL
WAY OF LAO TZU," OF A SOURCE BOOK IN CHINESE
PHILOSOPHY, PUBLISHED BY PRINCETON UNIVERSITY
PRESS, SEPTEMBER, 1963.

. . . .

Printed in the United States of America
31

ISBN 0-02-320700-0

Prentice-Hall International (UK) Limited,London
Prentice-Hall of Australia Pty. Limited, Sydney
Prentice-Hall Canada Inc., Toronto
Prentice-Hall Hispanoamericana, S.A., Mexico
Prentice-Hall of India Private Limited, New Delhi
Prentice-Hall of Japan, Inc., Tokyo
Pearson Education Asia Pte. Ltd., Singapore
Editora Prentice-Hall do Brasil, Ltda., Rio de Janeiro

Preface

No one can understand China or be an intelligent citizen of the world without some knowledge of the *Lao Tzu,* also called the *Tao-te ching* (The Classic of the Way and Its Virtue), for it has modified Chinese life and thought throughout history and has become an integral part of world literature. Therefore any new light on it, however little, should prove to be helpful.

There have been many translations of this little classic, some of them excellent. Most translators have treated it as an isolated document. Many have taken it as religious literature. A few have related it to ancient Chinese philosophy. But none has viewed it in the light of the entire history of Chinese thought. Furthermore, no translator has consulted extensively the many commentaries regarding the text, much less the thought. Finally, no translator has written a complete commentary from the perspective of the total history of Chinese philosophy. Besides, a comprehensive and critical account of the recent debates on Lao Tzu the man and *Lao Tzu* the book is long overdue. The present work is a humble attempt to fill these gaps.

I am grateful to Professor Derk Bodde of the University of Pennsylvania for his constructive criticisms and valuable comments. Professor C. C. Hamilton of Oberlin College has also offered helpful suggestions. My colleague, Professor Arthur Dewing, has always been ready to help when I interrupted him with questions on English usage. Mrs. Alice Weymouth helped me to prepare the manuscript. To all these people I am thankful.

Above all I am grateful to my wife, whose understanding and devotion, more than anything else, have made this book possible.

WING-TSIT CHAN

To Charles A. Moore

CONTENTS

· · · · · · · · · · · · · · · ·

Note on the Translation

The translation is based not on one particular text but on a constant consultation with the Wang Pi and Ho-shang Kung texts. The traditional order of chapters has been preserved, because, as is pointed out in footnotes, there is no objective standard by which to make alterations. Important alterations by commentators and translators are pointed out in footnotes. Obviously it is impossible to reproduce the rhymes, but I have put all chapters in verse form and arranged the sentences to show the rhyming pattern, if possible, in spite of the fact that some passages, including several whole chapters, are not rhymed. It is difficult to determine whether these are prose or blank verse. In the translation, because there are too many titles to cite, studies, commentaries, and translations of the *Lao Tzu* are referred to only by their authors and translators and not their titles except where one author had more than one title, in which case an abbreviated title is given in parentheses. Except for contemporaries, dates of authors are given in the Bibliography in Chinese and Japanese, where all titles and their translations are listed. Transliteration of Chinese titles follows the modified Wade-Giles system. Except for some contemporaries who, like myself, put their personal names before their family names, Chinese and Japanese names are given in the Chinese order, that is, with the family name first. Three abbreviations are used, namely, *SPPY* for the *Ssu-pu pei-yao* (Essentials of the Four Libraries) edition, *SPTK* for the *Ssu-pu ts'ung-k'an* (Four Libraries Series) edition, and *PNP* for the *Po-na-pen* (Choice Works Series).

W.T.C.

THE WAY OF LAO TZU

I. *The Philosophy of Tao*

Chinese civilization and the Chinese character would have been utterly different if the book *Lao Tzu* had never been written. In fact, even Confucianism, the dominant system in Chinese history and thought, would not have been the same, for like Buddhism, it has not escaped Taoist influence. No one can hope to understand Chinese philosophy, religion, government, art, medicine, and even cooking without a real appreciation of the profound philosophy taught in this little book. It is true that while Confucianism emphasizes social order and an active life, Taoism concentrates on individual life and tranquility, thus suggesting that Taoism plays a secondary role. But in opposing Confucian conformity with nonconformity and opposing Confucian worldliness with a transcendental spirit, Taoism is Confucianism's severe critic. In its doctrines on government, on cultivating and preserving life, and on handling things, it is fully Confucianism's equal.

1. HISTORICAL BACKGROUND AND THE TAOIST REACTION

In some respects Taoism goes even deeper into the way of life, so much so that while every ancient Chinese school taught its own Way (*tao*), Taoism alone is known by that name. And in spite of the fact that in the last twenty centuries the influence of Taoist philosophy has not been comparable to that of Confucianism or Buddhism, it has remained an important part of the backbone of every aspect of Chinese civilization. How this movement came to be strong and unique is still surrounded by mystery, for many questions about its historical origin, its founder, and the book in which its basic doctrines are set forth remain to be answered. The dispute continues as to whether Lao Tzu lived in the sixth or fourth century B.C., and whether the *Lao Tzu*, also called the *Tao-te ching* (The Classic of the Way and Its Virtue), is a product of the Spring and Autumn period (722-481 B.C.) or the Warring States times (403-222 B.C.). One thing is sure, however. Although the name "Taoist school" was not mentioned until the first century B.C.,[1] the movement must have been going on for centuries. Tradition says that ancient philosophical schools emerged from governmental offices, and Taoism in particular from that of the historian. What it really means is that they arose in response to actual historical situations. Unlike ancient Greek speculation on Nature or ancient Indian contemplation on the spirit, Chinese philosophies, whether Confucianism or Taoism, grew as a result of deplorable conditions of the time. Thus Taoism arose in opposition to existing practices and systems, on the one hand, and on the other, offered a new way of life that is as challenging as it is profound.

By the time of Confucius (551-479 B.C.), the house of Chou had been in power for more than half a millennium. It now showed many cracks and its foundation was shaking. Feudal lords began to usurp power, setting up virtually independent states, and war was rampant. Autocratic rulers indulged in extravagant ceremonial feasts, displayed fine weapons, and tried to outdo each other in cunning and strategy, all at the expense of the people. Laws and punishment were their last resort to handle the restless masses. A poet, echoing the real sentiment of the people, cried bitterly:

> Large rats! Large rats!
> Don't you eat our millet!
> We have endured you for three years.
> But you have shown no regard for us.
> We will leave you,
> And go to that happy land!
> Happy land! Happy land!
> Where we shall be at ease.[2]

[1] The footnotes follow each of the three parts of the Introduction. See p. 31.

At the same time Chinese society was entering upon a new era. Iron was more and more extensively used in place of bronze, thus putting the chief metal into the hands of more people and making it easier to produce utensils, weapons, and means of transportation. Agriculture and handicraft became gradually separated. Trade and business grew, and towns and cities developed. Feudal lords increasingly turned to the common people for talents to win wars and to put their own houses in order. Feudalism was unmistakably on the decline and the common man was definitely on the rise. It was a time for both destroying the old and constructing the new. Lao Tzu did both.[3]

On the destructive side, Lao Tzu launched severe attacks on political institutions and social mores. "The people starve because the ruler eats too much tax-grain," he declared (ch. 75). Such a ruler will bring his own collapse. "When gold and jade fill your hall," he said, "you will not be able to keep them. To be proud with honor and wealth is to cause one's own downfall" (9). It is futile to subjugate people with force, for "the more laws and orders are made prominent, the more thieves and robbers there will be" (57). Since "the people are not afraid of death," he asked, "why, then, threaten them with death?" (74). As to war, it is a symptom of the decline of man. "When Tao prevails in the world, galloping horses are turned back to fertilize (the fields with their dung). When Tao does not prevail in the world, war horses thrive in the suburbs" (46). There were those who offered the doctrines of humanity (*jen*), righteousness, rules of propriety (*li*) and wisdom as remedies for the degeneration, but he regarded these as no less symptoms of chaos. To him, "propriety is a superficial expression of loyalty and faithfulness, and the beginning of disorder" (38). "When the great Tao declined," he said, "the doctrine of humanity and righteousness arose. When knowledge and wisdom appeared, there emerged great hypocrisy" (18). Therefore, he said, "Abandon sageliness and discard wisdom; then the people will benefit a hundredfold. Abandon humanity and discard righteousness; then the people will return to filial piety and deep love. Abandon skill and discard profit; then there will be no thieves or robbers" (19).

These outcries have led Hu Shih (1891-1962) to call Lao Tzu a rebel.[4] If this sounds like an exaggeration, let us remind ourselves that throughout Chinese history Taoism has always been the philosophy of the minority and the suppressed, and that secret societies, in their revolt against oppressive rulers, have often raised the banner of Taoism.

2. THE MEANING OF TAO

The far more important element in Lao Tzu's teachings is, however, the constructive one. This is his formulation of the philosophy of Tao. In this he evolved a concept that had never been known in China before, a concept that served not only as the standard for man but for all things as well.

The word *tao* consists of one element meaning a head and another meaning to run. It means that on which something or someone goes, a path, or road, later extended to mean "method," "principle," "truth," and finally "reality." All of this is well summed up in the common English translation, "the Way." It is a cardinal concept in practically all ancient Chinese philosophical schools. Hitherto the connotation had been social and moral, but in Lao Tzu it connotes for the first time the metaphysical. It is the "mother" (1, 52) and "ancestor" (4) of all things. It exists before heaven and earth (25). It is the "storehouse" of things (62). It is at once their principle of being and their substance. "All things depend on it for life" (34). In its substance it is "invisible," "inaudible," "vague and elusive" (14, 35), indescribable and above shape and form (14, 41). It is one, a unity behind all multiplicity (14, 42). It is single like an uncarved block that has not been split up into individual pieces or covered up with superficial adornment (28, 32). It is everlasting and unchangeable (7, 16, 25). It is all-pervasive and "flows everywhere" (34). "It operates everywhere and is free from danger" (25). Use it and you "will never wear it out" (6). "While vacuous, it is never exhausted" (5). It depends on nothing (25). It is natural (25), for it comes into existence by itself and is its own principle for being. It is the "great form" (35). It is nameless (*wu-ming*) (1, 32, 37, 41), and if one is forced to give it a name, he can only call it "great," that is, unlimited in space and time (1, 25). It is nameless because it is not a concrete, individual thing or describable in particular terms. Above all, it is non-being (*wu*) (1, 40). "All things in the world come from being. And being comes from non-being" (40).

This concept of non-being is basic in Lao Tzu's thought. As Chuang Tzu (between 399 and 295 B.C.) said, the system of Lao Tzu is "based on the principles of non-being and being." [5] In a sense being and non-being are of equal importance. They complement and produce each other (12). "Let there always be non-being," Lao Tzu says, and "let there always be being" (1). As Fung Yu-lan has said, by non-being is not meant that there was a time when nothing but non-being existed, but logically non-being must be prior because before beings come into existence, there must be something before them. [6] In the final analysis, then, non-being is the ultimate, and in Chuang Tzu's statement it comes first.

On the surface non-being seems to be empty and devoid of everything. Actually, this is not the case. It is devoid of limitations but not devoid of definite characteristics. Han Fei Tzu (d. 233 B.C.), the first commentator on Lao Tzu, did not understand Tao in the negative sense of emptiness but in the positive sense of involving definite principles. He says:

> Tao is that by which all things become what they are. It is that with which all principles (*li*) are commensurable. Principles are patterns according to which all things come into being, and Tao is the cause of their being. Therefore it is said that Tao puts things in order (*li*). Everything has its own principle different from that of others, and Tao is commensurate with all of them. . . . According to definite principles, there are existence and destruction, life and death, and flourish and decline. . . . What is eternal has neither change nor any definite, particular principle itself. Since it

has no definite principle itself, it is not bound in any particular locality. This is why it is said that it cannot be told.[7]

Tao as non-being, then, is not negative but positive in character. This concept of non-being was absolutely new in Chinese thought and most radical. Other Chinese schools of thought conceived of non-being simply as the absence of something, but in Taoism it is not only positive; it is basic. This was epoch-making in the history of Chinese philosophy. According to Dubs, it is also new to Occidental thought. He says, "Here is a solution to the problem of creation which is new to Western philosophy: the universe can arise out of nothing because nonexistence itself is not characterless or negative." In his opinion, "here is a metaphysical system which starts, not with matter or with ideas, but with law (*Tao*), nonexistence, and existence as the three fundamental categories of reality." He found nothing similar in Occidental philosophy. "After Parmenides declared that nonexistence cannot exist," he says, "Western philosophers never attempted to challenge his dogma. The non-being of Plato and Plotinus, like the empty space of Greek atomists, was given no positive character. Only Einsteinian space-time—which is nothing, yet directs the motion of particles—comes at all close to the *Lao Tzu*'s concept of nonexistence."[8]

This positive character can be seen not only in the substance of Tao. It can also be seen in its function. Just as its nature is characterized by having no name, so its activity is characterized by taking no action (*wu-wei*). Taking no action does not mean to be "dry wood and dead ashes," to use the metaphors of Chuang Tzu.[9] Rather, it means taking no artificial action, noninterference, or letting things take their own course. Tao invariably "takes no action" (37) but "supports all things in their natural state" (64) and thus "all things will transform spontaneously" (37). As things arise, Tao "does not turn away from them" (2). "It produces them, but does not take possession of them," and "accomplishes its task, but does not claim credit for it" (2, 10, 34, 51). It "benefits all things and does not compete with them" (8). At the same time, things are governed by it and cannot deviate from it. Following it, a thing will flourish and "return to its root and destiny" (16). With it, heaven becomes clear, the earth becomes tranquil, spiritual beings become divine, the valley becomes full, and all things live and grow, but without it they will be exhausted, crumble, and wither away (39). In the production of things, it proceeds from the one to the many. "Tao produced the One. The One produced the two. The two produced the three. And the three produced the ten thousand things" (42). In its own activities, it always returns to the root (16, 40) or the non-ultimate (28). It operates in cycles.

From the above, it is not an exaggeration to say that Tao operates according to certain laws which are constant and regular. One may even say there is an element of necessity in these laws, for Tao by its very nature behaves in this way and all things, in order to achieve their full realization, have to obey them. Tao, after all, is *the* Way. In the words of Han Fei Tzu, it is the way in which things are ordered. Needham is fundamentally correct in equating Tao with the Order of Nature and in saying that Tao "brought all things into existence and governs their every action, not so much by force as by a kind of natural curvature in space and time." [10] When things obey its laws, all parts of the universe will form a harmonious whole and the universe will become an integrated organism.[11] One is tempted to compare Taoism with the organicism of Whitehead, but that would be putting too much modern philosophy into ancient Chinese thought. One thing is sure, however. Because Tao operates in a regular pattern, it is nothing mysterious. It is deep and profound (*hsüan*), to be sure, and it is described as subtle and elusive (1, 14). But it is neither chaotic nor unpredictable, for it is the "essence" which is "very real," and "in it are evidences" (21). It is popular, especially in the West, to describe Tao as mysterious, and there seems to be a special attraction to translate *hsüan* as mystery. It is mysterious only in the sense of subtlety and depth, not in the sense of irrationality.

The above description of Tao is inadequate but sufficient to indicate its novel and radical character. Its inception definitely marked a great advance in Chinese thought. Hu Shih thinks that Lao Tzu's conception of Tao as transcending heaven, earth, and all things is his greatest contribution.[12] Other schools of thought confined their thought and interest to the mundane world, whereas Lao Tzu extended his concern beyond the realm of human affairs to include the natural and the metaphysical. The human is no longer the criterion of what is good or true. The traditional idea that a supreme supernatural being, Heaven, is the ruler of the universe is replaced by the doctrine that the universe exists and operates by itself. When he says that "Heaven and Earth are not humane" (5), he means in a narrow sense that they are impartial, but in a broader sense that Nature is no longer governed according to human standards. And if there is a Lord, he says, Tao existed before him (4). In one stroke he removes Heaven and man as the standards of things and replaces them with Nature. Instead of the will of Heaven or human desires, there is now the law of Nature. As Needham has noted, to declare independence from the ethical judgment of men, in spite of the ethical character of the culture in which Taoism emerged and thrived, is the great credit of the Taoist movement.[13]

3. THE EMPHASIS ON MAN AND VIRTUE

This is by no means to suggest that Taoism is a dehumanizing philosophy, as is so often understood in the West. Like Confucius and other ancient philosophers, Lao Tzu's main concern is still man. Eighty per cent of the *Lao Tzu* is devoted not to the substance of Tao but to its function, particularly to its operation in society. The chief subject of the book is how to live, including ethics, government, and diplomacy. Lao Tzu may or may not have been a recluse. The fact remains that whereas other ancient recluses ridiculed reformers and retired to farms,[14] Lao Tzu came forward with a comprehensive program for social and political reconstruction for the happiness of all.

Waley thinks that the *Lao Tzu* is "not in intention a way of life for ordinary people," but a description of how the sage "through the practice of Tao acquires the power of ruling without being known to rule." [15] Ch'ien Mu also contends that Lao Tzu, in his political theories at least, speaks only in the interest of the ruling sage but not that of the masses.[16] This is most unfair. Although about half of the chapters deal with the sage and how he should rule, the other half do not, and it is here that the most important ideas are expressed. Furthermore, the sage is no more than an ideal person, which everyone could become through the practice of Tao. In the Chinese tradition in general and in Taoism in particular, everyone has the potentiality to become a sage. There is not the slightest hint in the *Lao Tzu* that the sage is of a different species.[17] Besides, as indicated above, the *Lao Tzu* puts forth some of the most vigorous protests against government. These protests and attacks can hardly convince people that Lao Tzu speaks for the ruler. If the sage is singled out as the one fit to rule, it is because he has cultivated virtue according to Tao. In short, the main objective of the book is the cultivation of virtue or *te*.

What is *te*? The traditional interpretation is a pun, namely, *te* ("virtue") is "to obtain" (*te*), that is, what one has obtained, in this case what one has obtained from Tao. Therefore, in explaining Lao Tzu, Han Fei Tzu says, "*Te* means the perfection of personality. In other words, to obtain *te* is to make one's person virtuous (*te*)." [18] Elsewhere he says, "*Te* is that in which principles are evident and which is found in all things." [19] Put differently, *te* is Tao endowed in the individual things. While Tao is common to all, it is what each thing has obtained from Tao, or its *te*, that makes it different from others. *Te* is then the individualizing factor, the embodiment of definite principles which give things their determinate features or characters. When Legge translated *te* as "characteristic," [20] he was essentially correct. But there is nothing wrong with the common translation "virtue." Waley objects to this translation because, he says, *te* can be good or bad, but there is no bad virtue.[21] Evidently he has forgotten that while there is no bad virtue, the absence of virtue is quite possible, and that is the term used in ancient texts. He prefers to translate it as "power," because, according to him, it is bound with potentiality or latent power. So far as potentiality is concerned, there is really no difference between "power" and "virtue." As the *Webster's International Dictionary* defines it, virtue is "active quality or power; capacity or power adequate to a production of a given effect." If it is objected that "virtue," to ordinary people, does not mean this, but means moral excellence, the answer is that ordinary people do not understand "power" in this sense but in the sense of force, which is diametrically opposed to the teachings of the *Lao Tzu*. The *Lao Tzu* itself says that "the all-embracing quality of the great virtue follows alone from the Tao" (21). If in one's life one follows Tao, that is virtue indeed.[22]

What is the life of virtue? It requires the usual moral qualities taught in almost all ethical systems. To Lao Tzu, deep love, frugality, and not daring to be ahead of the world are "three treasures," and because of them one becomes courageous, generous, and leader of the world (67). He urges us to love the earth in our dwelling, love what is profound in our hearts, love humanity in our associations, love faithfulness in our words, love order in government, love competence in handling affairs, and love timeliness in our activities (8). He wants us to maintain steadfast quietude and to be tranquil, enlightened, all-embracing, impartial, one with Nature, and in accord with Tao (16). He teaches us to "benefit all things" (8), to "treat those who are good with goodness" and "also to treat those who are not good with goodness" (49), and to "repay hatred with virtue" (63).[23] He admonishes us not to have ulterior motives (38), to show or justify ourselves or to boast (24), to be proud, to hoard things, or to be extravagant (44). He advises us to know the subtle and the eternal (16) but when we do not know anything, know that we do not know (71).

Virtually all the ingredients of a virtuous life, including the golden rule, are included.

4. WEAKNESS AND SIMPLICITY

But there is in the *Lao Tzu* a peculiar emphasis on what is generally regarded as negative morality, such as ignorance, humility, compliance, contentment, and above all, weakness. Lao Tzu is very insistent that we avoid the extreme, the extravagant, and the excessive (29), do away with desires (3, 19, 37), knowledge (10), competition (8), and things of the senses (12). He wants us to be "contented with contentment" (46) and "know when to stop" (44).[24] He encourages us to "keep to humility" and accept disgrace (28), to be willing to live in places which others detest (8), to be low and submissive, to be behind others but never ahead of them (7, 61, 67), and to "become one with the dusty world" (4)—in short, to be weak (30, 76).

In the *Lao Tzu*, water, the infant, the female, the valley, and the uncarved block are used as models for a life according to Tao.[25] No other school has deliberately selected these as symbols for a good life. Practically all of these symbolize the life of simplicity. Some people have therefore regarded the teaching of Lao Tzu as negative and defeatist. But this is not the case. Take the doctrine of having no desires, for instance. The virtue of having no desires is a current theme in the *Lao Tzu*, but as will be pointed out later, having no desires simply means having no impure or selfish desires, but not having no desires at all.[26] While desires should be few (19), good ones are to be fulfilled (61). This is also true of knowledge. Knowledge in the sense of cleverness and cunning is to be discarded, but knowledge of harmony and the eternal (16, 55), contentment (44), where to stop (32), and the self (33) is highly valued. Or take simplicity. The symbol for it is the uncarved block which is not spoiled by artifice. Metaphysically it stands for the original purity and unity of Tao (28, 32, 37) and ethically it stands for a simple life that is free from cunning and cleverness, is not devoted to the pursuit of profit or marked by hypo-critical humanity and righteousness, but is characterized by plainness, tranquility, and purity (15, 19, 57). Lao Tzu wants us to return to the life of a single and simple community where people do not use their utensils, weapons, or carriages, and where they "grow old and die without visiting one another" (80).

This sounds like primitivism and renunciation of civiliza-tion. Taken literally, this kind of simple life is entirely con-trary to modern civilization. Not even the most devout fol-lower of Lao Tzu would withdraw from civilization to this extent. Some modern writers in mainland China have seized upon this description of a primitive society, and other sayings of Lao Tzu, to say that he was advocating a communal life. To Hou Wai-lu, for example, *wu* does not mean non-being but the absence of private property; the simplicity that is not split up means a communal society; becoming one with the dusty world means the abolition of classes; noncompetition means the elimination of class struggle.[27] Following Hou, Needham has interpreted simplicity or the uncarved block as "the soli-darity, homogeneity, and simplicity of primitive collectivism," and becoming one with the dusty world as uniting "the rank and file for the community." [28] The primitive community de-scribed above not only becomes to him a "primitive agrarian collectivism" but also provides the clues for the opposition to feudal nobility and to the merchant alike.[29] The fact is that there is no evidence whatsoever in the *Lao Tzu* of collectivism, antifeudalism, or opposition to merchants, nor is there any condemnation of kings and barons (see 37, 39, 42). What Lao Tzu advocated is a life of plainness in which profit, cleverness, selfishness, and evil desires are all forsaken (12, 19).[30]

Is this primitivism a desertion of civilization? It is not. In the primitive society described above, Lao Tzu wants people to "relish their food, beautify their clothing, be content with their homes, and delight in their customs." Taken literally, primitivism is decidedly a deterrent to progress and amounts to renunciation. But if the spirit is correctly understood, it is simplicity and not renunciation that is desired. Unless we understand this, we shall not be able to appreciate why Taoism has become the central principle in Chinese aesthetic enjoyment. Tea drinking, landscape painting, poetry, the landscape garden, and the like, are not to be deserted but to be enjoyed in their simplicity.

As in the case of simplicity, weakness is not to be taken onesidedly or literally. Weakness is advocated for at least three reasons. One is that it is a virtue in itself, that is, as necessary in life as strength. "He who knows the male (strength) and keeps to the female (weakness) becomes the ravine of the world" (28). Secondly, weakness is often an outward expression of real strength. "What is most full seems to be empty" and "the greatest eloquence seems to stutter" (45). Thirdly, weakness overcomes strength in the long run. "There is nothing softer and weaker than water, and yet there is nothing better for attacking hard and strong things" (78). The life Lao Tzu advocates, totally speaking, is one of producing and rearing things without taking possession of them (10, 51), a life that is "as pointed as a square but does not pierce," "as acute as a knife but does not cut," "as straight as an unbent line but does not extend," and "as bright as light but does not dazzle" (58). In short, it is the life of "taking no action."

5. UNORTHODOX TECHNIQUES

Applied to government, this doctrine becomes that of laissez faire. The sage takes no action and does not interfere with the people, and they will transform spontaneously and the world will be at peace of its own accord (37). "I take no action and the people of themselves are transformed. I love tranquility and the people of themselves become correct" (57). The sage will rule "like cooking a small fish," firm in his conviction that much handling will spoil it (60). He "has no fixed (personal) ideas" but "regards the people's ideas as his own" (49). He embraces the One and becomes the model of the world (22). He leads the people but does not master them (10). He does not exalt the worthy (3). He does not seek to enlighten the people but makes them ignorant (65). He governs the state with correctness and operates the army with surprise tactics (57), but does not dominate the world with force (30).

This philosophy of laissez faire is a logical application of the doctrine of not taking action, but as the application of Tao several elements are difficult to explain. Why should the sage refuse to exalt the worthy? To say that the sage does not want others to share his power is to speak the language of the Legalists who advocated dictatorship, a system clearly out of tune with the tenor of Taoist philosophy. Lao Tzu's own explanation is that if the worthy is not exalted, the people will not compete (3). This sounds like giving up food because of a cough, as the Chinese common saying has it. More likely, the idea is part of a general opposition to political theories of the time, for one of the common tenets of political thought, in nearly all schools, is the exaltation of the worthy. Possibly Lao Tzu's opposition is due to the fact that the worthies of his time were advocates of ceremonies and music of which he disapproved. In any case, Lao Tzu contradicts himself, for inasmuch as the sage is but a higher stage of the worthy, in not exalting the worthy he is really not exalting the sage.[31]

Another puzzling point is the doctrine of keeping the people ignorant—a doctrine, emphasized by the Legalists and employed by more than one despot, which has been severely denounced. Lao Tzu frankly says that if people have too much knowledge they will be difficult to rule (65). But it is inconsistent with laissez faire deliberately to make people ignorant. As will be pointed out later, it may be part of his general condemnation of cunning and cleverness, or it may be a desire for the people's spontaneous compliance with Tao without deliberation or thought.[32] This explanation, however, is not satisfactory enough to remove the suspicion of Legalistic tendencies in Lao Tzu. One interesting question should be asked at this point. Lao Tzu says, "The best (rulers) are those whose existence is (merely) known by the people" (17). According to another reading, the best government is that whose existence is not known by the people. Could it be that making the people ignorant means making them ignorant of the existence of the ruler?

The most troublesome element is Lao Tzu's advocacy of devious tactics. They concern not only military operation (69). If they did, they would be easier to explain, for the opposition of Taoism to the use of force is well known, and the most bitter attack on militarism is found in the *Lao Tzu*.[33] It can then be argued that Lao Tzu uses warfare to illustrate his principles of taking no action and weakness because warfare is among the most dynamic and critical of human experiences, just as the Indian classic, the *Bhagavadgita*, chooses fighting as the theme on which to discuss the terrible dilemma whether one should fulfill his duty, as in the case of a soldier, and kill, or should fail in his duty and refrain from killing. But Lao Tzu's tactics seem to apply to life in general. "In order to destroy," he says, "it is necessary first to promote. In order to grasp, it is necessary first to give" (36). Undeniably there is an element of deceit involved. What is worse, if these tactics are the true Way in general or the way of taking no action in particular or an honorable activity of the sage, then they are morally questionable. The Confucianists are to be excused for having severely condemned them.[34] Confucius would never have tolerated such doctrine.

6. LAO TZU AND CONFUCIUS COMPARED

This is only one point at which Confucius and Lao Tzu are diametrically opposed. They differ in many other respects. While Lao Tzu stresses taking no action, Confucius stresses doing something. Lao Tzu focuses his attention largely on the individual, whereas Confucius focuses his on society, although the contrast must not be pushed too far. For the individual, Lao Tzu emphasizes peace of mind and tranquility of the spirit, but Confucius emphasizes moral perfection and social adjustment. Lao Tzu would nourish one's nature, but Confucius would fully develop it. With regard to one's destiny, Lao Tzu aims at returning to it, while Confucius aims at establishing it. Metaphysically, the basic concept of Lao Tzu is non-being while that of Confucius is being. Politically, Lao Tzu leaves people to their own transformation, whereas Confucius insists on transforming them through education, moral guidance, and personal influence. Lao Tzu wants us to become one with Nature, while Confucius wants us to become one with Heaven. Both seem to advocate forming one body with all things, but while in Lao Tzu the subject and all objects are to be interfused and unified, in Confucius there is a gradation from being affectionate to relatives, being humane to all people, and finally being kind to all things.[35] All in all, it is not incorrect to say, as popular writers do say, that the philosophy of Lao Tzu is for the individual while that of Confucius is for society, and that the former is for the aged while the latter is for the young. Surely the Taoism of Lao Tzu is more feminine and Confucianism more masculine. One is unmistakably more passive and the other, more active. Lao Tzu did not even mention any ancient king,[36] while Confucius loved and eulogized them. Lao Tzu rejected ceremonial and musical institutions, but Confucius promoted them. This is interesting because Lao Tzu, according to tradition, was an expert on these matters, on which Confucius went to consult him. Some scholars have tried to explain these differences by saying that while Lao Tzu came from Ch'u, south of the Yellow River, where culture was characterized by the ideal of weakness, Confucius grew up and taught in Lu, north of the river, where the ideal was strength. This geographical factor is one of those on which Hu Shih has based his theory that Lao Tzu was a *ju* (literati) of the old type, that of the weak, whereas Confucius was a *ju* of a new type, that of the strong.[37] Perhaps the differences are due to the fact that Lu was historically, politically, and culturally a strong center, whereas although Lao Tzu served as a curator of archives in the capital of Chou, he originally came from the small and oppressed state of Ch'en. Consequently, Lao Tzu took the attitude of protest against government and criticism

of institutions, whereas Confucius directed his efforts to partici-
pation in government and promoting culture. It may have
been that, having been keeper of records at the capital, Lao
Tzu saw at close range the vices of social and political institutions more clearly than did Confucius.

All these suggestions are no more than idle speculation, however. It is more profitable to note the similarities between them
in order to offset the possible impression that the teachings of
Lao Tzu and Confucius are irreconcilable. A number of similarities are pointed out in the comments on the various chapters. Suffice it to mention here that both are primarily interested in moral, social, and political reform, that both cherish
the same basic values such as humanity, righteousness,[38] deep
love, and faithfulness. Both oppose the use of force and punishment. Both avoid extremes and teach the golden rule. Both
highly esteem the integrity of the individual and social harmony, although their approaches are different. By implication,
at least, both emphasize the goodness of human nature and
the potentiality of all to become sages. It is because of these
and other similarities that Taoism and Confucianism run
harmoniously parallel throughout Chinese history so that every
Chinese is at once a Taoist and a Confucianist.

Another similarity between Lao Tzu and Confucius is that
just as Confucius' teachings were developed by Mencius (371-
289 B.C.), so those of Lao Tzu were developed by Chuang Tzu.
Mencius and Chuang Tzu were contemporaries but were probably not aware of each other. Instead of comparing these two,
however, it is more necessary here to compare Lao Tzu and
Chuang Tzu. They are often referred to as Lao-Chuang, as if
their doctrines were the same or those of Chuang Tzu but an
elaboration of Lao Tzu's philosophy. In fact, there are vast differences between them.

7. LAO TZU AND CHUANG TZU COMPARED

In every aspect Chuang Tzu carried Taoism to a higher stage
of development. Lao Tzu's "One" becomes in Chuang Tzu the

"great One." [39] Lao Tzu urges us to be infants, but Chuang Tzu wants us to be "a newborn calf." [40] Lao Tzu urges us to return to destiny or fate, whereas Chuang Tzu urges us to be contented with it.[41] To Lao Tzu, it is most important for the mind to be pure and tranquil, but to Chuang Tzu, it is most important for it to be vacuous and empty.[42]

These are but minor differences. Of far greater significance is the development of epistemology, metaphysics, and cosmology. Lao Tzu says nothing about the nature of knowledge but only about what one should know (44, 55). Chuang Tzu, however, distinguishes "great knowledge," which is "leisurely and at ease," and "small knowledge," which is "inquisitive." [43] The former is all-embracing, extensive, and synthetic, while the latter is partial, discriminative, and analytic. Lao Tzu's Tao is still vague, but that of Chuang Tzu "has reality and evidence." [44] Lao Tzu's cosmology (1, 25) is quite simple and elementary, whereas that of Chuang Tzu is much more refined, involving not only being and non-being but the state of neither being nor non-being.[45] In Lao Tzu, self-transformation concerns only man and operates in the social and moral spheres. In Chuang Tzu, it concerns all things and operates in the sphere of their nature.[46] Thus both the scope and character of self-transformation are greatly expanded, and naturalism is carried to a higher degree. Likewise the concept of change takes a great step forward. In Lao Tzu, the major notes are constancy and eternity while that of change is but a minor one. In Chuang Tzu, however, change is a main theme.[47] He conceives of the universe as a great current in which one state succeeds another in an endless procession, and in which things are in a perpetual flux. Life goes on "like a galloping horse." [48] Things not only develop from the simple to the complex as in Lao Tzu (42), but acquire an evolutionary character, for all things grew from germs through various stages of life to that of horse and then to that of man.[49] In these constant changes and rapid transfigurations, "all things are one," [50] for Tao embraces all of them and combines them into a unity. "Heaven and earth and I coexist," he says, "and all things and I are one."[51] Lao Tzu has stressed the unity of Tao, but it is a newer note to stress the oneness of all things. Within this unity, all differences and contraries disappear. Lao Tzu still sharply distinguishes black and white, glory and disgrace, and the front and the back (2, 28),[52] but to Chuang Tzu life and death, construction and destruction, beauty and ugliness, possibility and impossibility, and right and wrong are but differences in points of view, or merely relative, or causes of each other. In any case, Tao identifies them all as one.[53]

It can readily be seen that the arena of Chuang Tzu's philosophy is much greater than that of Lao Tzu and the action much faster. In fact, Chuang Tzu thinks of life as a play, with the universe as the stage. He therefore wants life to be like leisurely roaming and wandering in the universe.[54] If Lao Tzu treasures the tranquility of the spirit (10, 16), Chuang Tzu treasures its freedom. Chuang Tzu is therefore comparatively more romantic and otherworldly, while Lao Tzu is more realistic and mundane. Lao Tzu aims at handling human affairs and mastering worldly situations, but Chuang Tzu prefers to transcend them and go along with the transformation of heaven and earth. To Lao Tzu, the ideal man is the sage who is a practical man not above resorting to various tactics to handle human affairs.[55] To Chuang Tzu, the ideal man is the pure man who "did not know what it was to love life or to hate death." [56] Creel is essentially correct in maintaining that Chuang Tzu is primarily "contemplative," interested in an intoxication with the wonder and power of Nature, whereas Lao Tzu is primarily "purposive," chiefly interested in how to govern.[57] Lao Tzu speaks only of everlasting life (59), but Chuang Tzu tells stories about a man of the spirit who lives in a certain mountain, eats no grains, thrives on wind and dew, rides the clouds, and roams the universe,[58] and a perfect man who does not feel the heat of fire or the cold of frozen rivers, but rides on the sun and moon and rambles at ease beyond the seas.[59] There is very little mysticism in Lao Tzu, unless one considers union with Tao (56) as necessarily a mystical experience.[60] Chuang Tzu, however, speaks of "the fasting of the mind" in which "the mind is empty to receive all things" [61] and "sitting down and forgetting everything" in which "the body is abandoned, the intelligence is discarded, one is separated from the body and free from knowledge, and one becomes identical with a great penetration." [62] Such an experience is definitely mystical. There is nothing like this in the *Lao Tzu*. Every passage of it can be understood in terms of ordinary human experience, whereas many in the *Chuang Tzu* deal with pure experience that transcends the mundane. Many writers, especially translators, have presented Lao Tzu as almost the greatest mystic in Chinese history. They have either confused him with Chuang Tzu or have taken any intuitive philosophy as mysticism.

It should be emphasized that, broadly speaking, the differences between Lao Tzu and Chuang Tzu are a matter of degree rather than kind. The differences are far outweighed by the similarities, which are too many to mention. It is enough to point out that the doctrines of both are exclusively devoted to Tao and its virtue. It is interesting to note, too, that Chuang Tzu also came from south of the Yellow River and shared Lao Tzu's spirit of the frontier, the unorthodox, the minority, and the oppressed.

8. INFLUENCES ON NEO-TAOISM, BUDDHISM, AND NEO-CONFUCIANISM

Both of their philosophies were raised to a higher level in the Neo-Taoism of the third and fourth centuries. We shall bypass the *Huai-nan Tzu* and the *Lieh Tzu*. The former is by Liu An (d. 122 B.C.) whose originality is negligible. Aside from a reiteration and elaboration of earlier Taoism, his only contribution is a rational approach to metaphysics and cosmogony that helped to usher in the rationalism of Neo-Taoism. The *Lieh Tzu* is probably a product of the third century. Its ideas of the equality of things, indifference to life and death, following one's nature, and accepting one's fate are all original ingredients of Taoism, especially that of Chuang Tzu. But the

Taoist doctrine of taking no action is degenerated into a complete abandonment of effort, spontaneity is confused with resignation, and having no desire is replaced by hedonism. It represents no development of Taoism at all.

The most important development of Taoism in the history of Chinese thought is that of Neo-Taoism. It finds its expressions in the commentaries on the *Lao Tzu* and the *Book of Changes* (*I ching*) by Wang Pi (226-49) and the commentary on the *Chuang Tzu* by Kuo Hsiang (d. 312). In them, non-being is no longer essentially in contrast to being, but is the ultimate of all, or pure being (*pen-wu*), the One and undifferentiated. According to Wang Pi, original non-being transcends all distinctions and descriptions. It is the pure being, original substance (*pen-t'i*), and the One in which substance and function are identified. It is always correct because it is in accord with principle. Where Lao Tzu had destiny, Wang would substitute principle, thus anticipating the development in Neo-Confucianism.

Just as Wang Pi went beyond Lao Tzu, so Kuo Hsiang went beyond Chuang Tzu. The major concept is no longer Tao, as in Chuang Tzu, but Nature (*tzu-jan*). Things exist and transform themselves spontaneously and there is no other reality or agent to cause them. Things exist and transform according to principle, but each and every thing has its own principle. Compared with Wang Pi, he emphasizes being rather than non-being and the many rather than the one. To Wang Pi, principle transcends things, but to Kuo Hsiang it is immanent in them.

These major Taoist concepts of being and non-being were carried over to Buddhism from Neo-Taoism. In the third and fourth centuries, Buddhist thinkers practiced "matching the concepts" of Buddhism and Taoism, in which a Buddhist concept is equated with one in Taoist thought. Following Taoism, the early Buddhist philosophical schools centered their thoughts on being and non-being, some even calling their own schools "School of Original Non-being," "School of Non-being of Mind," and so forth. Like the Neo-Taoists, the Buddhists regard ultimate reality as transcending all being, names, and forms, and as empty and quiet in nature.

But the greatest Taoist influence on Buddhism lies in the Chinese development of Ch'an (Zen). It is generally recognized that Zen, which means meditation, is fundamentally Chinese, and there is no doubt that Taoism provided the stimulation as well as the climate for this development. According to the basic tenets of Zen, the Buddha-mind is everywhere and the Buddha-nature is in all men. As ultimate reality, the Buddha-mind is indescribable by words and inconceivable in thought, but as endowment in man, the Buddha-nature can be discovered. The only way to discover it is through enlightenment. Therefore the standard sayings of Zen are: "Point directly to the human mind," and "See one's nature and become a Buddha." To help achieve enlightenment to this end, Zen Masters have taught "the absence of thought," "forgetting one's feelings," and "letting the mind take its own course."

It does not take any scrutiny to see that many of these elements have come from, or at least have been promoted by, Taoism, especially Chuang Tzu, for Tao is everywhere and in all men and is indescribable but discoverable through enlightenment, if one discards thought, forgets personal feelings, and lets things take their own course. In point of fact, many early Buddhist thinkers were experts on Taoist philosophy and throughout history many Zen Masters were personal friends of Taoists.

Just as Taoism contributed to the development of Zen in the seventh and eighth centuries, so it contributed to the development of Neo-Confucianism in the eleventh. The philosophy of Chou Tun-i (1017-73) is set forth in the *T'ai-chi-t'u shuo* (Explanation of the Diagram of the Great Ultimate). According to it, the whole process of creation begins with the Non-ultimate which is also the Great Ultimate. The Great Ultimate generates yin, the cosmic passive force, and yang, the cosmic active force, through the transformation of which all things are produced. To some extent this scheme comes from the Confucian classic, the *Book of Changes,* on which the whole movement of Neo-

Confucianism is based. Whether he obtained the diagram from a Taoist priest is uncertain, but the idea of the Non-ultimate definitely comes from the *Lao Tzu*.[63] Furthermore, one of the cardinal doctrines of Confucianism has been sincerity. Chou Tun-i made it a central point in his philosophy, but he defines it as "having no desire," [64] which idea also comes from the *Lao Tzu*. In short, he assimilated the Taoist concept of non-being into Confucian thought. Also, to conceive of a universal scheme in which man plays only a part, though the most important part, clearly shows Taoist influence.

This universal outlook is also central in the philosophy of Shao Yung (1011-77), another outstanding Neo-Confucianist. Shao's fundamental concepts are three. First, there are the supreme principles governing the universe. Secondly, these principles can be discerned in terms of numbers. And thirdly, the best knowledge of them is the objective.[65] Like philosopher Chou, Shao has derived his ideas chiefly from the *Book of Changes*, but the striking similarity between his ideas and those in the *Lao Tzu*—that Tao is the universal principle, that Tao produces the One and the One produces the two and the two produces the three (42), and that things should be viewed as they are (54)—cannot be dismissed as coincidental. Because of these ideas, other Neo-Confucianists have criticized Shao as Taoistic. In another Neo-Confucianist, Chang Tsai (1020-77), we also see definite connections with Taoism. He says, "The Great Vacuity of necessity consists of material force. Material force of necessity integrates to become the myriad things. Things of necessity disintegrate and return to the Great Vacuity." [66] This is Lao Tzu's doctrine of Tao as the universal principle, that it operates through being and non-being, and that it always returns to its root, all in a nutshell. The term "vacuity," it should be added, originated in the *Lao Tzu* (5, 16).[67]

Although these Neo-Confucianists were influenced by Taoism, they were critical of it. Their followers, notably Ch'eng Hao (1032-85), Ch'eng I (1033-1107), and Chu Hsi (1130-1200), were even more so. But in all of them, and indeed in the entire Neo-Confucian movement, the Taoist concept of Tao as the natural and universal principle of existence has been borrowed and made the backbone of the system, so much so that the school is called the School of Principle.

The above survey is intended to give an outline of the development of Taoist philosophy and its influence on Chinese thought. Parallel with it was another development, namely, that of the Taoist religion. In reality it was a degeneration rather than a development, for the religion appropriated some Taoist ideas, twisted its doctrines, made Lao Tzu its spiritual founder, and turned the *Lao Tzu* into its Bible for a purpose alien to the philosophy of Lao Tzu. The Taoist religion and Taoist philosophy are entirely different things, called by different names in Chinese, the one *Tao-chia* or the Taoist school, and the other *Tao-chiao* or the Taoist religion. Unfortunately, they are both called Taoism in the West, thus confusing the two and giving rise to wrong interpretations of Taoist philosophy.

9. THE TAOIST RELIGION

The origin of the Taoist religion is still not clear. The practices of divination, astrology, faith healing, witchcraft, and the like had existed from very early days. By the fourth century B.C., there was, in addition, the belief in immortals who were supposed to live in islands off the China coast. The belief was so widespread and so firm that feudal lords sent missions there to seek elixir from them. On top of this effort, the ancient Chinese resorted to sitting in meditation, concentration of thought, dietary techniques, medicine, breathing exercises, bathing of all sorts, including sun bathing, various kinds of gymnastics, such as extending and contracting the body, sexual techniques, and alchemy, all directed to the search for the preservation of life, that is, longevity, and for immortality. Priest-magicians, called *fang-shih* or practitioners with special formula, went around to offer their services. By the early first century of our era these *fang-shih* came to be known as *tao-shih*, that is, practitioners of the Way.

In the meantime, a cult emerged bearing the names of the legendary Yellow Emperor of antiquity and Lao Tzu, most probably because their teachings of everlasting life, or similar teachings attributed to them, were a great help to preserving life and to achieving immortality. In spite of the supremacy of Confucianism as the state doctrine since 140 B.C., when non-Confucian scholars were dismissed from office, this cult continued to grow. In 103 B.C., Taoist scholars were again allowed to serve in the government, thus raising the prestige of the Yellow Emperor and Lao Tzu. In A.D. 167, the emperor even sacrificed to them in the capital. Needless to say, by this time the word *Tao* had assumed a special significance and possessed, especially for the masses, almost a magical meaning.

In the middle of the second century, a rebel by the name of Chang Ling (*fl.* A.D. 156), who had established a semi-independent state on the borders of Szechuan and Shensi, attracted many followers through faith healing and other magical practices. He charged five bushels of rice for membership in his group. Consequently his movement has been known as the Tao or Way of Five Bushels of Rice and eventually became the Taoist religion with practitioners of the Way as its priests. His name came to be known as Chang Tao-ling. He may have been the first to use the name Tao-chiao.[68] If so, did he purposely coin the term to stress the fact that his movement was a religion to be sharply distinguished from the Taoist school?

Chang Ling's movement was carried on and spread by his grandson, Chang Lu (*fl.* 188-220), who called Chang Ling the Celestial Teacher. For thirty years he maintained an independent state on the border of Szechuan and Hupei and promoted the Way of Five Bushels of Rice. Following the practices of his grandfather and also other rebels who had spread their own cults with similar practices, Chang Lu enforced prohibition, gave away food and practiced other charities, encouraged moral deeds, especially filial piety, prescribed repentance, meditation, and the use of charms as means to heal illness, exhorted people to honor Lao Tzu, and taught novices of his cult to read the *Lao Tzu.*

It is easy to understand why the *Lao Tzu* was turned into the Bible of the new religion. Its spirit of revolt gave the rebels a strong support. Lao Tzu was enjoying great popularity among both the masses and the rulers. In many places the *Lao Tzu* is difficult to understand so that the Taoist priests could interpret it to suit their own purposes. It is rhymed and therefore easy to recite and to be transmitted from mouth to mouth. Most important of all, it promises that "a good preserver of life will not meet tigers" and "the wild buffalo cannot butt its horns against him" (50). Many passages seem to assure an everlasting life on earth. "The spirit of the valley never dies," it says (6). It talks about one who "dies but does not really perish" (33) and about "long life and everlasting vision" (59). The "profound female" (6), "the role of the female in the opening and closing of the gates of Heaven" (10), "the union of the male and the female," and the infant's organ being aroused (55) all suggest sexual techniques to achieve immortality. "Keeping the spirit," "embracing the One" (10), and "maintaining steadfast quietude" (16) resemble yoga concentration. "Keeping the hearts vacuous" while "filling the bellies" (3) and "concentrating the vital force" (10) appear to describe breathing exercises. No wonder the priests of the new religion took full advantage of the book and made it virtually the manual for the preservation of life and for the search for immortality. In all probability, they and their followers honestly believed that Lao Tzu actually taught these techniques, in spite of the fact that he uttered not a single word about artificial methods to prolong life, physical ascension to heaven, or immortals roaming the universe. The *Chuang Tzu* is a better source for this type of thing, and the priests drew from it even more heavily.

As the search for immortality on earth was intensified, the cleavage between the Taoist religion and the Taoist school widened.[69] The religious development corrupted the Taoist philosophy, particularly that of leaving things to take their own course. But it did show an interesting sidelight on the scientific character of Taoist thought. Alchemy, medicine, the pill for immortality, and so forth, were definitely pseudo-scientific adventures. What is really significant is, as Needham has very well brought out, that the Taoist concepts of the order, unity, and uniformity of Nature, of Tao as the very structure of particular and individual types of things, of following objective instead of human standards for truth, and the spirit of observation are essentially scientific.[70]

As the search for immortality failed, the Taoist priests concentrated their efforts on seeking longevity through physical health and spiritual tranquility. As a result, commentators on the *Lao Tzu* interpreted it in the light of yoga. This tendency began with Ho-shang Kung's commentary, probably of the fourth century. From then on, this interpretation became increasingly popular until the rationalistic Neo-Confucianists of the eleventh century restored in their commentaries the philosophical character of the classic. Ever since then, the philosophical commentary by Wang Pi has been in ascendency.[71]

The amazing thing is that in recent years more modern writers have gone out of their way to find yoga in the *Lao Tzu*. The phrase "long life and everlasting vision" (59) simply means longevity, but "everlasting vision" has become for Waley "fixed staring." [72] This is putting much yoga into the mouth of Lao Tzu.[73] He is right, however, in stressing the fact that the Taoist religious practitioners understood the *Lao Tzu* in this spirit.

10. TAOISM IN CHINESE LIFE

The Taoist religion has continued to this day, while Taoist philosophy has been assimilated into Buddhism and Neo-Confucianism. It no longer exists as an independent philosophical system. In the last thousand years there has not been a Taoist school or a single outstanding Taoist philosopher, book, or theory. This does not mean, however, that Taoist philosophy is dead. One finds it everywhere, for it is tightly woven into the fabric of Chinese life. It is found in Neo-Confucianism, which has been the dominant philosophy in China in the last eight hundred years. One finds it in the rugged individualism of the Chinese which is sometimes expressed in the sense of contentment, fatalism, and retirement, and sometimes in nonconformity and revolt.[74] One finds it in the love of spiritual tranquility and mental peace, and in the transcendental outlook and broad perspective that are the basis of tolerance, patience, and indifference to things. One finds it in the enjoyment of the simplicity of life, in spontaneity and noninterference, in the tactic of withdrawal in order to advance, a tactic frequently used in the handling of ordinary affairs as well as in military operations and politics. One finds it in the concealment of wisdom in silence, and wealth in seeming poverty, and in the love of nature that takes the Chinese to the garden and to the mountains. And one finds it in all sorts of ways and means to preserve life and to nourish the spirit. Whether in conversation or in tea drinking, whether in arranging flowers or in writing poems, and whether in the landscape garden or in landscape painting, these aspirations are evident, for there one's spirit should be pure, one's mind should be free of selfish desires, simplicity should be the keynote, and Nature should be allowed to take its own course.

Does this still hold true in mainland China? From every indication it does. The study of the *Lao Tzu* is as lively as ever. A new development there has been the effort to make Lao Tzu an advocate of materialism. The concept of Tao has been reinterpreted in materialistic terms on the grounds that Tao is the basic substance of all things, their necessary nature, their law of change, their condition of existence, and their sum total.[75] Whether the arguments are sound or not, the fact remains that even in the midst of a gigantic revolution, Taoist thought continues to provoke thinking.

Much of this inspiration comes from the *Lao Tzu,* or *Tao-te ching,* a classic of about 5250 words. No other Chinese classic of such a small size has exercised so much influence over such a long period of time. About 950 commentaries have been written on it and more than 40 English translations made of it, in both respects more than any other Chinese classic, including the Confucian *Analects*. Regardless of what shapes things in China may take in the future, the *Lao Tzu* will continue to be a source of inspiration for the Chinese and perhaps for the rest of the world as well.

NOTES

1. In the *Shih chi* (Records of the Historian) by Ssu-ma Ch'ien (145-86 B.C.), 130:4b.
2. *Book of Odes,* Ode 113.
3. In view of the controversial nature of the person of Lao Tzu, perhaps one should use "the *Lao Tzu*" instead of "Lao Tzu," but that would be very clumsy.
4. *Chung-kuo che-hsüeh shih ta-kang* (Outline of the History of Chinese Philosophy), p. 50.
5. *Chuang Tzu,* ch. 33, *SPTK,* 10:35a. Cf. Giles (tr.), *Chuang Tzu* (1961 edn.), p. 319.
6. *The Spirit of Chinese Philosophy* (tr. Hughes), p. 62.
7. *Han Fei Tzu,* ch. 20, *SPTK,* 6:7a-8a. Cf. Liao (tr.), *The Complete Works of Han Fei Tzu,* I, 191-95.
8. "Taoism," in Harley Farnsworth MacNair (ed.), *China,* p. 272.
9. *Chuang Tzu,* ch. 2, *SPTK,* 1:18a. Cf. Giles, p. 34.
10. *Science and Civilisation in China.* Vol. II, *History of Scientific Thought,* pp. 36-37.
11. See discussion on this point by Chang Chung-yüan, "The Concept of Tao in Chinese Culture," *Review of Religion,* XVII (1953), 127-28.
12. Hu Shih, *Chung-kuo che-hsüeh shih ta-kang,* p. 56.
13. Needham, p. 49.
14. See the Confucian *Analects,* 18:6-7.
15. *The Way and Its Power,* p. 92.
16. *Chuang-Lao t'ung-pien* (General Discussions on Lao Tzu and Chuang Tzu), p. 123.

17. For further remarks on the sage, see comments on chapters 19 and 26.
18. *Han Fei Tzu*, ch. 20, *SPTK*, 6:1a. Cf. Liao (tr.), *The Complete Works of Han Fei Tzu*, I, 170.
19. *Ibid.*, ch. 8, *SPTK*, 2:7a. Cf. Liao, I, 55.
20. Legge (tr.), "The Tao Teh King: The Tao and Its Characteristics," in *The Texts of Taoism*.
21. *The Way and Its Power*, p. 31.
22. On *te*, see comment on chapter 51.
23. See comment on chapter 63, on the golden rule.
24. On contentment, see comment on chapter 46.
25. For remarks on some of these models, see comments on chapters 8, 15, 52, and 55.
26. See comment on chapter 64.
27. Hou Wai-lu *et al.*, *Chung-kuo ssu-hsiang t'ung-shih* (General History of Chinese Thought), I, 278, 288, and 290.
28. *History of Scientific Thought*, pp. 114 and 113, respectively.
29. *Ibid.*, p. 100.
30. On primitivism, see comment on chapter 80.
31. See comment on chapter 3 for a further discussion.
32. See comment on chapter 65.
33. See comment on chapter 31.
34. See comment on chapter 36.
35. For a discussion of this point see Chang Chung-yüan, "Tao and the Sympathy of All Things," *Eranos-Jahrbuch*, XXIV (1955), 409-10.
36. See comment on chapter 19.
37. *Shuo ju* (On the Literati), *Hu Shih lun-hsüeh chin-chu* (Recent Essays on Learned Subjects by Hu Shih), pp. 69-75.
38. There is no inconsistency between Lao Tzu's attack on humanity and righteousness (18, 19) and his esteem of them (38). What is attacked is the hypocritical and what is esteemed is the "superior."
39. *Chuang Tzu*, ch. 24, *SPTK*, 8:42a. Cf. Giles (tr.), *Chuang Tzu*, pp. 246-47.
40. *Ibid.*, ch. 22, *SPTK*, 7:45a. Cf. Giles, p. 212.
41. *Ibid.*, ch. 11, *SPTK*, 4:27b (Giles, p. 107).
42. *Ibid.*, ch. 4, *SPTK*, 2:13a (Giles, p. 54).
43. *Ibid.*, ch. 2, *SPTK*, 1:21b. Cf. Giles, p. 35.

44. *Ibid.*, ch. 6, *SPTK*, 3:10a (Giles, p. 76).

45. *Ibid.*, ch. 2, *SPTK*, 1:33b (Giles, p. 41).

46. *Ibid.*, chs. 11 and 17, *SPTK*, 4:38b and 6:20b (Giles, pp. 113 and 165, respectively).

47. *Ibid.*, ch. 13, *SPTK*, 5:27a (Giles, p. 134); ch. 14, *SPTK*, 5:39a (Giles, p. 144).

48. *Ibid.*, ch. 17, *SPTK*, 6:20a-b (Giles, p. 165).

49. *Ibid.*, ch. 18, *SPTK*, 6:36a-37a (Giles, p. 177).

50. *Ibid.*, ch. 12, *SPTK*, 5:3b (Giles, p. 118).

51. *Ibid.*, ch. 2, *SPTK*, 1:34a. Cf. Giles, p. 41.

52. See D. C. Lau, "The Treatment of Opposites in Lao Tzu," *Bulletin of the School of Oriental and African Studies*, XXI (1958), 344-60. For his theory, see below, chapter 40, note 2.

53. *Chuang Tzu*, ch. 2, *SPTK*, 1:27b-31a (Giles, pp. 37-39).

54. *Ibid.*, ch. 1.

55. For an interesting contrast between the sage of Lao Tzu and that of Chuang Tzu, see Ch'ien Mu, *Chuang-Lao t'ung-pien*, pp. 114-26.

56. *Chuang Tzu*, ch. 6, *SPTK*, 3:3b. Cf. Giles, p. 72.

57. "On Two Aspects in Early Taoism," in Kaizuka Shigeki (ed.), *Silver Jubilee Volume of the Zinbun-Gagaku-Kenkyusyo*, pp. 50-52.

58. *Chuang Tzu*, ch. 1, *SPTK*, 1:11b-12a (Giles, p. 31).

59. *Ibid.*, ch. 2, *SPTK*, 1:40a-b (Giles, p. 44).

60. See comment on chapter 56. For a discussion of the absence of mysticism, in the Western sense at least, in Lao Tzu, see Welch, *The Parting of the Way*, pp. 58-64.

61. *Chuang Tzu*, ch. 4, *SPTK*, 2:13a. Cf. Giles, p. 54.

62. *Ibid.*, ch. 6, *SPTK*, 3:26a-b. Cf. Giles, pp. 84-85.

63. Ch. 28. See comment.

64. See his *T'ai-chi-t'u shuo* (Explanation of the Diagram of the Great Ultimate).

65. *Huang-chi ching-shih shu* (Supreme Principles Governing the World), 7A:1a, 6:26a-b, 8B:9b.

66. *Cheng-meng* (Correcting Youthful Ignorance), ch. 1, in *Chang Heng-ch'ü chi* (Collected Works of Chang Tsai), 2:3b.

67. See comment on ch. 5.

68. Jao Tsung-i thinks so. See his *Lao Tzu hsiang-erh chu chiao-chien* (A Study of Chang Tao-ling's Hsiang-erh Commentary of *Tao Te Ching*), p. 58. No one knows what the term *hsiang-*

erh means. For a discussion of this term, see Shih-hsiang Chen, "Hsiang-erh Lao-tzu Tao-ching Tun-huang ts'an-chüan lun-cheng" (On the Historical and Religious Significance of the Tun-huang MS of *Lao Tzu*, Book I, with Commentaries by "Hsiang-erh"), *Tsing-hua Journal of Chinese Studies*, I (1957), 49-50, 61.

69. Creel correctly distinguishes philosophical Taoism and *hsien* (immortals) Taoism, the latter denoting the search for immortality. See his "What Is Taoism?" *Journal of the American Oriental Society*, LXXVI (1956), 143.

70. For discussions of the scientific character of Taoist philosophy, see Needham, *History of Scientific Thought*, pp. 36-68, and Wing-tsit Chan, "Neo-Confucianism and Chinese Scientific Thought," *Philosophy East and West*, VI (1957), 312-14.

71. For these commentaries, see below, pp. 78-82.

72. *The Way and Its Power*, pp. 213-14. Chang Chung-yüan has not gone quite so far. For him, breathing leads to enlightenment and interfusion with the Real Being. See his "An Introduction to Taoist Yoga," *Review of Religion*, XX (1956), 131-33.

73. See comment on chapter 59, and chapter 62, note 5.

74. For an excellent discussion on this point, see Lin Tung-chi, "The Chinese Mind: Its Taoist Substratum," *Journal of the History of Ideas*, VIII (1947), 259-73.

75. See *Lao Tzu che-hsüeh t'ao-lun chi* (Symposium on the Philosophy of Lao Tzu), pp. 16, 40, 147-49, 167. Opinions are by no means unanimous. Some writers have argued that the concept of Tao is idealistic, because Tao is indescribable, transcends space and time, comes from non-being, is the One and therefore abstract, and an absolute spirit (pp. 16, 176, 184-85, 300), but these writers represent a small minority.

II. *Lao Tzu, the Man*

Few controversies in modern Chinese history have lasted longer and involved more scholars than that concerning Lao Tzu, the man, and *Lao Tzu*, the book. It has lasted for forty years, engaged dozens of debaters, and produced half a million words. And the battle is still continuing, both in China and in the West.

1. TRADITIONAL ACCOUNTS

Ever since Ssu-ma Ch'ien wrote in his *Records of the Historian* that Lao Tzu was a contemporary of Confucius and the author of a book expounding the doctrine of the Way and its virtue, for centuries the Chinese accepted this account without question. However, as the new rationalistic spirit grew in the Sung dynasty (960-1297), a number of Neo-Confucianists began to question the tradition.[1] Yeh Shih (1150-1223) definitely rejected the tradition [2] and Chu Hsi was puzzled.[3] In the eighteenth century, as the critical and skeptical spirit grew in strength among Chinese scholars, many of them, especially Wang Chung (1744-94) and Ts'ui Shu (1740-1816), revolted against the traditional account. But it was Liang Ch'i-ch'ao's (1873-1929) publication, in a newspaper in 1922, of a critical review of Hu Shih's *Chung-kuo che-hsüeh shih ta-kang* (Outline of the History of Chinese Philosophy) that touched off the long and bitter controversy. Hu Shih had upheld the tradition about the man and the book, but Liang threw it overboard. Since then, hardly a scholar with anything to say about them has not taken a position. The point has been reached that in some circles in the West, as well as in China, a scholar is considered outdated if he upholds the tradition.

Before we proceed any further, we need to know what Ssu-ma Ch'ien has to say. This is what the historian wrote:

Lao Tzu was a native of Ch'ü-jen hamlet in Li county, in the K'u district [4] of the state of Ch'u. His surname was Li, private name Erh, courtesy name Po-yang, and posthumous name Tan. He was an official of the archives in Chou [the capital].

Confucius went to Chou to consult Lao Tzu about rules of propriety. Lao Tzu said, "Those whom you talk about are dead and their bones have decayed. Only their words have remained. When the time is proper, the superior man rides in a carriage, but when it is not, he covers himself up and staggers away. I have heard that a good merchant stores away his treasures as if his store were empty and that a superior man with eminent virtue appears as if he were stupid. Get rid of your air of pride and many desires, your insinuating manners and lustful wishes. None of these is good for you. That is all I have to tell you."

Confucius left and told his pupils, "I know birds can fly, fish can swim, and animals can run. That which runs can be trapped, that which swims can be netted, and that which flies can be shot. As to the dragon, I don't know how it rides on the winds and clouds and ascends to heaven. Lao Tzu, whom I saw today, is indeed like a dragon!"

Lao Tzu practiced the Way and its virtue. His learning aims at self-effacement and possessing no fame. Having lived in Chou for a long time, he realized that it was in decline and left. As he reached the pass, the pass-keeper, Yin-hsi, said, "You are about to retire. Please try your best to write a book for me." Thereupon Lao Tzu wrote a book in two parts, expounding the ideas of the Way and its virtue in over five thousand words and then departed. None knew how he ended.

Some say that Lao Lai Tzu was also a native of Ch'u. He wrote a book in fifteen parts on the application of Taoist doctrines. It is said that he was a contemporary of Confucius.

Probably Lao Tzu lived to be more than one hundred and sixty years—some say more than two hundred years—because he practiced the Way and nourished his old age.

One hundred and twenty-nine years after the death of Confucius, as historians have recorded, Grand Historian TAN of Chou had an audience with Duke Hsien [reigned 384-362 B.C.] of Ch'in saying, "First Ch'in joined with Chou and then separated. After five hundred years they were united again. Then in seventy years a king of feudal lords appeared." Some say TAN was Lao Tzu while others say no. People today do not know who are right.

Lao Tzu was a recluse gentleman. Lao Tzu's son was named Tsung. Tsung became a general in the state of Wei, and was enfeoffed at Tuan-kan. Tsung's son was Chu and Chu's son was Kung. Kung's great-great-grandson was Chia, who was an official under Emperor Hsiao-wen [reigned 179-157 B.C.] of the Han dynasty [206 B.C.–A.D. 220]. Chia's son, Chieh, became grand tutor to Ch'iung, prince of Chiao-hsi, and so made his home in Ch'i.

Today followers of Lao Tzu degrade Confucianism and students of Confucianism also degrade Lao Tzu. "People going different ways do not take counsel from one another." [5] Is this referring to this fact?

Li Erh takes no action and spontaneously transforms himself. He was pure and tranquil and was naturally correct.[6]

The historian gathered his material from his extensive travels. There are actually three separate accounts—one about Lao Tzu whom Confucius visited, one about Lao Lai Tzu, and one about Grand Historian TAN and Lao Tzu's son. The fact that Ssu-ma Ch'ien was himself uncertain about his material is indicated by the expressions "probably," "it is said," "none knew," "some say," and the like. His mention of an exceptionally long life may have been an attempt to reconcile the three separate and conflicting stories.

2. LAO TZU'S BIRTHPLACE AND NAMES

Of the three separate accounts, the first, which deals with Lao Tzu's personal data, his meeting with Confucius, and his authorship, is the most important and most troublesome. There is no question about his native district. Technically, Ssu-ma Ch'ien is wrong in saying that the K'u district was in the state of Ch'u, for it was in the state of Ch'en until Ch'en was captured by Ch'u in 535 B.C. But it is not really an error because it was a general practice for Han dynasty writers to refer to places by their current names rather than by their ancient names.[7] But Lao Tzu's names are surrounded with mystery.

In both his biography of Lao Tzu and in his autobiography,[8] Ssu-ma Ch'ien refers to him as Li Erh. The private name Erh, meaning "ear," has been generally accepted. The surname Li, ordinarily meaning "plum," however, has led to both amusement and puzzlement. It has given rise to stories that he was born under a plum tree and that he obtained the surname because he ate bitter plums when he was a refugee. These are amusing stories but the humor is more than offset by the puzzlement. For one thing, there was no such surname before the fourth century B.C. Furthermore, during the Warring States period (403-222 B.C.) none referred to him as Li.

To avoid the difficulty, Yao Nai (1731-1815) has suggested that his original surname was Tzu, but because of its similarity in pronunciation with *li* in ancient times, he was known as Li.[9] Ma Hsü-lun thinks Yao is near the truth.[10] But as Kao Heng has pointed out, Yao has presented no evidence for his theory.[11] Ma has suggested that it is possible that Li was originally *LI* (meaning a hamlet) which was known as a surname, and a certain LI mentioned in the *Tso chuan* (Tso's Commentary) [12] was later referred to as Li,[13] thus indicating that Li and LI were interchangeable. But as Kao Heng has also said, that was simply a change made by someone at a much later time.[14] Kao himself believes the man's real surname was Lao but because its pronunciation is similar to that of *li,* he came to be known as Li.[15] It is interesting that Kao has argued along the same line as Yao Nai and has offered no more evidence than Yao did.

No one doubts the name Tan itself or its meaning (long ear). The question is whether Li Erh and Lao Tan refer to the same person. The *Chuang Tzu* refers to Lao Tzu and Lao Tan many times.[16] In three places it relates the story of Confucius visiting Lao Tan.[17] In another place, it records an additional conversation between Confucius and Lao Tan.[18] Four times it speaks of Lao Tzu and Lao Tan as one person.[19] It also quotes twice from the *Lao Tzu* as the words of Lao Tan.[20]

Likewise, the *Han Fei Tzu* quotes twice from the *Lao Tzu* as words of Lao Tan.[21] The *Huai-nan Tzu*, too, quotes two passages from the *Lao Tzu* and says they are the words of Lao Tan [22] while other quotations from the *Lao Tzu* are stated as from Lao Tzu. Clearly Lao Tzu and Lao Tan are treated as one man in these books. The *Lü-shih ch'un-ch'iu* (Mr. Lü's Spring and Autumn Annals) mentions Lao Tan in a number of places.[23] In two of these, however, the Chinese character is *tan* rather than *Tan*.[24] Since the two characters were pronounced the same and meant the same thing, as Pi Yüan (1730-97) has pointed out,[25] evidently they were used interchangeably. In fact, the name, TAN, of the Grand Historian in the third account was also pronounced the same and meant "long ear." This immediately raises the question whether Grand Historian TAN was not the same person as Lao Tzu. This is a complicated problem which cannot be dealt with until we come to the third account.

The courtesy name Po-yang is definitely false. As Wang Nien-sun (1744-1832) has pointed out, the original edition of the *Records of the Historian* reads, "His private name was Erh, courtesy name Tan, and surname Li." Since Ssu-ma Chen (*fl.* 727) explicitly says in his *Shih chi so-yin* (Tracing the Hidden Meanings of the *Records of the Historian*) that the words "courtesy name Po-yang" were not correct, Wang has concluded that the name is a later addition.[26] In point of fact, the name comes from the *Shen-hsien chuan* (Biographies of Immortals), attributed to Ko Hung (253-333?).[27] It was added because there was a Po-yang in the eighth century B.C. who was reputed to have supernatural power and foreknowledge of the end of the Chou dynasty (1111-249 B.C.), and followers of the Taoist religion attempted to attribute this power and foreknowledge to Lao Tzu by giving him the name.[28]

The statement that Lao Tzu had a posthumous name is also false. Not only is there no posthumous name in the original edition of the *Records of the Historian;* it was also improper to confer a posthumous name on Lao Tzu because he was a commoner and not eligible for one, as Yao Nai has said.[29]

Even if his followers wanted to honor him by giving him such a name, Yao Nai has added, they would have given him a name describing his eminent virtue instead of his long ears.

Why has he been called Lao Tzu? Many attempts have been made to answer the question but none is really conclusive. The most common explanation is that of Cheng Hsüan (127-200), according to whom *lao* means "old age." [30] Ko Hsüan says that Lao Tzu was so called because when he was born, he was already old with white hair.[31] The latter theory is too fantastic to be taken seriously, whereas the former has been generally accepted.

There is also the theory that *lao* means "to inquire" and that Lao Tzu acquired his name because he penetrated and understood the principles of things.[32] This is a theory too speculative to be of any merit.

Modern scholars have not been satisfied with the interpretation of *lao* as meaning "old age," for there is no reason why of all old people this man alone was called Lao. Instead, Yao Nai thinks Lao was a surname because there was such a surname, in the state of Sung, which included P'ei where, according to the *Chuang Tzu*,[33] Confucius went to see Lao Tzu.[34] The trouble with this theory is that it does not explain why the *Records of the Historian* says his surname was Li. In trying to resolve the difficulty, Hu Shih suggests that Lao may have been the surname, and Li, the clan name. He thinks that although Lao Tzu was not a noble and was therefore not entitled to a clan name, he may have come from a large clan.[35] Hu also thinks that Lao may have been a courtesy name, for there was the practice, though unusual, in the Spring and Autumn period to put one's courtesy name before the honorific.[36] Ch'en Chu also believes Lao was a surname but for a different reason. He is of the opinion that *li* and *lao* were interchangeable because of their similar pronunciation and that is why he was called "Lao." [37] All these theories are speculative and have created as much uncertainty as they have attempted to remove.

As to the word *tzu*, aside from Yao Nai's theory that it is a surname, as noted above, Homer H. Dubs offers the novel interpretation that it may have the ordinary meaning of a viscount.[38] Evidently he was influenced by his belief that Lao Tzu's son was a general in the fourth century B.C. With these rare exceptions, scholars, both past and present, and both Asian and Western, are content with its being an honorific, meaning a gentleman, scholar, or master, as in the cases of Chuang Tzu, Hsün Tzu (fl. 298-238 B.C.), and the rest.

3. LAO TZU'S OCCUPATION

With reference to Lao Tzu's occupation, Ssu-ma Ch'ien says that he was a curator of archives (shou-ts'ang shih) in the Chou capital (present Loyang). The term the historian uses merely means a collector and curator, but Ssu-ma Chen in his Shih-chi so-yin says that it means a curator of books, evidently based on the story in the Chuang Tzu that Confucius wanted to deposit his writings in the capital through the good office of Lao Tzu.[39] Ssu-ma Chen further says that Lao Tzu was "a curator by the column" (chu-hsia shih) but K'ung Ying-ta (574-648), quoting the Records of the Historian, says that he was a "curator of books or a curator by the column." [40] There is no irreconcilable conflict between the two titles because the two offices were probably identical, for the phrase "by the column" may mean being near the columns of the palace, that is, an important office near the ruler, or it may literally mean that the collection was placed at the foot of the columns. Obviously in an unnecessary effort to reconcile the apparent conflict, the Lieh-hsien chuan (Biographies of the Many Immortals) says that he was first a curator of books and then "a curator by the columns." [41] According to Cheng Hsüan, he was a historian,[42] but as K'ung Ying-ta has pointed out, we don't know the basis for his assertion.

Most scholars have accepted the story that Lao Tzu was a curator of books, whether or not in an office by the columns. Wang Chung, however, is not willing to accept this story at all. He has rejected it because, he says, except in one case, people from the several states did not serve in the Chou capital, because books were in charge of historians whose positions were hereditary, and because an imperial officer cannot be called a recluse.[43] These arguments are not conclusive because, since he mentions one exception for people from the states serving in the capital of Chou, Lao Tzu could have been another. There is no evidence that books were exclusively in the care of historians, and it is not unreasonable to suppose that Lao Tzu became a recluse after he retired from office.

4. CONFUCIUS' VISIT TO LAO TZU

Wang's argument against certain aspects of Confucius' visit to Lao Tzu, however, is much more formidable. In the *Book of Rites,* there are four different passages quoting Lao Tan's words on funerals and mourning rites in which he is serious as well as meticulous.[44] The second passage says that when Confucius and Lao Tan were assisting at a funeral, there was an eclipse and Lao Tan told Confucius to have the bier stopped on the left of the road, for according to the rules of propriety, Lao Tan said, a superior man would not expose his relatives to darkness, which is evil. Wang Chung has noted [45] that Lao Tzu's serious regard for rules of propriety is entirely out of tune with his attack on them in chapter 38 of the *Lao Tzu.* Furthermore, Wang says, in the third passage Lao Tzu eulogizes the Duke of Chou (d. 1094 B.C.) and other wise men of the past, but in his writing he declares, "Unless sages are dead, great robbers will not stop." [46]

To Wang's argument Ts'ui Shu has added several more. He argues that Lao Tzu's lecture to Confucius during the visit is characterized by the literary style of the Warring States period rather than that of the Spring and Autumn period. He asks if Confucius was in fact a man of pride and many desires. And he wonders why the *Analects* makes no mention of Lao Tzu if Confucius had really praised him as a dragon.[47]

Whether there was a special literary style during the Warring States and what the absence of reference in the *Analects* means will be discussed later.[48] Clearly Ts'ui Shu had an entirely different image of Confucius as the sage from that of Lao Tzu. Confucius was not beyond criticism; for example, he was described as having good manners but no courage.[49] In the biography of Confucius, the *Records of the Historian* reports that Ching-shu asked the ruler of Lu to permit him to visit the capital of Chou with Confucius, that the ruler gave them a carriage with two horses and a page, and that their visit to the capital was for the purpose of consulting Lao Tzu on rules of propriety.[50] The *Records of the Historian* puts this story in the period between Confucius' ages of seventeen and thirty. Some writers have carelessly asserted that the visit took place when Confucius was seventeen, in 535 B.C. (Duke Chao, 7th year). As early as the eighth century, doubt was already expressed about this date. Ssu-ma Chen, commenting on the story, says that Confucius could not have visited Lao Tzu at that time because during his visit Confucius remarked to Lao Tzu, "It is difficult for the Way to prevail," [51] and this is not a likely expression of a seventeen-year-old but more appropriate after Confucius had served in the government.[52] Ssu-ma Chen's argument is based on the quotation from a spurious source and is therefore not dependable. That of Liang Yü-sheng (1745-1819), however, is more convincing, because he says that when Confucius was seventeen, Ching-shu had not yet been born.[53] It goes without saying that the theory that Confucius saw Lao Tzu at seventeen is untenable.

It has also been construed, from the story in the biography of Confucius, that he visited Lao Tzu at thirty, in 522 B.C. (Duke Chao, 20th year). But as Yen Jo-ch'ü (1636-1704) has pointed out, there was no eclipse in that year. He has therefore theorized that the visit took place in 518 B.C. (Duke Chao, 24th year), when Confucius was thirty-four, a year in which an eclipse did occur.[54]

One defect of Yen's theory, as Ts'ui has brought out, is that in that year Ching-shu was only thirteen and, furthermore, was in mourning. It is therefore most unlikely that he accompanied

Confucius on the journey.[55] Besides, during the reign of Duke Chao eclipses took place in 521 and 520, as well as in 518 B.C., and there is no reason why 518 had to be the year.

The *Chuang Tzu* says Confucius went at fifty-one, that is, in 501 B.C.[56] Many modern scholars have preferred this date.[57] As Ma Hsü-lun sees it, it fits in with a number of factors. Ching-shu was then thirty-one. Confucius had served in the government. And Lao Tzu was old and had retired, as the story in the *Chuang Tzu* says he did. Huang Fang-kuang (1901-45) has also pointed out [58] that the Confucian pupil, Tzu-kung (520-*c*.450 B.C.), was then thirty-one, which was why Lao Tzu called him a young fellow, according to the story in the *Chuang Tzu*. To the objection that Confucius was at that time a magistrate and could not very well travel, Ma replies that research has established that he did not become magistrate until the following year.[59] Nevertheless, one great difficulty remains, and that is, as Yen Jo-ch'ü has noted,[60] there was no eclipse in that year. The suggestion that perhaps Confucius saw Lao Tzu again in another year when there was an eclipse [61] seems to be assuming too much. Hu Shih thinks that the visit probably took place sometime between 518 and 511 B.C. when Confucius was thirty-four and forty-one, respectively.[62] As mentioned above, there were eclipses in both years.[63]

It is significant that in spite of these uncertainties about the date and the nature of the conversation, even rebels against tradition have not discarded the story of the visit entirely. Wang Chung is against Lao Tzu's lecture during the meeting but not the visit itself.[64] Ts'ui Shu rejects the meeting partly because of the lecture also, but he is willing to grant that Lao Tzu was an expert on ceremonies although he was skeptical even about that.[65] Both of them could not stand the thought that Confucius was taught a moral lesson; critical and independent thinkers as they were, they were not completely above partisanship. Hu Shih has not only accepted the story of the visit; he even thinks that Lao Tzu was a senior *ju* (literati), of which Confucius eventually became the leader of a new type.[66]

Those who have rejected the story of the visit have done so not so much on the basis of such details as the date and conversation but on the basis of the source of the story itself. Liang Ch'i-ch'ao was the one who led many writers in this direction. He presented six arguments against the whole biography of Lao Tzu. They are: (1) Lao Tzu's son, Tsung, lived too long after Confucius for Confucius and Lao Tzu to be contemporaneous. (2) Lao Tzu was never mentioned by Mo Tzu (*fl.* 479-438 B.C.) or Mencius. (3) Lao Tzu's words as recorded in the *Book of Rites* are inconsistent with those in the *Lao Tzu*. (4) A majority of the material in the biography comes from the *Chuang Tzu,* which is unreliable. (5) The ideas expressed in the *Lao Tzu* are too radical for the Spring and Autumn period. (6) There are many terms in the *Lao Tzu* belonging to the Warring States times.[67] The fifth and sixth arguments deal exclusively with the *Lao Tzu* and will be taken up later,[68] as will the first, which concerns Lao Tzu's genealogy.[69] In the third argument he repeats Wang Chung and Ts'ui Shu. His second argument, that Mencius and Mo Tzu have never mentioned Lao Tzu, is not conclusive because Mencius has never mentioned Hsün Tzu or Chuang Tzu either, and we cannot conclude for that reason that they were fictitious figures. Liang's strongest argument, and that which has been employed by many others, is the fourth, namely, that most of the material of the biography of Lao Tzu has been derived from the *Chuang Tzu.*[70] Scholars who have discarded either the story of the visit in particular, or of Lao Tzu as a person in general, have relied heavily on this argument.

The *Chuang Tzu* is held unreliable because it speaks of Confucius going west to deposit books in the imperial library,[71] suggesting, as Yao Nai has said, that it is a Han dynasty fabrication attempting to attribute to Confucius the foreknowledge of the Burning of Books in 213 B.C.[72] Furthermore, it mentions the "twelve classics" at a time when no book was known as a classic, much less a set of twelve. But Ssu-ma Ch'ien did not use this material at all. The *Chuang Tzu* says that at fifty-one Confucius went south to P'ei (in present Kiangsu) to see Lao

Tzu to learn the Way,[73] whereas Ssu-ma Ch'ien says he went before thirty to Chou to ask Lao Tzu about rules of propriety. The material about Lao Tzu's age and descendants did not come from the *Chuang Tzu*. One wonders if Ssu-ma Ch'ien did not purposely avoid the *Chuang Tzu* as the source. It is more probable that he derived his material from a long and general tradition about Lao Tzu and Confucius' visit to him. That Confucius learned from Lao Tzu is recorded many times in the *Chuang Tzu*,[74] once in the *Lü-shih ch'un-ch'iu*,[75] and four times in the *Book of Rites*.[76] That the two met is recorded three times in the *Chuang Tzu*,[77] and once in the *Book of Rites*.[78] These are sure indications that there was a widespread story about Lao Tzu from which Ssu-ma Ch'ien obtained the information which is not found in the *Chuang Tzu*. The most significant thing is that this tradition has been perpetuated by the Confucian school itself. Therefore we cannot dismiss it as a Taoist fabrication to glorify Lao Tzu as Confucius' teacher.

To accept the visit as true does not mean that Lao Tzu was necessarily the author of the *Lao Tzu*, of course. This question will be discussed in the next section on the book. Suffice it to say here that few scholars believe that Lao Tzu went through a pass and wrote a book at the request of the pass-keeper.[79]

5. LAO LAI TZU AND LAO P'ENG

Turning to the second account in the biography, that about Lao Lai Tzu, it does not present as much difficulty as the first. Why Ssu-ma Ch'ien included it in the biography is a mystery. Perhaps he meant to suggest that there was, at his time, some confusion about the two men. But certainly there was no confusion in his own mind, for not only does he tell of one as the author of a book in two parts dealing with the ideas of the Way and its virtue and the other as the author of a book in fifteen parts dealing with the applications of Taoist doctrines; he also clearly distinguishes them in his own *Records of the Historian*.[80]

Little is known of Lao Lai Tzu. Pi Yüan has asserted that

his surname was Lai, which was the surname of a number of people in ancient times,[81] and he was also called Lao because of his old age. Whether this is true or not, most authoritative Chinese scholars have been satisfied that Lao Tzu and Lao Lai Tzu were two different people.[82] Ch'ien Mu, however, contends that Lao Lai Tzu was the one whom Confucius visited. He based his contention on the account in the *Chuang Tzu* where Lao Lai Tzu is quoted as teaching Confucius to get rid of his pride and his air of wisdom.[83] But, as already indicated, Chuang Tzu often told imaginary tales. While this particular injunction is consonant with what Lao Tzu told Confucius, the rest of Lao Lai Tzu's words are not. Ch'ien himself is puzzled as to why, of the eleven worthies Confucius praised,[84] Lao Lai Tzu alone is not mentioned either in the *Analects* or in the *Tso chuan,* and his story appears for the first time in the *Chuang Tzu.*[85] Thus his own assertion has been made on shaky grounds. He also identifies Lao Lai Tzu with the old man, carrying across his shoulder on a staff a basket of weed, who advised Confucius to retire.[86] This identification is made on the flimsy ground that *lai* means "weeding," [87] which is hardly enough evidence to be convincing.

Lao Tzu has also been identified with the Lao referred to by Confucius when he compared himself with Lao P'eng.[88] Cheng Hsüan [89] and Wang Pi (226-49) [90] thought "Lao P'eng" was two persons instead of one, and identified "Lao" with Lao Tan and "P'eng" with P'eng-tsu, who lived many centuries earlier. These identifications are not supported by facts. Ma Hsü-lun thinks Lao P'eng was one man rather than two, but instead of P'eng-tsu, the legendary Methusaleh of China, as often understood, he believes he was Lao Tzu because, he says, the pronunciation of *p'eng* and *tan* was similar and he was called Lao Tan and Lao P'eng in two different dialects. In addition, he offers the argument that just as Lao P'eng is described by Confucius as a transmitter and not a creator, so Lao Tan, in quoting proverbs and ancient sayings, was not a creator.[91] Ma has to make a considerable effort in trying to establish that *p'eng* and *tan* were in fact similar in pronunciation. He has given some plausible examples but has not identified the dialects. As to Lao Tzu being a transmitter, by Ma's standard, anyone who quotes several ancient sayings becomes a transmitter and not a creator.[92]

6. THE GRAND HISTORIAN

The similarity of pronunciation has also played a great role in the discussions of the third account in the biography of Lao Tzu. This account deals with Grand Historian TAN and Lao Tzu's son, Tsung. Ssu-ma Ch'ien states that TAN had an interview with Duke Hsien of Ch'in in 374 B.C., but is not sure if TAN was Lao Tzu, for some people said yes and others said no. It has been two thousand years since Ssu-ma Ch'ien, but we are just as uncertain as he was. Some say TAN and Lao Tan were the same person, because the words TAN, *Tan* and *tan*, according to Pi Yüan, were all identical in pronunciation as well as in meaning and were interchangeable.[93] Others, however, have contended that they were two different people but because of the similarity of their names, plus the fact that both were officials and both traveled west, became confused as one.[94]

Wang Chung has maintained that Lao Tzu was none other than TAN. He says that according to the *Lieh Tzu*, there are three conversations between Lieh Tzu (450-375 B.C.) and Kuan Yin, keeper of the pass.[95] In the *Wen Tzu*, Lao Tzu is quoted as referring to the alliance between the states of Wei, Ch'u, and others.[96] Since Lieh Tzu lived in the fourth century B.C. and the alliance also took place in that period, Wang argues, Lao Tzu must have been TAN who interviewed Duke Hsien and could not have been Tan whom Confucius visited. Unfortunately for the argument, both the *Lieh Tzu* and *Wen Tzu* are spurious works and untrustworthy as evidence.

Whether Grand Historian TAN was Lao Tzu depends very much on whose son Tsung was. Ssu-ma Ch'ien merely says he was the son of Lao Tzu, and it can be taken to mean either Tan or TAN. From the context of the biography, and according to most scholars, he meant the former if the two men were different. But in this case we face a number of difficulties. It will be recalled that Liang Ch'i-ch'ao's first argument against the biography is that Lao Tzu's son lived too long after Confucius for Confucius and Lao Tzu to be contemporaneous. He says that since Lao Tzu's eight-generation descendant, Chia, was an official in about 160 B.C., it would mean there were only eight generations compared with thirteen generations in Confucius' family in the same period. This means an average of about half a century for each generation in the Lao family line, a most unlikely event.[97]

Actually, in many Chinese clans, generations overlap by as many as five generations. This is the case in my own clan, but it has taken eight hundred years for it to make the difference. We could accept Ssu-ma Ch'ien's report that Lao Tzu lived to be one-hundred-sixty or even two hundred years old, but even he was not sure of it. Any argument based on such an improbability is very weak indeed.

If Tsung was not the son of Lao Tzu, was he the son of Grand Historian TAN? The answer of Wang Chung,[98] Dubs,[99] Lo Ken-tse,[100] Kao Heng,[101] and others is affirmative. It is generally agreed that Tsung was none other than Ch'ung, whose clan name was Tuan-kan. According to the *Chan-kuo ts'e* (Strategy of the Warring States) [102] he was sent as a general to make peace with Ch'in a year after his state, Wei, was defeated by Ch'in in 273 B.C. This identification has been made by Yao Fan (1702-71) [103] and Wang Chung, and has been accepted by Kao Heng and Lo Ken-tse, among others. In an explanation of the identification, Yao says that *tsung* and *ch'ung* were pronounced alike and were interchangeable, and he quotes as evidence a passage from the *Book of History* in which the word *ch'ung* occurs and the same passage in the *History of the Former Han Dynasty* in which this *ch'ung* is replaced by *tsung*. Dubs has also made the identification independently. To him the fact that both were generals in the same state and bore the same clan name of a fief is compelling evidence that they were the same person.[104]

Some, like Ch'ien Mu,[105] have objected that between the peace conference in 273 B.C. and TAN's interview with Duke Hsien in 374 B.C., there was a lapse of one hundred and one years, and Tsung would have been too old to be a general. But Kao Heng has figured out that if the interview took place when TAN was thirty, and his son Tsung was born when TAN was sixty, Tsung would have been seventy-one when he sued for peace, not too old an age for a highly responsible general.[106]

Kao Heng's calculation is not too unreasonable. However, even if this calculation is accepted, another difficulty still remains. As Chang Ping-lin (1868-1936) has pointed out, the *Records of the Historian* mentions one Tuan-kan Mu as teacher of Duke Wen (reigned 410-387 B.C.) and one Tuan-kan P'eng.[107] Since Tuan-kan was a clan name given one when he was enfeoffed, and since Tsung was enfeoffed Tuan-kan, he must have been the first one to be so named and therefore he must have lived before Duke Wen's time.[108] According to Ch'ien Mu, Tuan-kan Mu lived about 465-395 B.C.[109] This means that Tsung lived in the fifth or sixth century B.C. and was, therefore, the son of Lao Tan instead of TAN. It is possible to suppose, as Bodde has said, that the first Tuan-kan line died off, thus permitting Tsung's enfeoffment with the same name for an entirely new family line.[110] But, as Bodde has added, until further proof can be advanced, this can only remain a hypothesis. If it is argued that Wei did not become a state until 403 B.C. and could not have had any general, much less a fief, the reply is that Wei was virtually a state during the reign of King Yüan (reigned 475-469 B.C.), and by 454 already had its own prime minister. It is therefore not unreasonable to suppose that it also had a general shortly before.[111]

7. SUMMARY AND CONCLUSION

Much of the above discussion is speculative. No argument on either side of the controversy is based on concrete evidence or is really conclusive. It is clear that none of the important facts about Lao Tzu's life—his curatorship, his meeting with Confucius, his identification with Grand Historian TAN, and his relationship with Tsung—can be completely affirmed or entirely denied on such a basis. Under such circumstances, scholars can accept the biography without question, on the assumption that Ssu-ma Ch'ien was in general a very reliable historian and was some two thousand years closer to the events, and that, essentially speaking, we have no more information than he had. Few modern scholars, if any, are faithful to tradition to this extent. Practically everyone has raised some question, however minor, about the biography. Scholars can also dismiss the entire biography as fiction. The first one to do so was the Japanese scholar Itō Rangu (1693-1778), who regarded the biography as fiction on the grounds that neither Confucius nor Mencius mentioned him and that the Lao Tzu mentioned in the *Hsün Tzu* [112] is a mistake for someone else. The latter statement is a purely arbitrary assertion and the first argument is inconclusive.[113] To be consistent, scholars who dismiss Lao Tzu as fictitious should also dismiss Chuang Tzu and many ancient philosophers, including Mo Tzu and perhaps Mencius, as fictitious, for the sources of their biographies are not much different from that of Lao Tzu, and as in the case of Lao Tzu, Ssu-ma Ch'ien was their first and chief biographer. In fact, much of ancient Chinese history would have to be rejected. No scholar has gone this far. Between these two extremes, scholars can accept certain parts of the biography that seem to them most reasonable or most suitable to their own theory, and then try to substantiate or justify them. This has been done by most scholars.

In any case, a decision has been arrived at chiefly through a willingness or unwillingness to accept certain sources as reliable and certain circumstances as evidential. In the final analysis, any theory about Lao Tzu is a matter of personal choice. It may be helpful to list the various choices and their outstanding representatives. The chosen theories are as follows:

A. Lao Tzu was Lao Tan of the sixth century B.C. whom Confucius visited.
   1. He was author of the *Lao Tzu* and was identical with Grand Historian TAN (Pi Yüan).[114]
   2. He was author of the *Lao Tzu* and a senior *ju* (literati) of the type of which Confucius eventually became the leader (Hu Shih).[115]
   3. He was author of the *Lao Tzu* (Huang Fang-kuang).[116]
   4. He was author of the *Lao Tzu* but different from TAN (Ma Hsü-lun,[117] Ch'en Chu,[118] Kao Heng [119]).
   5. His sayings were collected by someone later (Kuo Mo-jo).[120]

B. Lao Tzu lived in the Spring and Autumn period but was not author of the *Lao Tzu*.
   1. He lived before Mo Tzu (5th-4th centuries B.C.), but never wrote a book. Confucius never visited him, but he may or may not have been an expert on ceremonies (Ts'ui Shu).[121]
   2. He saw Confucius in 501 B.C., but the book was written toward the end of the Warring States period (Liang Ch'i-ch'ao).[122]
   3. He was identical with Lao Lai Tzu (6th century B.C.), but the author of the *Lao Tzu* was probably Chan Ho (350-270 B.C.) (Ch'ien Mu).[123]

C. Lao Tzu lived in the Warring States period (403-222 B.C.).
   1. He was identical with the Grand Historian TAN (Lo Ken-tse,[124] Dubs [125]).
   2. He was identical with TAN, author of the *Lao Tzu*, but different from Lao Tan whom Confucius visited (Wang Chung).[126]
   3. He was identical with Li Erh of the Warring States period, but it is not sure if there was a Lao Tan of Confucius' time (Fung Yu-lan).[127]
   4. He lived after Yang Chu (4th century B.C.) and was not author of the *Lao Tzu* (Ku Chieh-kang).[128]

D. Lao Tzu is legendary (Arthur Waley,[129] Itō Rangu,[130] Tsuda Sōkichi [1872-1961],[131] Hou Wai-lu [132]).

It may safely be said that those who believe Lao Tzu lived in the Spring and Autumn period and those who believe he lived in the Warring States period are about equal in number. Only a very, very small minority has treated him as a myth. I believe it is highly probable that Lao Tzu was a curator of archives, for I cannot think of any motive for the fabrication of the myth, if he was not. It is even more probable that Confucius visited him, or else the Confucian school would not have perpetuated the story. That Tsung was the son of a certain Lao Tzu seems to be quite sure, for the genealogy is clear and definite. It is not unreasonable to suppose that Grand Historian TAN was a historical figure, was Tsung's father, and because of his similarity with Lao Tan in more than one respect, was confused with him. As to the book, it is, as will be shown in the next section, a product of a long evolution, although it embodies the basic teachings of Lao Tan.

All this is no more than a belief, but so is every other theory.

NOTES

1. For an account of the opinions of these Neo-Confucianists, see Lo Ken-tse, *Chu-tzu k'ao-so* (Inquiry on Ancient Philosophers), pp. 258-61. Lo has written a comprehensive chronological account of the whole controversy (pp. 257-81). A shorter, systematic account is found in *Lao Tzu che-hsüeh t'ao-lun chi* (Symposium on the Philosophy of Lao Tzu), pp. 1-7.
2. *Hsi-hsüeh chi-yen* (Notes from Study and Recitation), 15:1b.
3. *Chu Tzu wen-chi* (Collection of Literary Works by Chu Hsi), 74:11b.
4. Modern Lu-i County in eastern central Honan province.
5. *Analects*, 15:39.
6. *Shih chi* (Records of the Historian), 63:1a-3b.

7. For detailed discussions on Lao Tzu's native district, see Ma Hsü-lun, *Lao Tzu chiao-ku* (*Lao Tzu* Collated and Explained), pp. 20-30, and Kao Heng, *Ch'ung-ting Lao Tzu cheng-ku* (Revised Collation of the *Lao Tzu*), pp. 153-60.

8. *Shih chi*, 130:93a.

9. *Lao Tzu chang-i* (Commentary on the *Lao Tzu*), Preface, 1a.

10. *Lao Tzu chiao-ku*, p. 21.

11. *Ch'ung-ting Lao Tzu cheng-ku*, p. 157.

12. Duke Min, 2nd year.

13. In the commentary on the *Lü-shih ch'un-ch'iu* (Mr. Lü's Spring and Autumn Annals), ch. 3, sec. 3, *SPPY*, 3:6a.

14. *Ch'ung-ting Lao Tzu cheng-ku*, p. 157.

15. *Ibid.*

16. In thirteen chapters, namely, 3, 5, 7, 11-14, 21-23, 25, 27, and 33.

17. Chs. 13, 14, and 21, *SPTK*, 5:29b-30b, 5:43b-51a, 7:33a. See Giles (tr.), *Chuang Tzu*, pp. 136, 147-49, and 202, respectively.

18. Ch. 22, *SPTK*, 7:45a; Giles, p. 213.

19. Chs. 14 (twice), 23, and 27, *SPTK*, 5:43b, 5:49b, 8:1a-6a, 9:17a. See Giles, pp. 147, 151, 221-24, and 269.

20. Ch. 27, *SPTK*, 9:17b (Giles, pp. 269-70), quoting from *Lao Tzu*, ch. 41. Ch. 33, *SPTK*, 10:35b (Giles, p. 320), quoting from *Lao Tzu*, ch. 28.

21. Chs. 31 and 46, *SPTK* 10:1a, 2b, 18:4a (Liao [tr.], *The Complete Works of Han Fei Tzu*, II, 1-6, 246), quoting from *Lao Tzu*, chs. 36 and 44, respectively.

22. *Huai-nan Tzu*, 1:10b and 12:2b (Morgan [tr.], *Tao, The Great Luminant*, pp. 17 and 105), quoting from the *Lao Tzu*, chs. 43 and 14, respectively.

23. Ch. 1, sec. 4; ch. 2, sec. 4; ch. 13, sec. 3; ch. 17, sec. 7; and ch. 18, sec. 2; *SPPY*, 1:9a, 2:9b, 13:6b, 17:15b, and 18:5a, respectively. See Richard Wilhelm (tr.), *Frühling und Herbst des Lü Bu We*, pp. 10, 24, 166, 285, and 297, respectively.

24. Chs. 17 and 18.

25. *Lao Tzu tao-te ching k'ao-i* (Inquiry into Variants in the *Lao Tzu*, the Classic of the Way and Its Virtue), Preface, 1a.

26. *Tu-shu tsa-chi* (Miscellaneous Notes from Reading), Bk. II, sec. 4, p. 78.

27. *Shen-hsien chuan*, ch. 1, Biography of Lao Tzu.

28. For the attribution of an earlier name of Po-yang to Lao Tzu, see Kao Heng, *Ch'ung-ting Lao Tzu cheng-ku*, pp. 159-60. See also Ma Hsü-lun, *Lao Tzu chiao-ku*, pp. 21-23, about the name.

29. *Lao Tzu chang-i*, Preface, 2b.

30. In his commentary on ch. 7 of the *Book of Rites*.

31. In his preface to the Ho-shang Kung text of the *Lao Tzu*.

32. A theory of one Chang Chun-hsiang, quoted in the biography of Lao Tzu in Chang Shou-chieh's *Shih chi cheng-i* (Correct Meanings of the *Records of the Historian*). Nothing is known of Chang Chun-hsiang.

33. *Chuang Tzu*, ch. 14, *SPTK*, 5:43b (Giles, p. 147).

34. Yao Nai, *Lao Tzu chang-i*, Preface, 2b.

35. *Chung-kuo che-hsüeh shih ta-kang*, p. 49.

36. *Ibid*.

37. *Lao-hsüeh pa-p'ien* (Eight Essays on the Study of Lao Tzu), p. 12. He has been followed by Kao Heng in his *Ch'ung-ting Lao Tzu cheng-ku*, p. 157.

38. "The Date and Circumstances of the Philosopher Lao-dz," *Journal of the American Oriental Society*, LXI (1941), 221.

39. Ch. 13, *SPTK*, 5:29b. See Giles, p. 136.

40. In his *Li chi cheng-i* (Correct Meanings of the *Book of Rites*), 18:11b. The quotation does not appear in the present *Records of the Historian* but may have in the original edition.

41. In its biography of Lao Tzu. The *Li-hsien chuan* is attributed to Liu Hsiang (77-6 B.C.).

42. Cheng Hsüan's commentary on the *Analects*, quoted by K'ung Ying-ta.

43. *Shu-hsüeh* (Notes from Studies), Supplement, 27b.

44. "Questions of Tseng Tzu," secs. 16, 32, 34, and 36. See Legge (tr.), *The Li Ki*, "Sacred Books of the East," XXVII, 325, 338-39, 340-41, 341-42, respectively.

45. *Shu-hsüeh*, Supplement, 27a.

46. This is from the *Chuang Tzu*, ch. 10, *SPTK*, 4:20a. Cf. Giles (tr.), *Chuang Tzu*, p. 102. For a similar but less emphatic saying, see *Lao Tzu*, chapter 19.

47. *Chu-Ssu k'ao-hsin lu* (Inquiry into the True Facts Concerning Confucius), 1:12b-13a.

48. See below, pp. 63, 65-66.

49. *Tso chuan*, Duke Ting, 10th year.

50. *Shih chi,* 47:3a-b. See Chavannes (tr.), *Les mémoires historiques de Se-ma Ts'ien,* V, 299-300, or Lin Yutang (ed. and tr.), *The Wisdom of Confucius,* pp. 57-58.

51. According to the *K'ung Tzu chia-yü* (School Sayings of Confucius), ch. 11, *SPTK,* 3:4b. See C. de Harlez (tr.), "Familiar Sayings of Kong Fu Tze," *The Babylonian and Oriental Record,* VII (1893), 69.

52. In his *Shih chi so-yin.* See *Shih chi,* 47:3b.

53. *Shih chi chih-i* (Doubts on the *Records of the Historian*), 25:6a.

54. *Ssu-shu shih-ti* (Explanations of Geographical Terms in the *Four Books*), Supplement, section on Confucius visiting Chou.

55. *Chu-Ssu k'ao-hsin lu,* 1:13b.

56. Ch. 14, *SPTK,* 5:43b (Giles, p. 147).

57. Including Liang Yü-sheng (*Shih chi chi-i,* 25:6b), Ma Hsü-lun (*Lao Tzu chiao-ku,* p. 29) and Kao Heng (*Ch'ung-ting Lao Tzu cheng-ku,* p. 166).

58. In *Ku-shih pien* (Discussion on Ancient History), IV, 380.

59. *Lao Tzu chiao-ku,* p. 29.

60. *Ssu-shu shih-ti,* Supplement, *ibid.*

61. Huang Fang-kuang in *Ku-shih pien,* IV, 380-81, and Kao Heng, *Ch'ung-ting Lao Tzu cheng-ku,* pp. 164-66.

62. *Chung-kuo che-hsüeh shih ta-kang,* pp. 47-48.

63. The suggestion by Ku Te-tseng that Confucius went at seventy-one is hardly worth considering. See Leng Ch'ing-hsiao, *Lao Tzu hsüeh-an* (Study on Lao Tzu), pp. 9-10.

64. *Shu-hsüeh,* Supplement, 28b.

65. *Chu-Ssu k'ao-hsin lu,* 1:14a.

66. *Hu Shih lun-hsüeh chin-chu* (Recent Essays on Learned Subjects by Hu Shih), pp. 69-72.

67. *Liang Jen-kung hsüeh-shu yen-chiang chi* (Collection of Liang Ch'i-ch'ao's Lectures on Learned Subjects), I, 18-19.

68. See below, pp. 68-71.

69. See above, pp. 48-50.

70. According to Liang, from chs. 13, 14, and 26, *SPTK,* 5:29b-31a, 43b-51a, 9:4b-6b. Giles, pp. 136-38, 147-51, 261-62.

71. Ch. 13, *SPTK,* 5:29b. Giles, pp. 136-37.

72. *Lao Tzu chang-i,* Preface, 2b. See also Wang Hsien-ch'ien (1842-1917), *Chuang Tzu chi-chieh* (Collected Explanations of the *Chuang Tzu*), p. 77.

73. Ch. 14, *SPTK,* 5:43b. Giles, p. 147.

74. Chs. 12, 13, 14, 21, and 22, *SPTK*, 5:9b, 29b, 43b, 7:33a, 46a. Giles, pp. 123, 136-37, 147, 202, and 213.

75. Ch. 2, sec. 4, *SPPY*, 2:9b. See above, note 23.

76. See above, note 44.

77. Besides chapters 13 and 14, already referred to (note 17 above), it is also mentioned in chapter 21, *SPTK*, 7:33a; Giles, p. 202.

78. "Question of Tseng Tzu," sec. 32. Legge, *The Li Ki*, pp. 338-39.

79. For good accounts of Lao Tzu's occupation and Confucius' visit, see Ma Hsü-lun, *Lao Tzu chiao-ku*, pp. 25-30; Kao Heng, *Ch'ung-ting Lao Tzu cheng-ku*, pp. 160-67; and Ch'ien Mu, *Hsien-Ch'in chu-tzu hsi-nien* (Chronological Studies of the Pre-Ts'in Philosophers), pp. 4-8.

80. *Shih chi*, 63:2b.

81. *Lao Tzu tao-te ching k'ao-i*, Preface, 1b.

82. See Ma Hsü-lun, *Lao Tzu chiao-ku*, pp. 10-11.

83. *Chuang Tzu*, ch. 26, *SPTK*, 9:5b. Cf. Giles, p. 261.

84. In *Ta-Tai li chi* (Book of Rites by the Elder Tai), ch. 60, *SPTK*, 6:8a-9b.

85. *Hsien-Ch'in chu-tzu hsi-nien*, p. 213.

86. *Analects*, 18:7.

87. *Hsien-Ch'in chu-tzu hsi-nien*, pp. 213-14.

88. *Analects*, 7:1.

89. Quoted by Lu Te-ming (556-627) in his *Ching-tien shih-wen* (Explanation of Words in the Classics), ch. 24, explaining *Analects*, 7:1.

90. Quoted by Hsing Ping (932-1010) in his commentary on *Analects*, 7:1.

91. *Lao Tzu chiao-ku*, pp. 13-18.

92. For further discussions on Lao P'eng, see Ch'ien Mu, *Hsien-Ch'in chu-tzu hsi-nien*, pp. 220-21.

93. *Lao Tzu tao-te ching k'ao-i*, Preface, 1a.

94. For this viewpoint, see Kao Heng, *Ch'ung-ting Lao Tzu cheng-ku*, pp. 186-87.

95. Chs. 2:2b and 8:1a-b. See Graham, *The Book of Lieh Tzu*, pp. 37, 158-61.

96. *Wen Tzu*, ch. 2, *SPPY*, Pt. I, 13b.

97. See above, note 67. The suggestion of Chang Hsü (*Ku-shih pien*, IV, 313) that the word *hsüan* (great-great-grandson) means distant is farfetched.

98. *Lao Tzu k'ao-i* (Inquiry into the Errors about Lao Tzu), in the Supplement to his *Shu-hsüeh*, p. 28b.

99. "The Date and Circumstances of the Philosopher Lao-dz," *Journal of the American Oriental Society*, LXI (1941), 215-21.

100. *Chu-tzu k'ao-so*, p. 225.

101. *Ch'ung-ting Lao Tzu cheng-ku*, pp. 186-87.

102. Compiled by Liu Hsiang.

103. *Yüan-ch'un-t'ang pi-chi* (Notes from the Quails-aiding Hall), 16:7b.

104. *Journal of the American Oriental Society*, LXI (1941), 219.

105. *Hsien-Ch'in chu-tzu hsi-nien*, p. 222.

106. *Ch'ung-ting Lao Tzu cheng-ku*, p. 187.

107. *Shih chi*, 44:3b and 46:11b. See Chavannes (tr.), *Les mémoires historiques de Se-ma Ts'ien*, V, 141, 240.

108. Chang Ping-lin, *Tao-han wei-yen* (Subtle Words of Chang Ping-lin), 29b-30a.

109. *Hsien-Ch'in chu-tzu hsi-nien*, p. 616.

110. "The New Identification of Lao Tzu Proposed by Professor Dubs," *Journal of the American Oriental Society*, LXII (1942), 11.

111. Ho Tun-weng, *Lao Tzu hsin-i* (New Explanation of the *Lao Tzu*), Supplement, p. 28.

112. *Hsün Tzu*, ch. 17, *SPTK*, 11:25a. See Dubs (tr.), *The Works of Hsüntze*, p. 184.

113. Itō's manuscript on Lao Tzu seen by Takeuchi and quoted in his *Rōshi no kenkyū* (Study of the *Lao Tzu*), I, 150-51.

114. *Lao Tzu tao-te ching k'ao-i*, Preface, 1a-b.

115. *Chung-kuo che-hsüeh shih ta-kang*, pp. 47-49; *Hu Shih lun-hsüeh chin-chu*, pp. 69-73.

116. In *Ku-shih pien*, IV, 362-63, 381.

117. *Lao Tzu chiao-ku*, pp. 11-13, 18-19.

118. *Lao Tzu*, pp. 10-11.

119. *Ch'ung-ting Lao Tzu cheng-ku*, pp. 186-87.

120. *Ch'ing-t'ung shih-tai* (Bronze Age), pp. 245-46. See also, below, p. 73.

121. *Chu-Ssu k'ao-hsin lu*, 1:14a.

122. *Lao Tzu che-hsüeh* (Philosophy of Lao Tzu), p. 1, and *Liang Jen-kung hsüeh-shu yen-chiang chi*, I, 18-21.

123. *Hsien-Ch'in chu-tzu hsi-nien,* pp. 212-13, 224. See also, below, p. 73.

124. *Chu-tzu k'ao-so,* p. 279.

125. *Journal of the American Oriental Society,* LXI (1941), 217-9. For further discussion, see the same journal, LXII (1942), 8-12, 300-4; LXIV (1944), 24-27.

126. *Shu-hsüeh,* Supplement, 28a-b.

127. *A History of Chinese Philosophy,* I, 172.

128. *Ku-shih pien,* IV, 500-1.

129. *The Way and Its Power,* pp. 106-8.

130. See Takeuchi, *Rōshi no kenkyū,* I, 150-51.

131. *Dōke no shisō to sono tenkai* (Taoist Thought and Its Development), p. 27. For a brief summary of Japanese scholars' theories on Lao Tzu, the person, see Yamada Sumeru, *Rōshi* (Lao Tzu), p. 33.

132. *Chung-kuo ku-tai ssu-hsiang hsüeh-shuo shih* (History of Ancient Chinese Thought and Theories), pp. 9-11, 159.

III. *Lao Tzu, the Book*

As an integral part of the problem of Lao Tzu, the problem of the book, called the *Lao Tzu,* or the *Tao-te ching* (Classic of the Way and Its Virtue), is equally complex and controversial. Perhaps it is more so because it deals with such intangibles as literary style and ideas, and as a book it has many irregularities. The number of its words varies from 5227 to 5722, although it is usually called the 5000-word classic and followers of the Taoist religion have actually made attempts to reduce the number to exactly 5000.[1] Most of the variants concern only auxiliary words, interchangeable terms, and synonyms, it is true, but as we shall see, certain discrepancies have created serious problems. The style of the book is most indefinite. Almost all the chapters are rhymed,[2] but the rhyming scheme comes in many patterns.[3] Its sentences, containing many couplets,[4] may be long or short, difficult or easy, simple or complex, and its expressions may be concise or elaborate. Its several quotations[5] complicate rather than simplify matters because their sources are not certain and they may not be quotations at all. There is not a single dialogue, historical event, or proper noun to provide a clue for its date or author. Instead, it contains many repetitions and contradictions to increase our difficulty.[6] Many sayings attributed to Lao Tzu in other books are not found here.

1. REACTIONS AGAINST TRADITION

All these complications have provided a fertile ground for endless debate. As in the case of Lao Tzu, the man, for centuries the tradition that the book was written by Lao Tzu of the sixth century B.C.[7] was accepted without question. However, skepticism about the book grew much earlier than that about the man, for as early as the fifth century its authorship was questioned.[8] Later, when Neo-Confucianists raised doubts about the date of Lao Tzu, they doubted the date of the book also.[9] Wang Chung, Ts'ui Shu, and other eighteenth-century critical scholars carried the skepticism to a higher degree. How, Wang asks, could Lao Tzu, an advocate of rules of propriety, have been the author of a book that attacks them? [10] To Ts'ui Shu, the style of the book is similar to that of the Warring States period (403-222 B.C.) and utterly different from that of the *Analects* of the Spring and Autumn period (722-481 B.C.).[11]

In Japan, Saitō Setsudō (1787-1865) said the book could not have been earlier than the Warring States period because it contains the combined term "humanity and righteousness," which was not used earlier, and also because it opposed ruinous wars and oppressive laws, which were current at the time.[12]

These observations had subjected the tradition to serious questioning, but it was not until 1922, when Liang Ch'i-ch'ao threw overboard the whole tradition about Lao Tzu, that the foundation of the tradition about the book was thoroughly shaken.

Liang directed two of his six arguments against tradition specifically at the book. One is that the ideas in the *Lao Tzu* are too radical for the Spring and Autumn period and the other is that the book contains terms which surely date it in the Warring States times.[13] Since his famous attack, scholars have been divided into two camps, those who put the book in the Spring and Autumn days and those who assign it to the age of the Warring States.

Scholars who have favored the later period have each chosen their own date within that period. They have tried to outbid each other in being as late as possible. Some, like Lo Ken-tse [14] and Hou Wai-lu,[15] have put the *Lao Tzu* after Confucius (551-479 B.C.) and Mo Tzu (*fl.* 479-380 B.C.) but before Mencius (371-289 B.C.) and Chuang Tzu (between 399 and 295 B.C.). Others have assigned it to the latter part of the Warring States period, or about 250 B.C. This group includes prominent scholars like Liang Ch'i-ch'ao, Ch'ien Mu, Fung Yu-lan, Duyvendak

(1889-1954), and Arthur Waley. Ch'ien specifically puts it after the completion of the "inner chapters" of the *Chuang Tzu*.[16] Fung Yu-lan at first dated it after Mencius, or about 300 B.C., but later postponed it to the time after Hui Shih (308-305? B.C.). and Kung-sun Lung (b. 380? B.C.), or about 250 B.C.[17] Duyvendak dates it after 300 B.C., and Waley puts it about 240 B.C.[18] Ku Chieh-keng [19] has gone so far as to place it between the *Lü-shih ch'un-ch'iu* (Mr. Lü's Spring and Autumn Annals) and the *Huai-nan Tzu*, or between 200 and 150 B.C.[20] On the other side, Hu Shih,[21] Kuo Mo-jo,[22] Ma Hsü-lun,[23] and others have upheld the tradition that the *Lao Tzu* is a product of the Spring and Autumn period.[24]

2. ARGUMENTS ABOUT CONTEMPORARY REFERENCES

Arguments on both sides surround the questions of contemporary reference, style, terminology, individual authorship, and ideas. We shall take them up one by one.

With regard to contemporary reference, it is not denied that the sayings of Lao Tzu were widely known in ancient China. Twenty-two of them are quoted in the *Chuang Tzu*.[25] Hsün Tzu does not quote any, but criticizes Lao Tzu for "having insight about bending but not about expending," [26] indicating that he was familiar with the thoughts of Lao Tzu. Han Fei wrote two chapters commenting on Lao Tzu's sayings [27] and quotes him several times.[28] The *Chan-kuo ts'e* [29] and the *Lü-shih ch'un-ch'iu* [30] also quote him. But all these works belong to the Warring States period, not to the Spring and Autumn period in which tradition has dated the *Lao Tzu*. One of Ts'ui Shu's arguments against the traditional date of the *Lao Tzu*, it will be recalled, is its lack of contemporary reference. Liang Ch'i-ch'ao has repeated the argument. "Why is there no trace of it in the *Analects*, the *Book of Mencius*, and the *Mo Tzu?*" he asks.[31]

The answer is that if one argues that the *Lao Tzu* did not exist because the *Analects*, for example, contains no trace of it, one can also argue the other way, that the *Analects* did not exist because the *Lao Tzu* makes no mention of it. Besides, parts of many ancient works, which might have referred to it, have been lost. The *Mo Tzu,* for example, once had 71 chapters [32] but now has only 53. It happens, however, that a missing part of it did quote the *Lao Tzu.*[33] There are also cases where quotations are not included in the present text. Mencius quotes Confucius' sayings, a number of which are not found in the *Analects.*[34] Quite aside from this, the absence of quotation from a work or reference to it in contemporary texts does not necessarily mean that it did not exist. We are sure that Mencius and Chuang Tzu lived at the same time but neither one refers to the other. Nor does Mencius mention Hsün Tzu although Hsün Tzu criticizes him at length.[35] Neither Mencius nor Chuang Tzu is quoted or mentioned in the *Han Fei Tzu* or the *Chan-kuo ts'e.*

Ch'ien Mu's chief argument is that quotations of Lao Tzu in the "inner chapters" of the *Chuang Tzu* [36] are not found in the present *Lao Tzu.*[37] All quotations from the present *Lao Tzu* occur in the "outer" and "miscellaneous" chapters (8-33), which are generally considered as later works. But whether the outer chapters are authentic or not is still an open question. Ku Chieh-kang considers quotations in the *Lü-shih ch'un-ch'iu* as unreliable because, he says, it is a "rule" in that book that whenever a quotation is made, its source or author is always mentioned, but no such mention is made of Lao Tzu even though "two-thirds" of the *Lao Tzu* has been incorporated into it.[38] But as Hu Shih has convincingly shown, there is no "rule" of any kind in the *Lü-shih ch'un-ch'iu* about quotations. It mentions the *Book of Filial Piety* in connection with one quotation from it but not with another. Of the 53 passages which Ku has claimed to be identical with or similar to Lao Tzu's sayings, actually only three are quotations from the *Lao Tzu.*[39]

From the above, it is clear that it is incorrect to conclude that a work did not exist simply because contemporary works do not refer to it.

3. ARGUMENTS ABOUT STYLE

Both Ku Chieh-kang and Fung Yu-lan depend heavily on style for their arguments. Ku contends that the *Lao Tzu* is in the style of a prose-poem,[40] and Fung contends that it is not in the dialogue form but in the simple style of a classic.[41] These styles, they say, show that it is a product of the Warring States period. As Hu Shih has clearly demonstrated, these scholars are simply begging the question. Their major premise that these styles belong to the Warring States period is by no means proved. Furthermore, no one really knows what a "simple style of a classic" is. If chapter 1 of the *Lao Tzu* is of such a style, Hu argues, then *Analects*, 2:3, is also of this same style. If, as Fung says, the *Lao Tzu* must be later than the *Analects* and the *Book of Mencius* because it is not in the dialogue style, then, Hu counters, the ancient odes must also be later. Besides, most of the *Analects* is not in the dialogue form. As Hu has pointed out, only one of 16 chapters in Book I, one out of 26 in Book II, and seven out of 37 in Book IV are conversations. As to Ku's prose-poem style, which he conceives to consist of rhyme, description, and the use of the exclamatory particles of *hsi* and *hu*, Hu reminds us that many ancient odes are rhymed descriptions [42] and that descriptions and exclamatory particles are also employed in the *Analects*.[43] Hu is certainly sound when he states that it is not easy for us to determine just when a certain style comes into use, for it goes through a long period of evolution.[44]

It is also contended that the employment of rhyme and the practice of stating the subject in the beginning sentence originated in the age of the Warring States. Since these are features of the *Lao Tzu*, it is argued, it must be a product of that period. But it is not sure that the use of rhyme started in the Warring States period. Aside from ancient odes, many passages in the *Book of History* and in the text of the *Book of Changes*,[45] and even some chapters in the *Analects*,[46] are rhymed. As to stating the subject, many of Mo Tzu's essays do so in the beginning. But the point is that the first sentence of the *Lao Tzu* does state the subject of the book.

4. ARGUMENTS ABOUT TERMINOLOGY

Turning to terminology, some scholars, like Waley, have argued that certain words used in the *Lao Tzu* prove it to be a third-century B.C. product. In this they have relied on Karlgren. By using nine tests, Karlgren has found that the *Chuang Tzu,* the *Lü-shih ch'un-ch'iu,* the *Chan-kuo ts'e,* the *Hsün Tzu,* and the *Han Fei Tzu* have a common language. (1) It has both *jo* and *ju* for "like" and "as." (2), (3) It has neither *ssu* for "then" and "thereupon" nor the same *ssu* for "this," both of which are salient features of the Lu dialect in which, he says, the *Analects* and the *Book of Mencius* were written. (4) It has the preposition *hu* and (5) to a small extent the final interrogative article *yü.* (6) It lacks the preposition *chi* for "and" and (7) it has no trace of the peculiar distinction between *YÜ* (on, with) and *yü* (at, to, in). (8) Its first person pronoun is the same as that of the Lu district. He found (9) their language possesses the final interrogative article *yeh,* which is entirely unknown in the Lu dialect. He says that these facts make it possible to speak of a general third-century literary language.[47]

By applying these nine tests, Waley has found that in grammar the *Lao Tzu* is typical of the third century, except *ssu* in chapter 2.[48] But as Erkes has pointed out, *hu* is not used in the *Lao Tzu* as a preposition at all.[49] As to the final interrogative particle, *yeh,* it appears only once in the *Chuang Tzu,*[50] not enough to be typical. Furthermore, Karlgren himself has admitted that the *Mo Tzu,* a book earlier than these texts by more than a century, has very much the same grammar. To explain this contrary evidence to his theory, he has suggested that it might have been edited in the third century.[51] Even if we accepted this extraordinary solution, the fact still remains that, according to Karlgren, the language of the *Hsün Tzu* and the Lu dialect in which the *Book of Mencius* was written were fundamentally different.

Some Chinese scholars have held that *yü* was originally used as a preposition and *YÜ* as an exclamation, that beginning in the Spring and Autumn times both were used interchangeably as a preposition, that *yü* becomes more and more infrequently used, and that by tabulation of their instances it can be shown that the later the work, the less frequently *yü* is used. Since *YÜ* occurs 52 times in the *Lao Tzu* and *yü* not at all, the argument goes, this is unmistakable evidence that it was written in the Warring States period.[52] If the argument is carried to its logical conclusion, the *Book of Mencius* must have preceded the *Analects* since the latter uses fewer *yü*'s and the *Lao Tzu* must have come even after the *Huai-nan Tzu* of the second century B.C., since *yü* is used in it but not in the *Lao Tzu*.[53] With all these inconsistencies, where can one find the "typical grammar" of the third century B.C.?[54]

Liang Ch'i-ch'ao maintains that the terms "kings and barons" (32, 37, 39), "kings and lords" (42), "lord with ten thousand chariots" (26), and "taking over the empire" (29, 48, 57) prove the late date of the *Lao Tzu* because they describe a political situation which did not exist until the Warring States period.[55] But as Hu Shih has pointed out, terms like "putting the empire in order," "possessing the empire," and "declining the empire," appear in the *Analects*,[56] and "kings and barons" and "kings and lords" are found in the older section of the *Book of Changes*.[57] If the *Analects* can speak of "a country of a thousand chariots,"[58] Hu asks, why can't the *Lao Tzu* speak of a king of ten thousand chariots?[59]

It is also asserted that the term "three ministers" (62) was not known before the Warring States period. But we encounter it many times in the *Mo Tzu*.[60] It is true that there was neither lieutenant general nor senior general (mentioned in chapter 31) in the Spring and Autumn period, but the term "general" was used many times.[61] It is also true that the custom of honoring the right (31) did not begin in the Warring States period, but in the *Tso chuan* it is remarked that the people of Ch'u, who were barbarians, honored the left,[62] implying that the Chinese honored the right. Besides, it is stated in the older portion of the *Book of Changes* that when an army operates toward the left, there will be no error.[63] This defense of the titles of generals and the custom of honoring the right is admittedly weak. However, they concern a chapter which may be a commentary, a corrupted passage, or an outright interpolation, in part or in total.

Ku Chieh-kang thinks the word *kung* was a title, as "kings and lords," in the Warring States period, and that its use as "impartial" (16) came into use in this period, as in the *Hsün Tzu*.[64] But, asks Hu Shih, since the *Analects* also uses *kung* in the sense of impartial,[65] should it then be dated three hundred years later along with the *Lao Tzu*? [66]

5. ARGUMENTS ABOUT IDEAS

With regard to ideas, opponents of tradition feel they are on an absolutely sure ground. Liang Ch'i-ch'ao was perfectly confident when he said that the attack on filial piety and deep love (18) and the like are "too radical" for the Spring and Autumn period. He believes that the combined term "humanity and righteousness" was initiated by Mencius and therefore its use in the *Lao Tzu* (18, 19) reveals its date to be later than Mencius.[67] He claims that the opposition to the exaltation of the worthy (3), the attack on law and punishment (57-60, 74-75), and the criticism of rules of propriety (38) seem to be specifically directed against the Moists, Legalists, and Confucianists of the Warring States period, respectively.[68] But as Hu Shih has said, Mencius had no monopoly on the combined term "humanity and righteousness," for it also appears in the *Tso chuan*.[69] Because Confucius taught correcting oneself as the best way to govern [70] and because the *Lao Tzu* teaches the same (57), Ku Chieh-kang has concluded that the *Lao Tzu* must have derived the idea from Confucius.[71] But as Hu Shih has said, one can argue just as well that Confucius learned from Lao Tzu.[72] Fung Yu-lan postponed the date of the *Lao Tzu* after Hui Shih and Kung-sun Lung because the *Lao Tzu* contains considerable discussion about the nameless, and in order to do this, he says, it would seem that men should "first have become conscious of the existence of names themselves." [73] He seems to imply that Hui Shih and Kung-sun Lung were the first to become conscious of them. Evidently he has forgotten the Confucian doctrine of the rectification of names, a doctrine he has stressed very strongly.[74] Quite aside from this, his shift is puzzling. Hui Shih and Chuang Tzu were contemporaries. If Fung puts the *Lao Tzu* between the times of Hui Shih and Chuang Tzu and calls the Taoism of Chuang Tzu a later phase than that of the *Lao Tzu,* does that mean that the Taoism of the *Lao Tzu* was formulated or came into maturity some time between Hui Shih's pronouncement of his theories in his youth and Chuang Tzu's pronouncement of his in his old age? Is this assumption reasonable?

While Liang, Ku, Fung, and many others have advanced the argument of ideas, the one who has pushed it most vigorously is Ch'ien Mu. He has selected 33 concepts from the *Lao Tzu,* like Tao, Heaven, the One, name, and the eternal. In each case, he has attempted to prove that the concept developed from primitive beginnings to its maturity in the *Lao Tzu,* with the *Chuang Tzu* as the transition. Take Tao, for example. According to Ch'ien, *tao* or the Way, to Confucius, only concerns human affairs. In Mo Tzu it is seldom discussed and then only superficially. In the *Lao Tzu,* however, it becomes profound and subtle. It is well developed in the *Chuang Tzu,* it is true, but it is still not yet well defined. Hence the *Chuang Tzu* serves as a transition.[75]

Ch'ien has presented his case with profound erudition and extensive learning, as is usual with him, but his thesis that concepts evolve systematically and chronologically remains to be proved. By Ch'ien's formula, one can claim that the *Lao Tzu* appeared long before the *Chuang Tzu* because certain concepts are absent in the former but are fairly well developed in the latter. Take that of principle (*li*), for example. It is not mentioned in either the *Lao Tzu* or the *Analects.* In the *Book of Mencius* it is understood as order.[76] But in the *Chuang Tzu* it occurs in many places and is understood in a higher sense, namely, that of principle. The same things can be said about concepts of nature (*hsing*) and feelings (*ch'ing*), both of which are not found in the *Lao Tzu* but are much discussed in the *Chuang Tzu*.[77] One may add that the terms "the Great One" (*t'ai-i*), "perfect man" (*chih-jen*), and so forth are not found in the *Lao Tzu* but are prominent in the *Chuang Tzu*[78] and therefore one could argue that the second must be later.

Such systematic interpretation of intellectual history is neat and attractive but is not supported by facts. Ch'ien contends that Confucius and Mo Tzu should come before Lao Tzu and Chuang Tzu. Otherwise, he says, since Lao Tzu had already originated the doctrine of Tao preceding the Lord (4), Confucius and Mo Tzu should not have still held the doctrine of the order of Heaven[79] and the will of Heaven.[80] This is so, he adds, because the thread of thought does not run this way.[81] Hu Shih's response to this contention is worth quoting:

> According to your way of inference and conclusion, is it to be declared that after the birth of Lao Tzu and Chuang Tzu there should be no more talk of Heaven's order and Heaven's will? Is it conceivable that those who in the last two thousand years have talked of Heaven's order and Heaven's will—Tung Chung-shu [*c.* 179–*c.* 104 B.C.], Pan Piao [A.D. 3–54] and the rest—should all be regarded as prior to the time of Lao Tzu and Chuang Tzu?[82]

Ch'ien holds that the *Lao Tzu* is later than Chuang Tzu and Kung-sun Lung and therefore it has taken the concepts of Tao and name from them respectively and combined them.[83] But by his own reckoning, Kung-sun Lung died about 257 B.C. Between this date and the death of Han Fei in 233 B.C., there were only 24 years, hardly enough time for the doctrines to develop to such a point that Han Fei could comment on them extensively.[84]

Ch'ien and those who argue like him do not realize that most ideas are not limited to any particular period. The exaltation of the worthy, the use of law and punishment, and so forth, were also current in the Spring and Autumn period, though perhaps not so much as in the age of the Warring

States. If a contrary idea necessarily means opposition and therefore must occur later in time, one can argue that Confucius lived after Mo Tzu because the latter advocated serving spiritual beings,[85] whereas Confucius puts serving human beings first and prefers not to talk about spiritual beings.[86] The progression from the individual through the family, the community, and the country to the world seems to be a systematic development. This concept is not found in the *Analects*, is only hinted at by Mencius,[87] but is quite clear in the *Lao Tzu* (54). For this reason it has been maintained that the *Lao Tzu* is later than the time of Mencius.[88] But it must not be forgotten that Mencius was quoting what he himself said was a common saying. Who can tell how long it takes for a saying to become common? So far as the basic concepts of the *Lao Tzu* are concerned, they were already known in the Spring and Autumn days. Those of taking no action, Tao, vacuity, and repaying evil with virtue, for example, are all found in the *Analects*.[89]

6. THE QUESTION OF AUTHORSHIP

We shall now come to the question of individual authorship. One of Fung Yu-lan's well-known arguments is that before Confucius no one had written a book in his private capacity. He was repeating the argument of Chang Hsüeh-ch'eng (1738-1801) who said that the purpose of writing in ancient times was fulfilled in writing down governmental records and that writing was never employed in a private capacity.[90] Fung has added that ancient aristocrats did not write because they had to govern and therefore had no time. Besides, he says, there was no need for any writing since their ideals were to be carried out in governmental measures.[91] Therefore he dismisses all private writings attributed to ancient writers before Confucius as spurious and comes to the bold conclusion that there was no private writing before Confucius.[92] Obviously Fung is begging the question. As Hu Shih has pointed out, "Mr. Fung ought to have proved first that the *Lao Tzu* actually came out after Confucius' time before he advanced the premise that before Confucius' time there was no such thing as individual authorship." [93]

Going beyond Fung, Lo Ken-tse has presented four "evidences" to prove the absence of individual authorship before the Warring States period. He says there is no mention of any private writing in the *Chuang Tzu, Hsün Tzu, Han Fei Tzu,* and other books of the period, that the private writings before the period recorded in the bibliographical section of the *History of the Former Han Dynasty* are false, that no books in the early Warring States period quote any private writing before the period, and that no private writing was used in the Spring and Autumn days for public instruction. The reasons for the absence of individual authorship, according to him, are that before Confucius all books were kept in official archives and that before the Warring States period all philosophers emphasized rules of propriety as a means for social reform and there was no need of any writing.[94] Later he has added the reason that aristocrats had no need of writing and even opposed it, while serfs were too ignorant to write.[95] Not that ancient writers or books were not mentioned, or ancient philosophers quoted, in the books of the Warring States period. But the books are regarded by him either as official documents or as forgeries, and the quotations as from oral transmission instead of private writings. He is virtually saying, "There was no private writing, for all private writings are false!"

Actually, throughout the whole controversy, it has not always been clear whether the debaters were talking about doctrines, sayings transmitted orally or written down and circulated separately, or sayings collected in book form. The time that had elapsed between the enunciation of the doctrines and the compilation of the book may have been centuries. Certainly that was the case with the *Analects,* the *Mo Tzu,* the *Chuang Tzu,* the *Book of Changes,* and many others. In the process extraneous material, whether ideas or words, must have crept in, through unintentional mistakes and sometimes through deliberate forgery. Practically no ancient Chinese classic is free from these.

This raises the question whether the *Lao Tzu* is from one hand or many. Those who believe in a single author emphasize certain consistent features like rhyme and the use of the pronoun "I." These scholars have naturally placed the author in the particular period they have chosen.[96] Thus Pi Yüan,[97] Hu Shih, Kao Heng,[98] and others have insisted that the author was Lao Tzu, contemporary of Confucius. Ts'ui Shu, as stated above, thought he was a follower of Yang Chu at the end of the Spring and Autumn period. And Kuo Mo-jo believes the book actually contains the sayings of Lao Tzu which were collected by his follower Huan Yüan, a contemporary of Mencius. Kuo's argument is that the *Records of the Historian* says Lao Tzu and Huan Yüan each wrote a book in two parts and that Lao Tzu saw Kuan Yin, the officer at the pass which Lao Tzu was supposed to have gone through. Kuo thinks that Kuan Yin and Huan Yüan were actually the same person, the two names being pronounced almost alike.[99] Whoever these scholars believe the author to be, he lived in the Spring and Autumn days. Almost without exception, scholars who believe the book was written by one man in the Warring States period have assigned it to Lao Tan, the fourth-century historian. These scholars include Yeh Shih [100] and Wang Chung before our time and many contemporary scholars like Lo Ken-tse. Ch'ien Mu is of the opinion that the author was perhaps Chan Ho or an unknown person who lived in the early third century B.C. The pronunciation of *chan ho* in ancient times was similar to *tan* and he was therefore confused by historians with Lao Tan.[101] Ch'ien was at pains to put the author in this period in order to conform to his theory that the book is later than the "inner chapters" of the *Chuang Tzu*, and he did so reluctantly.

It may be assumed that those who have not definitely identified the author believe that the book is a collective or evolutionary product, although few have explicitly stated this position. It is interesting that in 1959 some writers in Peking came out for this theory.[102] My own belief is that the *Lao Tzu* embodies the basic ideas of Lao Tzu but took a long period, some time before Chuang Tzu, to become a book. In other words, the doctrines are products of the sixth century B.C., but the book as such may be of the fourth century. This is no more than a theory, which, like every other theory, starts with certain assumptions or beliefs, without scientific proof, such as whether any ancient reference is acceptable or whether certain ideas or literary styles were decisive. This condition applies to other ancient texts like the *Chuang Tzu* and the *Book of Mencius*. I am willing to accept them as embodying the teachings of Chuang Tzu and Mencius, but believe that the formation of the books as we have them took place after their time.

7. TITLES AND STRUCTURE

The *Lao Tzu* has even continued to change since the Warring States days, although only in a minor way. We no longer know how early editions looked. The *History of the Former Han Dynasty* mentions the *Lao Tzu* in the ancient script,[103] but we have no idea of what it was like. When Liu Hsiang and his son Liu Hsin (*c.* 46 B.C.–A.D. 23) compiled the first Chinese bibliography in the first century B.C., the *Lao Tzu* was included,[104] but we know nothing of its text or structure. The oldest text in existence is inscribed on a tablet in the Lunghsing Temple in I-chou, Hupei province, which was inscribed in 708.[105] The book as it stands now is divided into two parts, the first consisting of 37 chapters, and the second, of 44 chapters. Of the two common texts, the one used by Wang Pi for his commentary has no titles for either the two parts or the chapters. The one used by Ho-shang Kung for his commentary, however, calls the two parts "Classic of Tao" and "Classic of Te," respectively, and has a title for each chapter.[106]

The book was merely called the *Lao Tzu* and not a classic (*ching*) up to the beginning of the Han dynasty (206 B.C.–A.D. 220). According to Chiao Hung, it was called a classic during the reign of Emperor Ching (reigned 156-141 B.C.).[107] Whether this is true or not, it is a fact that the bibliography compiled by Liu Hsiang lists three commentaries on the *Lao Tzu* as those on the "classic," although the *Lao Tzu* itself is not listed.[108] This is repeated in the bibliographical section of the *History of the Former Han Dynasty* by Pan Ku (32-92). Yang Hsiung (53 B.C.–A.D. 18) has been quoted as saying that Lao Tzu wrote the *Classic of Tao*.[109] Ma Hsü-lun says that the title *Tao-te ching* appears in a number of works in the Former Han pe-period (206 B.C.–A.D. 8).[110]

The division into two parts goes back to early times. As already indicated, in his biography of Lao Tzu, Ssu-ma Ch'ien refers to it as consisting of two parts.[111] The "Hsiang-erh" commentary, which may antedate Wang Pi's commentary, divides the text into two parts.[112] Some say Wang Pi did not divide the text into two parts, but in his commentary on chapter 20, he specifically mentions "Part Two." It is possible that up to the Sung period (960-1279), the Wang Pi text was so divided in some editions but not in others.

As to the division into chapters, since the bibliography section of the *History of the Former Han Dynasty*, in mentioning the Ho-shang Kung commentary, does not give the number of chapters and since in Lu Te-ming's (556-627) *Lao Tzu yin-i* (Pronunciation and Meanings of the *Lao Tzu*) there is no chapter division, many scholars believe the division originated in the Sui (581-618) or T'ang (618-907) dynasty. According to tradition, Ho-shang Kung divided Part One into 37 chapters to conform to the odd number of heaven, and Part Two into 44 chapters to conform to the even number of earth.[113] Yen Tsun (*fl.* 53-24 B.C.) divided the book into 72 chapters, because, he said, it is the product of eight, which is the way of yin (the cosmic passive force), and nine, which is the way of yang (the cosmic active force).[114] Thus he had 40 chapters for Part One, and 32 for Part Two. The Taoist philosopher Ko Hung went further. Because he thought heaven consisted of the four seasons and earth of the Five Agents or Elements (Water, Fire, Wood, Metal, and Earth), he assigned 36 chapters (4 × 9) to

Part One, and 45 (5 × 9) to Part Two, thus achieving 81, the product of 9 × 9. This scheme was followed by Emperor Ming-huang (reigned 713-55), who, in his *Tao-te ching chu* (Commentary on the *Classic of the Way and Its Virtue*), further grouped chapters 1-9, 10-18, 19-27, and 28-36 of Part One to correspond to the four seasons, respectively, and chapters 37-45 of Part Two to correspond to humanity, propriety, righteousness, wisdom, faithfulness (which correspond to the Five Agents). It is said that he was the first to fix the order of the chapters and their sentences.[115]

Unlike these fantastic schemes, that of Wu Ch'eng (1249-1333) is more logical. In his commentary he combines chapters 5 and 6, 17 to 19, 23 and 24, 30 and 31, 39 and 40, 42 and 43, 57 and 58, 63 and 64, 66 and 67, 68 and 69, 70 and 71, and 73 and 74, because they deal with similar subjects, thus totaling 68 chapters. In the *Tao-te chen-ching chu* (Commentary on the *Pure Classic of the Way and Its Virtue*) by Emperor T'ai-tsu (reigned 1368-98) of the Ming dynasty (1368-1644), there are 67 chapters. In Yao Nai's *Lao Tzu chang-i* (Commentary on the *Lao Tzu*), there are still 81 chapters, but Part One has 31 and Part Two, 50, the shortest having only four words (the fifth saying in present chapter 63) and the longest having several hundred. More radically, Ma Hsü-lun has divided the book into 114 chapters, the shortest having six words (line 3, present chapter 70) and the longest having 104.[116] The most recent arrangement, by Yen Ling-feng, has 54 chapters (chapters 1-4 on the substance of Tao, 5-8 on the principle of Tao, 9-23 on the function of Tao, and 34-54 on the technique of Tao).[117]

8. COMMENTARIES

Much more constructive than these rearrangements have been the commentaries. They are indispensable to the understanding of the text itself, and as elaborations on the teachings of the book they are often helpful.

The first commentator on the *Lao Tzu* was Han Fei Tzu.

He both expounded the meanings of Lao Tzu's sayings and cited historical events to illustrate them.[118] Being a Legalist, he naturally interpreted Lao Tzu in the light of his own philosophy. For example, in commenting on chapter 26, he says that "the heavy" means the ruler controls the government himself and "the tranquil" means the ruler's not departing from his seat of authority.[119] This is, of course, a farfetched interpretation.

Appearing after Han Fei were the three commentaries recorded by Liu Hsiang and in the bibliographical section of the *History of the Former Han Dynasty*. These have disappeared long ago. We do not know the dates of the commentators mentioned, except that they existed before the early first century B.C., when the Lius lived. Nor do we know the text Han Fei or these commentators used, although we know the number of chapters Han Fei commented on is 55, and the other three commentaries consisted of 4, 6, and 37 chapters. The oldest extant commentary as such is probably the "Hsiang-erh" commentary. It is a manuscript discovered in a Tun-huang cave in 1900, and brought back to the British Museum in 1907 by Auriel Stein.[120] It was an important book in the Taoist religion in the second and subsequent centuries. But its date and authorship are uncertain.[121] The commentary is incomplete, for only Part One has survived. Most important of all, it is not a study or clarification of the text or thought of the *Lao Tzu*, but an effort to use it to promote the chief objective of the Taoist religion at that time, namely, the search for earthly immortality through the nourishment of the vital force, the control of breathing, and other similar occult practices.[122] The oldest extant complete commentaries on the book are those by Wang Pi and Ho-shang Kung. Since Wang's time, there have been about 700 commentaries and annotations in China, of which 350 are still in existence, besides fragments of many more. There have been about 250 in Japan.[123] Tu Kuang-t'ing (*fl.* 901) has selected comments from more than 60 commentators [124] and Chiao Hung has selected from 64, which are among the best.[125]

Among the commentaries, those by Wang Pi and Ho-shang Kung are the most common, and the former is generally considered the oldest and the best. The Wang commentary has obviously gone through some changes. Its title recorded in the bibliographical sections of the *Sui shu* (History of the Sui Dynasty) and the *Sung shih* (History of the Sung Dynasty) agrees with the work we have today,[126] but it is recorded in the *Chiu T'ang shu* (History of the T'ang Dynasty) under a different title.[127] Furthermore, certain quotations from his commentary are no longer found in the present work.[128] However, quotations from it in the commentary on the *Lieh Tzu* by Chang Chan of the Eastern Chin dynasty (317-420)[129] tally with the present work. Evidently, the commentary was rare during the Sung dynasty, but from the Ming dynasty on, there have been more and more editions.[130]

As to the Ho-shang Kung commentary, the *Sui shu* lists a commentary by Ho-shang Chang-jen ("man with a walking staff on the bank of the Yellow River") who lived in the Warring States period and another one by Ho-shang Kung ("old man on the bank of the Yellow River") who lived during the reign of Emperor Wen (reigned 179-157 B.C.). The former commentary, if it ever existed, has long been lost. The original Ho-shang Kung commentary may have antedated the Wang Pi commentary but the present version is certainly later.

Little is known about Ho-shang Chang-jen. The *Records of the Historian* mentions him as a teacher of the *Lao Tzu*.[131] As to Ho-shang Kung, Ko Hung claims that when Emperor Wen could not understand certain passages of the *Lao Tzu*, he went to the old man for help. The latter jumped up in the air and, while holding himself aloft, gave the explanation.[132] To this fantastic account, the preface to the commentary, ascribed to Ko Hsüan (*fl.* 210), has added that the emperor went at the recommendation of his vice minister P'ei K'ai and that the old man gave the emperor a copy of the *Lao Tzu*. The whole account is fictitious and is not worth serious attention. There is no record in the *History of the Former Han Dynasty* that the emperor ever made the journey. Though the *Records of the Historian* mentions Ho-shang Kung's name, it does not say that he ever wrote a commentary. Liu Hsin, Liu Hsiang, and the *History of the Former Han Dynasty* list three commentaries, but not his. And P'ei K'ai (*fl.* 267) lived two centuries later than Emperor Wen.

As to the commentary bearing Ho-shang Kung's name, it cannot have existed during Emperor Wen's time. For one thing, the custom of incorporating commentary into the text did not begin until the first century,[133] but in this commentary they are incorporated. Furthermore, the idea of the gates of Heaven in chapter 10 as referring to the place in the Polar Star where the Lord of Heaven lives did not prevail in the early Han dynasty.[134]

Erkes has offered three proofs that the commentary existed before the second century. Kao Yu (*fl.* 205) has interpreted the word *hsüan* in the term *hsüan-t'ung* (mysterious union or profound identification) in the *Huai-nan Tzu* as equivalent to heaven.[135] Erkes argues that this term comes from the *Lao Tzu* (chapter 56), and since Ho-shang Kung identifies *hsüan* with heaven, Kao Yu "must have known Ho-shang Kung." [136] This proof is unsound because we are not sure the *Huai-nan Tzu* is quoting the *Lao Tzu,* for so far as *hsüan-t'ung* is concerned, the two books deal with entirely different subjects. Furthermore, Ho-shang Kung's reason for identifying *hsüan* with heaven is because man can practice "blunting the sharpness," "softening the light," and so forth, whereas Kao Yu's reason is that "Heaven makes no demands." Even if a connection between the two writers is assumed, how do we know that Ho-shang Kung did not borrow from Kao Yu? Erkes' answer is that this is impossible because Kao Yu merely mentions *hsüan* as heaven whereas Ho-shang Kung makes the concept a complete system. It is true that he understands *hsüan* in chapters 1, 6, and 65 as heaven, but he does not do so in chapters 10 and 51. Erkes is wrong in asserting that *hsüan* always means heaven to Ho-shang Kung. Granted such an idea is more prominent in him than in Kao Yu, it does not follow that the latter borrowed from the former. Erkes also implies that Ho-shang Kung originated this new meaning of *hsüan* in *hsüan-t'ung*, for, Erkes says, this meaning had only been found in the combination *hsüan-huang* or heaven and earth. He has overlooked the fact that the term *hsüan-t'ien* appears in the *Chuang Tzu*.[137] There it means nature or heaven.[138]

Erkes offers as the second proof that the Ho-shang Kung commentary existed before the third century the fact that Mou Tzu mentions that the *Classic of Te* has 37 chapters,[139] which is the arrangement of the Ho-shang Kung commentary.[140] However, the date of Mou Tzu is by no means certain. Scholars are inclined to believe he existed in the third century. Erkes offers the preface ascribed to Ko Hsüan as the third proof,[141] but any writing that includes fantastic accounts and anachronisms is not reliable enough to be a proof.

According to Ma Hsü-lun, since parts of chapter 31 are commentaries on the Wang Pi text mixed up with the text itself, and since Ho-shang Kung has commented on them, it shows that his commentary came after the corruption of the Wang Pi commentary, that is, after the third century. According to Ma, the first mention of the Ho-shang Kung commentary by title did not take place until the fourth century, it was not quoted until the fifth or sixth century (by Huang K'an, 448-545), and it was not listed in a catalogue until the Liang period (502-57). Ma has therefore concluded that the commentary did not become current until Liang times.[142]

This commentary contains archaic as well as colloquial words of later times. Its style is crude. It shows extensive influence of popular religion, as it refers to a Taoist god (10), hell ("yellow spring," 45), protection by gods (32, 55), nourishing the essence and the spirit (33, 59, 72), yoga breathing (5, 10), and, most important of all, immortality on earth (1, 4, 5, 7, 16, 39, 54). Buddhist influence is also evident, as it uses the Buddhist term "ten directions" (10).[143] In contrast, Wang Pi's commentary is in refined language and elegant style. It is a clear and consistent expression of his own Neo-Taoist philosophy. And it is free from religious superstition. For these reasons, the former commentary may be regarded as representing the masses while the latter represents the intellectual.

Both commentaries existed throughout the centuries, each in slightly varying versions. However, since the Taoist religion was dominant in the T'ang dynasty, enjoying personal encouragement by emperors and empresses and a considerable following among the masses, there is no doubt that the Ho-shang Kung commentary was more popular. This explains why T'ang dynasty inscriptions and manuscripts of the *Lao Tzu* agree with its text. The Wang Pi text, being less popular, was not current. As late as the eighteenth century it was still difficult to find.[144] Since then, however, more editions of the Wang Pi commentary have appeared than the Ho-shang Kung one. At present there are 34 editions of the former and 33 of the latter.[145] The *Ssu-pu pei-yao* (The Essentials of the Four Libraries) edition (1929) of the Wang Pi text and his commentary is a reproduction of an edition of the middle of the Wan-li period (1573-1619). The *Ssu-pu ts'ung-k'an* (The Four Libraries Series) edition (1929) of the Ho-shang Kung text and his commentary is a reproduction of an edition of the Northern Sung dynasty (960-1126). It is safe to say that Wang's commentary is still favored by intellectuals while Ho-shang Kung's is favored by popular religionists.

The increasing popularity of the Wang Pi commentary reflects a growing philosophical interest in the *Lao Tzu*. The fervent religious sentiment for the book had disappeared by the tenth century. With the emergence of Neo-Confucian philosophy in the eleventh century, more and more commentaries were devoted to philosophical deliberations. Wang An-shih (1021-86) punctuates sentences in chapter 1 to mean "being" and "non-being" rather than "having" or "not having" desires.[146] Su Ch'e (1039-1112) interprets the named and the nameless (1) in terms of substance and function, understands the Invisible, the Inaudible, and the Subtle (14) not as mysterious, but as the function of the nature of reality, and considers the spirit of the valley (6), not as supernatural, but as pure formlessness beyond life and death.[147] Likewise, Lü Hui-ch'ing (*fl.* 1078) regards the valley as that with form, and spirit as that without form.[148]

This rationalistic tendency persisted throughout the centuries. Wu Ch'eng expounds the *Lao Tzu* in the light of Confucian and Buddhist thought.[149] And Chiao Hung injects much Confucian philosophy into his commentary. He takes the gate of Heaven and its opening and closing (10) as the mind and its function, respectively, and like Su Ch'e, takes "returning to the root" (16) to mean the Confucian investigation of principle, full development of one's nature, and fulfilling one's destiny.[150] In his collection of commentaries, Chiao lays special emphasis on philosophical commentators like Su Ch'e, Lü Hui-ch'ing, and Wu Ch'eng.[151] This rationalistic trend was continued, notably by Wang Fu-chih (1619-92), who understands the immortality of the spirit of the valley in terms of the perpetual progress from the past to the present.[152]

In expounding their philosophical views different commentators have different emphases.[153] Generally speaking, however, they have presented their own ideas rather than those of the *Lao Tzu,* or have read Confucianism and Buddhism into it.[154] It is no wonder that, in the twentieth century, Yen Fu (1853-1921), who introduced evolutionism into China by translating Darwin's works into Chinese, put evolutionism into the mouth of Lao Tzu.[155] In consequence, the philosophy of Lao Tzu itself did not develop. In the case of the *Chuang Tzu,* its commentator, Kuo Hsiang, the Neo-Taoist, developed Taoist philosophy to new heights.[156] But there has been no commentator on the *Lao Tzu* comparable to Kuo Hsiang.

9. TRANSLATIONS

As to translations of the *Lao Tzu,* the first was in Sanskrit by the famous Buddhist priest, Hsüan-tsang (596-664) who made the translation by imperial command.[157] More than a thousand years later, a Latin version was brought to London and presented at a meeting in 1788.[158] A Russian version followed in 1828.[159] Three years later, G. Pauthier made the first French version, and in 1868, John Chalmers, Protestant missionary in China, made the first English translation.[160] Since then more than 40 English versions have appeared, almost half of them in London. The first American translation was by Paul Carus in 1898, and the first Chinese to make his own translation was Au-young Sum Nung, in 1938. In the last twenty years, a new version has appeared about every other year, with half of them in the United States.[161] Two American versions, those by Bynner and Bahm, are interpretations. Arthur Waley reflects much of critical Chinese scholarship in the 1920's and early 1930's and makes some original historical and textual criticisms of his own.[162] Ch'u Ta-kao, following the contemporary commentator, Ma Hsü-lun, almost exclusively, has transposed a number of sayings. Duyvendak, following Ma and Kao Heng a great deal, has transposed even more. Curiously, both of them have kept the traditional order of chapters, which is more incoherent than the order of those sayings they have rearranged. The only commentary on the *Lao Tzu* rendered into a Western language is that by Erkes, *Ho-shang-kung's Commentary on the Lao-tse.* Lin Yutang has not only put the *Lao Tzu* into beautiful English, but has also translated long passages of the *Chuang Tzu* for elaboration and support. It is highly desirable to have a translation of Wang Pi's commentary and a selection from the best of the hundreds of other commentaries.

NOTES

1. For the variation of the numbers, see Chiao Hung (1541-1620), *Lao Tzu i* (Aids to the *Lao Tzu*), 5:13a; Kimura Eiichi, *Rōshi no shinkenkyū* (New Study of the *Lao Tzu*), pp. 219-220; Takeuchi Yoshio, *Rōshi no kenkyū* (Study of the *Lao Tzu*), I, 127, 131, 136, 220; and Kojima Kenkichirō, *Shina shoshi hyakkakō* (Inquiry on the Hundred Schools of Ancient Chinese Philosophy), p. 142. The Ho-shang Kung text,

SPTK (1929), has 5268 words, and the Wang Pi text, *SPPY* (1927), has 5281. In reducing the total number to 5000, Taoist followers replaced the phrase *san-shih* ("thirty") with the colloquial *sa* ("thirty") in the *Lao Tzu* (ch. 11). For further information on the reduction to 5000 words, see Jao Tsung-i, *Lao Tzu hsiang-erh chu chiao-chien* (A Study on Chang Tao-ling's Hsiang-erh Commentary of *Tao-te ching*), p. 4.

2. Chapters 31, 49, 50, 61, 74, and 75 are not rhymed, while only small parts of chapters 7, 11, 23, 32, 34, 42, 60, 66, 72, and 81 are rhymed. Hu Yüan-chun, in his *Lao Tzu shih-ki* (Explanation of the *Lao Tzu,* p. 3) goes so far as to say that the whole book is in rhyme.

3. For a complete list of rhymes, see B. Karlgren, "The Poetical Parts in Lao-Tsi," *Göteborgs Högskolas Årsskrift,* XXXVIII (1932), 6-20, and Ch'en Chu, *Lao Tzu chi-hsün* (Collected Explanations on the *Lao Tzu*), *passim.* For some examples of the rhyming scheme, see Ch'en Chu, *Lao-hsüeh pa-p'ien* (Eight Essays on the study of Lao Tzu), pp. 29-34.

4. For examples and an analysis, see T'an Cheng-pi, *Lao Tzu tu-pen (Lao Tzu* Reader), pp. 10-12, and Kojima, pp. 143-47.

5. Chapters 22, 36, 41, 42, 57, 69, 78, and 79.

6. These repetitions have been pointed out in footnotes. For a good list of contradictions, real or imagined, see Tsuda Sōkichi, *Dōke no shisō to sono tenkai* (Taoist Thought and Its Development), pp. 34-35.

7. See above, p. 35.

8. By Ts'ui Hao (d. 450), according to Wang Shih-p'eng (1112-71), *Mei-hsi Hsien-sheng wen-chi* (Collection of Literary Works by Wan Shih-p'eng), 13:17a.

9. For the opinion of these Neo-Confucianists, see Lo Ken-tse, *Chu-tzu k'ao-so* (Inquiries on Ancient Philosophers), pp. 258-61.

10. See his *Lao Tzu k'ao-i* (Inquiry into the Errors about Lao Tzu), in the supplement to his *Shu-hsüeh* (Notes from Studies), 27a-28b.

11. *Chu-Ssu k'ao-hsin lu* (Inquiry into the True Facts Concerning Confucius), 1:13a-14a.

12. *Rōshi ben* (An Examination on the *Lao Tzu*), sec. 5.

13. In his review of Hu Shih's *Chung-kuo che-hsüeh shih ta-kang* (Outline of the History of Chinese Philosophy), which is found in *Liang Jen-kung hsüeh-shu yen-chiang chi* (Collec-

tion of Liang Ch'i-ch'ao's Lectures on Learned Subjects), I, 1-41. The arguments are presented on pp. 19-21. For Liang's attack on the traditions about Lao Tzu, see above, p. 45.

14. Lo Ken-tse, *Chu-tzu k'ao-so*, pp. 267-81.

15. Hou Wai-lu, *Chung-kuo ku-tai ssu-hsiang hsüeh-shuo shih* (History of Ancient Chinese Thought and Theories), pp. 11-17, 159-61, and *Chung-kuo ssu-hsiang t'ung-shih* (General History of Chinese Thought), I, 257.

16. *Hsien-Ch'in chu-tzu hsi-nien* (Chronological Studies on the Pre-Ts'in Philosophers), p. 224.

17. *A History of Chinese Philosophy*, I, 170; *A Short History of Chinese Philosophy*, pp. 93-94. Fung's dates for Hui Shih, *fl.* 350-260 B.C., and for Kung-sun Lung, *fl.* 284-259 B.C.

18. Duyvendak, *Tao Te ching*, p. 6; Waley, *The Way and Its Power*, p. 86.

19. "Ts'ung Lü-shih ch'un-ch'iu t'ui-ts'e Lao Tzu chih ch'eng-shu nien-tai" (Inferring the Date of the *Lao Tzu* from *Mr. Lü's Spring and Autumn Annals*), in *Ku-shih pien* (Discussions on Ancient History), IV, 462-520.

20. Kimura even says that the present text of the *Lao Tzu* did not appear until about 150 B.C. See his *Rōshi no shin kenkyū* (New Study on the *Lao Tzu*), p. 164. A similar view is expressed in *Lao Tzu che-hsüeh t'ao-lun chi* (Symposium on the Philosophy of Lao Tzu), p. 5.

21. *Chung-kuo che-hsüeh shih ta-kang*, pp. 49-50, and "A Criticism of Some Recent Methods Used in Dating Lao Tzu," *Harvard Journal of Asiatic Studies*, II (1937), 373-97.

22. *Ch'ing-t'ung shih-tai* (Bronze Age), pp. 241-54.

23. *Lao Tzu chiao-ku* (*Lao Tzu* Collated and Explained), pp. 18-19.

24. Many more scholars have been involved in the dispute, each offering his own date. For general accounts of the whole controversy, see Lo Ken-tse, *Chu-tzu k'ao-so*, pp. 257-81. See also *Lao Tzu che-hsüeh t'ao-lun chi*, pp. 1-7.

25. Yen Ling-feng, *Lao-Chuang yen-chiu* (Studies on Lao Tzu and Chuang Tzu), pp. 209-12, lists 29, but 7 of them are at best paraphrases.

26. *Hsün Tzu*, ch. 17, *SPTK*, 11:25a. Cf. Dubs (tr.), *The Works of Hsüntze*, p. 184.

27. *Han Fei Tzu*, chs. 20-21.

28. In ch. 31, *SPTK*, 10:1a, alluding to *Lao Tzu*, ch. 36 (see Liao (tr.), *The Complete Works of Han Fei Tzu*, II, 1); ch. 38,

SPTK, 16:3a (twice), 4b, quoting from *Lao Tzu*, chs. 63, 17, and 65 (Liao, II, 178, 179, 183); and ch. 46, *SPTK*, 18:4a, quoting from *Lao Tzu*, ch. 44 (Liao, II, 246).

29. At 11:5a, quoting from *Lao Tzu*, ch. 39, and 22:3a, quoting from *Lao Tzu*, ch. 81. The *Chan-kuo ts'e* was compiled by Liu Hsiang (77-6 B.C.), but much of the material long antedated him.

30. Ch. 6, sec. 4, *SPPY*, 6:7a, quoting from *Lao Tzu*, ch. 58; ch. 16, sec. 5, *SPPY*, 16:10a, quoting from *Lao Tzu*, ch. 41; ch. 17, sec. 2, *SPPY*, 17:4a, quoting from *Lao Tzu*, ch. 47. See Wilhelm (tr.), *Frühling und Herbst des Lü Bu We*, pp. 74, 248, 266, respectively. The *Huai-nan Tzu* quotes the *Lao Tzu* 89 times—ch. 1 (15 times), 2 (3), 6 (2), 7 (3), 8 (2), 9 (5), 11 (4), 12 (52), 14 (1), and 18 (2)—but this book appeared in the early Han period. According to Karlgren, no less than 1767 words out of a version of 5247 are quoted in pre-Han and Han texts ("The Poetical Parts in Lao-Tsi," *Göteborgs Högskolas Årsskrift*, XXXVIII (1932), 26).

31. *Liang Jen-kung hsüeh-shu yen-chiang chi*, I, 18-19.

32. According to *History of the Former Han Dynasty* (*Han shu*), ch. 30, section on the Moist School.

33. According to the *T'ai-p'ing yü-lan* (Imperial Collection of the T'ai-p'ing Period), 322:5b, a saying from *Lao Tzu*, ch. 4, was quoted in the *Mo Tzu*.

34. *Book of Mencius*, 2A:1, 4; 4A:7, 8; 4B:21; and 5A:6.

35. See *Hsün Tzu*, especially ch. 23.

36. *Chuang Tzu*, chs. 5, 7, *SPTK*, 2:36b-37b and 3:31a, respectively (Giles [tr.], *Chuang Tzu* pp. 66 and 87-88).

37. *Hsien-Ch'in chu-tzu hsi-nien*, p. 224.

38. *Ku-shih pien*, IV, 447.

39. "A Criticism of Some Recent Methods Used in Dating Lao Tzu," *Harvard Journal of Asiatic Studies*, II (1937), 387-97.

40. *Ku-shih pien*, IV, 481.

41. *A History of Chinese Philosophy*, I, 170.

42. *Book of Odes*, Odes 40, 57, 106, as examples.

43. *Analects*, 8:18-19, are Hu's examples.

44. *Harvard Journal of Asiatic Studies*, II (1937), 375-76, 383-85.

45. Many examples are given in Ho Tun-weng, *Lao Tzu hsin-i* (New Explanations of the *Lao Tzu*), Supplement, p. 2.

46. *Analects*, 2:1, 5; 11:19, for examples.

47. B. Karlgren, "On the Authenticity and Nature of the *Tso chuan*," *Göteborgs Högskolas Årsskrift*, XXXII (1926), 63.

48. Waley, *The Way and Its Power*, pp. 127-28.

49. Erkes, "Arthur Waley's Laotse-Übersetzung," *Artibus Asiae*, V (1935), 295. Erkes has added *chi* (and) as another ancient usage found in the *Lao Tzu* (chs. 13 and 48), but he is wrong in this case, because *chi* here does not mean "and," but "when" or "if."

50. Ch. 21, *SPTK*, 7:31a. See Giles (tr.), *Chuang Tzu*, p. 201.

51. Karlgren, p. 63.

52. See *Ku-shih pien*, IV, 326-30. The tabulation there does not agree with the Harvard-Yenching Institute Sinological Index Series, but it is still true that the *Analects*, *Book of Mencius*, and *Chuang Tzu* use very few *yü*'s but many *YÜ*'s.

53. Both Erkes (p. 295) and Ho Tun-weng (*Lao Tzu hsin-i*, Supplement, p. 10) say that *yü* is used twice in *Lao Tzu*, ch. 64. This is not the case in either the Wang Pi or the Ho-shang Kung text. It is possible that it is used in a text which they saw, for the two words are interchangeable and copyists used them interchangeably.

54. For further statistics on the use of grammatical terms in the *Lao Tzu*, and their use in comparison with the *Analects*, see Kojima, *Shina shoshi hyakkakō*, pp. 150-51.

55. *Liang Jen-kung hsüeh-shu yen-chiang chi*, I, 20-21.

56. *Analects*, 14:18, 14: 6, and 8:1, respectively.

57. Hexagram nos. 18, 29, and 30. See Legge (tr.), *Yi King*, pp. 96, 236, and 305, respectively.

58. *Analects*, 1:5.

59. *Harvard Journal of Asiatic Studies*, II (1937), 383-87. See also Chang Hsü's refutation of Liang in *Ku-shih pien*, IV, 307-17, or in Miu Erh-shu, *Lao Tzu hsin-chu* (New Annotations of the Lao Tzu), pp. 78-81.

60. *The Concordance to Mo Tzu* of the Harvard-Yenching Institute Sinological Index Series gives 15 instances. For other examples, see Ho Tun-weng, *Lao Tzu hsin-i*, Supplement, p. 9.

61. See *Tso chuan*, Duke Chao, 28th year. For other examples, see Ho Tun-weng, pp. 9-10, and Kanō Naoki, *Chūgoku tetsugaku shi* (History of Chinese Philosophy), p. 179.

62. *Tso chuan*, Duke Huan, 8th year.

63. Hexagram no. 7. Cf. Legge, pp. 72 and 275. Legge's translation does not bring out the idea of the left.

64. *Ku-shih pien*, IV, 483.

65. *Analects*, 20:1.

66. *Harvard Journal of Asiatic Studies*, II (1937), 386. There is also an instance of *kung* used in the sense of impartiality in the *Mo Tzu*, ch. 8, *SPTK*, 2:3a. See Mei (tr.), *Works of Motse*, p. 33, where it is translated as "public."

67. *Liang Jen-kung hsüeh-shu yen-chiang chi*, I, 19-20. Also his *Ku-shu chen-wei chi ch'i nien-tai* (Authenticity of Ancient Texts and Their Dates), pp. 7, 56.

68. See his *Hsien-Ch'in cheng-chih ssu-hsiang shih* (History of Political Thought before the Ch'in Dynasty), p. 110. This part is not translated in L. T. Chen's translation, *History of Chinese Political Thought During the Early Tsin Period*.

69. Hu, in *Harvard Journal of Asiatic Studies*, II (1937), 386. See *Tso chuan*, Duke Chuang, 22nd year, and Duke Hsi, 14th Year. Hsü Ti-shan (1893-1941), *Tao-chiao shih* (History of the Taoist Religion), p. 26, mentions many ancient texts that quote Confucius discussing humanity and righteousness, but he considers these quotations as forgery.

70. *Analects*, 12:17.

71. *Ku-shih pien*, IV, 488.

72. *Harvard Journal of Asiatic Studies*, II (1937), 377.

73. *A Short History of Chinese Philosophy*, p. 94.

74. *Ibid.*, pp. 41-42.

75. *Chuang-Lao t'ung-pien* (General Discussion on Lao Tzu and Chuang Tzu), pp. 21-102, 287-314. See especially pp. 22-23.

76. *Book of Mencius*, 5B:1.

77. These concepts have been advanced by Yen Ling-feng, *Lao-Chuang yen-chiu*, pp. 227-31. In connection with the concept of *li*, it may be added that in the *Han Fei Tzu*, ch. 20, *SPTK*, 6:7a-8a (Liao [tr.], *The Complete Works of Han Fei Tzu*, I, 191-94), it has developed to an even higher point, for here principle is definitely a metaphysical concept and has acquired specific characteristics.

78. Chs. 1, 4, 24, 32, 33, *SPTK*, 1:9b; 2:8a; 8:42a; 10:17a; 35a, etc. See Giles (tr.), *Chuang Tzu*, pp. 29, 51, 246, 307, and 319.

79. See *Analects*, 2:4, etc.

80. *Mo Tzu*, chs. 26-28.

81. *Chuang-Lao t'ung-pien*, pp. 26-37.

82. *Harvard Journal of Asiatic Studies*, II (1937), 377-78.

83. *Chuang-Lao t'ung-pien*, Preface, p. 11.

84. *Han Fei Tzu*, chs. 20-21. This difficulty has been pointed out by Hsü Fu-kuan in his *Chung-kuo ssu-hsiang shih lun-chi* (Collected Essays on the History of Chinese Thought), p. 95.

85. *Mo Tzu*, ch. 31.

86. *Analects*, 11:11 and 7:20.

87. *Book of Mencius*, 4A:5.

88. This is the claim of Ts'ao Ju-lin, in his *Chou-Ch'in chu-tzu k'ao* (Inquiry on the Philosophers of the Chou and Ch'in Dynasties), pp. 52-53.

89. *Analects*, 15:4, 14:38, 8:5, and 14:36, respectively.

90. Fung, *A History of Chinese Philosophy*, I, 7.

91. *Ibid.*, p. 8.

92. *Ibid.*, pp. 7, 170.

93. *Harvard Journal of Asiatic Studies*, II (1937), 374-75.

94. *Chu-tzu k'ao-so*, pp. 13-61.

95. *Ibid.*, p. 62.

96. Welch suggests that "the absence of proper names is evidence that it bears the impress of a single mind" (see his *The Parting of the Way*, p. 190). It is difficult to follow the logic of this statement. Hou Wai-lu even goes so far as to say that the author purposely omitted proper names in order to conceal its actual date! See Hou, *Chung-kuo ku-tai ssu-hsiang hsüeh-shuo shih*, p. 11.

97. *Lao Tzu tao-te ching k'ao-i* (Inquiry into Variants in the *Lao Tzu, Classic of the Way and Its Virtue*), Preface, 1b.

98. *Ch'ung-ting Lao Tzu cheng-ku* (Revised Collation of the *Lao Tzu*), pp. 153-67.

99. *Ch'ing-t'ung shih-tai*, pp. 245-49, 253.

100. *Hsi-hsüeh chi-yen* (Notes from Study and Recitations), 15:1b.

101. *Hsien-Ch'in chu-tzu hsi-nien*, pp. 205 and 224; *Chung-kuo ssu-hsiang shih* (History of Chinese Thought), p. 51.

102. *Lao Tzu che-hsüeh t'ao-lun chi*, pp. 6-7.

103. *Han shu*, ch. 53, second biography.

104. In his *Ch'i-lüeh* (Bibliography in Seven Brief Sections). This was completed by his son, Liu Hsin. It now exists only in fragments.

105. For a list of inscriptions on the *Lao Tzu* on tablets, see Yen Ling-feng, *Chung-wai Lao Tzu chu-shu mu-lu* (Bibliography

on the *Lao Tzu* in Chinese and Foreign Languages), pp. 371-73. Ho Shih-ch'i, *Ku-pen tao-te ching chiao-k'an* (Old Texts of the *Classic of the Way and Its Virtue* Collated), Vol. III, contains photographic reproductions of the I-chou and other tablets.

106. These titles have been translated by Wilhelm, Carus, Heysinger, Au-young Sum Nung, Old, Lin Yutang, etc., in their translations.

107. *Lao Tzu i*, 5:11b.

108. *Han shu*, ch. 30, section on the Taoist school.

109. *T'ai-p'ing yü-lan*, 191:7a.

110. *Lao Tzu chiao-ku*, p. 7

111. See above, p. 36.

112. See below, note 120.

113. See Tung Ssu-ching, *Tao-te ching chi-chieh* (Collected Explanations of the *Classic of the Way and Its Virtue*), Preface.

114. In the preface of his commentary.

115. Chiao Hung, *Lao Tzu i*, 5:15b.

116. This rearranged text is found in his *Lao Tzu chiao-ku*, pp. 203-16.

117. See his *Lao Tzu chang-chü hsin-pien tsuan-chieh* (New Arrangement and Commentary of the *Lao Tzu*), pp. 170-84.

118. In chapters 20 and 21 of the *Han Fei Tzu*, respectively. See Liao (tr.), *The Complete Works of Han Fei Tzu*, Vol. I.

119. *Han Fei Tzu*, ch. 21, *SPTK*, 7:1b. Cf. Liao (tr.), *The Complete Works of Han Fei Tzu*, I, 210.

120. This has been reproduced in Jao Tsung-i's *Lao Tzu "hsiang-erh" chu chiao-chien* (A Study of Chang Tao-ling's "Hsiang-er" Commentary of *Tao Te Ching*).

121. Jao Tsung-i has accepted the traditional attribution of the authorship to Chang Tao-ling (*fl.* 156); see p. 4. Chen Shih-hsiang, in his "Hsiang-erh Lao Tzu Tao-ching Tun-huang ts'an-chüan lun-cheng" (On the Historical and Religious Significance of the Tun-huang MS of *Lao Tzu*, Book I, with Commentary by "Hsiang-erh"), *Tsing-hua Journal of Chinese Studies*, Vol. I, no. 2 (1957), makes a thorough examination of the commentary, noting that its literary and calligraphic styles are indisputably those of the early third century of our era, that the *Lao Tzu* itself had not yet been divided into chapters, and that the text and the commentary had not yet been distinguished in any way. Chen concludes

that the *Lao Tzu* with the "Hsiang-erh" commentary was an important scripture of the Taoist religion from the third century on (pp. 42-50), although he is not sure that the commentary was written by Chang Ling's grandson, Chang Lu (*fl.* 188-220) to whom the commentary has also been attributed. No one knows what *hsiang-erh* means. For a discussion of the term, see Chen, pp. 49-50.

122. For example, "filling the belly" (ch. 3) is understood as filling it with the vital force for immortality; "holding and filling" (ch. 9) is understood as keeping the energy and returning it to the brain; the "thirty spokes" in chapter 11 is taken to mean the thirty different forces of the five visceras; and "essence" in chapter 21 is regarded as the essence of man's spiritual energy. See also below, ch. 10, note 2.

123. According to the lists in Yen Ling-feng, *Chung-wai Lao Tzu chu-shu mu-lu,* which runs to 1956. There have been several commentaries since then. For a selected list of Japanese commentaries and annotations, see Takeuchi, *Rōshi no kenkyū* (Study on the *Lao Tzu*), I, 233-35. Tu Tao-chien (*fl.* 1306), in the Preface of his *Tao-te hsüan-ching yüan-chih* (Original Meanings of the *Profound Classic of the Way and Its Virtue*), says there have been 3000 commentators altogether, obviously an exaggeration.

124. In his *Tao-te ching kuang sheng-i shu* (Commentary Elaborating the Imperial Commentary on the *Classic of the Way and Its Virtue*). The names of these commentators are found in Chiao Hung's work, 5:13a-14b.

125. In his *Lao Tzu i.*

126. *Sui shu,* ch. 34, and *Sung shih,* ch. 205, sections on the Taoist school.

127. *Ch'iu T'ang shu,* ch. 47, section on the Taoist school.

128. According to Hung I-hsüan (b. 1765), *Tu-shu ts'ung-lu* (Notes from Reading), section on Lao Tzu.

129. See *Lieh Tzu,* ch. 1, *SPTK,* 1:1b.

130. For a discussion on this commentary, see the *Ssu-k'u ch'üan-shu tsung-mu t'i-yao* (Essentials of the Complete Catalogue of the Four Libraries), pp. 3032-33, and Wang Chung-min, *Lao Tzu k'ao* (Bibliography of the *Lao Tzu*), pp. 86-87.

131. *Shih chi,* 80:8b.

132. *Shen-hsien chuan* (Biographies of Immortals), ch. 3.

133. According to the *Ssu-k'u ch'üan-shu tsung-mu t'i-yao,* p. 3031.

134. According to Ma Hsü-lun, *Lao Tzu chiao-ku,* p. 2.

135. *Huai-nan Tzu,* ch. 16, *SPPY,* 16:6a.

136. *Ho-shang-kung's Commentary on Lao-tse,* p. 10.

137. *Chuang Tzu,* ch. 11, *SPTK,* 4:37b. Cf. Giles (tr.), *Chuang Tzu,* p. 113.

138. Erkes rejects the assumption of a common source unless special proof is available (see his "Arthur Waley's Laotse-Übersetzung," *Artibus Asiae,* V [1935], 301-2), but the proof he gives here is very weak.

139. *Hung-meng chi* (Essays Elucidating the Doctrine), 1:12b.

140. Erkes, *Ho-shang-kung's Commentary on Lao-tse,* p. 11.

141. *Ibid.*

142. *Lao Tzu chiao-ku,* pp. 2-3.

143. Erkes thinks the word *fa* in chapter 4 may be the Buddhist equivalent to *dharma.* (Erkes, *Ho-shang-kung's Commentary on Lao-tse,* p. 19). He is wrong because, although *dharma* is translated as *fa* (element of existence), the *fa* in the commentary cannot have any other than the ordinary meaning of "method."

144. See Ch'ien Chi-po, *Lao Tzu tao-te ching chieh-t'i chi ch'i tu-fa* (About the Text of the *Lao Tzu, Classic of the Way and Its Virtue,* and How to Study It), p. 29.

145. According to the lists in Yen Ling-feng, *Chung-wai Lao Tzu chu-shu mu-lu,* pp. 373-77.

146. In his *Lao Tzu chu* (Commentary on the *Lao Tzu*).

147. In his *Lao Tzu chu.*

148. In his *Tao-te chen-ching chuan* (Commentary on the *Pure Classic of the Way and Its Virtue*).

149. See his *Tao-te ching chu* (Commentary on the *Classic of the Way and Its Virtue*).

150. See his *Lao Tzu i.*

151. *Ibid.*

152. *Lao Tzu yen* (Elucidation of the *Lao Tzu*).

153. For these different emphases, see Chiao Hung, *Lao Tzu i,* 5:15a.

154. For Chu Hsi's criticism of Su Ch'e's mixture of Confucianism, Buddhism, and Taoism, see *Chu Tzu wen-chi* (Collection of Literary Works by Chu Hsi), 72:16b.

155. See his *P'ing-tien Lao Tzu tao-te ching* (*Lao Tzu, The Classic of the Way and Its Virtue,* Commented on and Punctuated), chs. 5, 15, and 74.

156. For Kuo Hsiang, see Fung Yu-lan, *A History of Chinese Philosophy*, II, 205-36, and Wing-tsit Chan, *A Source Book in Chinese Philosophy*, ch. 19, sec. 6.

157. *Hsü kao-seng chuan* (Supplement to the Biographies of Eminent Monks), ch. 4. See *Taishō Daizōkyō* (Taishō Edition of the Buddhist Canon), L, 455. The date of the translation is uncertain. For a discussion of it, see Inoyue Shūten, *Rōshi no shinkenkyū* (New Study of the *Lao Tzu*), Introduction, pp. 50-52.

158. James Legge, *The Texts of Taoism*, p. 58.

159. For a historical survey of the study of the *Lao Tzu* in Russia, see Yang Hsing-shun, *Chung-kuo ku-tai che-hsüeh-chia Lao Tzu chi ch'i hsüeh-shuo* (China's Ancient Philosopher, Lao Tzu, and His Doctrines), pp. 89-98.

160. See Henri Cordier, *Bibliotheca Sinica*, I, 722-23.

161. Lists of English translations are found in Wang Chung-min, *Lao Tzu k'ao*, pp. 497-501; Yen Ling-feng, *Chung-wai Lao Tzu chu-shu mu-lu*, pp. 306-10; Welch, *Parting of the Way*, pp. 4-5; and Bahm (tr.), *Tao Teh King*, pp. 121-26. They are all incomplete. The list in Bahm is the latest, and longest, but it is already outdated.

162. For a critical review of his translation, see Eduard Erkes, "Arthur Waley's Laotse-Übersetzung," *Artibus Asiae*, V (1935), 288-307.

THE
Lao Tzu

(Tao-te ching)

1

THE TAO *that can be told of is not the eternal* [1] *Tao;*
The name that can be named is not the eternal name.
The Nameless [2] *is the origin of Heaven and Earth;* [3]
The Named is the mother of all things.

Therefore let there always be non-being, so we may
  see their subtlety, [4]
And let there always be being, [5] *so we may see their outcome.* [6]
The two are the same,
But after they are produced, they have different names. [7]
They both may be called deep and profound. [8]
Deeper and more profound,
The door of all subtleties! [9]

COMMENT

This is the most important of all chapters, for in one stroke the basic characteristics of Tao as the eternal, the nameless, the source, and the substance of all things are explicitly or implicitly affirmed. It is no wonder the opening sentences are among the most often quoted or even chanted sayings in Chinese.

The key Taoist concepts of the named and the nameless are also introduced here. The concept of name is common to all ancient Chinese philosophical schools, but Taoism is unique in this respect. Most schools insist on the correspondence of names and actualities and accept names as necessary and good; Taoism, on the contrary, rejects names in favor of the nameless. This, among other things, shows its radical and unique character. To Lao Tzu, Tao is nameless and is the simplicity without names; when names arise, that is, when the simple oneness of Tao is split up into individual things with names, it is time to stop. [10]

The cardinal ideas of being and non-being are also important here, for in Taoism the nameless (*wu-ming*) is equiva-

97

lent to non-being and the named (*yu-ming*) is equivalent to being. For this reason, when he comments on the saying about the named and the nameless, Wang Pi says, "All being originated in non-being." As students of Chinese thought well know, the ideas of being and non-being have been dominant throughout the history of Chinese philosophy. They are central concepts in Neo-Taoism, Chinese Buddhism, and also Neo-Confucianism. It was the importance of these concepts, no doubt, that led the Neo-Confucianist Wang An-shih to deviate from tradition and punctuate the phrases "always be no desires" and "always be desires" to read "Let there always be non-being, so we may . . . ," and "Let there always be being, so we may. . . ."

Wang's punctuation not only underlines the importance of these ideas; it also shows the new metaphysical interest in Neo-Confucianism. Confucianism had been fundamentally ethical in tradition, but under the impact of Buddhist and Taoist metaphysics, the Neo-Confucianists developed Confucianism along metaphysical lines. In this case, in substituting the ideas of being and non-being for the ideas of having desires and having no desires, Wang shows a greater recognition of the philosophical content of the *Lao Tzu*, as it deserves.

NOTES

1. On the basis of some ancient texts, Yü Yüeh equates *ch'ang* (eternal) with *shang* (high), but few commentators have followed him.

2. It is possible to punctuate *wu-ming* (nameless) and *yu-ming* (named) to mean "non-being is the name of" and "being is the name of," respectively. This is the reading by Cheng Lin (p. 1, sec. 6), and Duyvendak. Duyvendak refers to Ma Hsü-lun as authority; indeed, he depends chiefly on Ma. Ma did punctuate in this way in 1924 but in the revised edition of his book (1956), he has discarded the punctuation and has reverted to the generally accepted way as we have it. *Wu-ming* and *yu-ming* are key terms in the *Lao Tzu*, and are found also in chapters 32, 37, and 41.

3. On the basis of Wang Pi's commentary, which mentions "the origin of all things," Ma Hsü-lun contends that "Heaven and Earth" must have been originally "all things." Chiang Hsi-ch'ang supports him, and says that similar ideas appear in chapters 40 and 52. Such evidences are hardly strong enough to alter the text.

4. This translation of *miao* as "subtlety" rather than "mystery" is according to Wang Pi.

5. Both Wang Pi and Ho-shang Kung punctuate *yu-yü* and *wu-yü* to mean "having desires" and "having no desires." These are the traditional interpretations. Wang An-shih, however, punctuates them after *wu* and *yu*, thus making the phrases mean "there is always being," and "there is always non-being." Several Neo-Confucianists, notably Ssu-ma Kuang, Su Ch'e, and Fan Ying-yüan, and many modern writers such as Ma Hsü-lun, Kao Heng, and Ting Fu-pao, and some translators, like Medhurst, Old, Ch'u Ta-kao, Duyvendak, Cheng Lin (p. 2, sec. 7), and Mei have followed him. I have also departed from tradition because the idea of desires interrupts the thought of the chapter. To say that "the two" in the next line means desires and absence of desires, as Ho-shang Kung says, is forced; even in Wang Pi's own explanation about desires, he has to resort to the ideas of being and non-being. As Chiang Hsi-ch'ang has pointed out, we may grant that the term *wu-yü* (having desires) is a technical term in the *Lao Tzu* and appears in chapters 3, 37, and 57; as Ch'en Ching-yüan has said, we should read the *Lao Tzu* in its own light. But the term *yu-yü* does not appear anywhere else, whereas the terms *yu* and *wu* are found in chapters 2, 11, and 40. Besides, as Ch'en himself has noted, Chuang Tzu says that Lao Tzu "established his doctrines on the principles of eternal being and non-being" (ch. 33, *SPTK*, 10:35b. Cf. Giles [tr.], p. 319).

6. The word *chiao* (outcome) is open to many interpretations. Two of the variants, *chiao* (bright) in a Tun-huang manuscript, and *ch'iao* (hole) in the Huang Mao-ts'ai text, may readily be ruled out, since they do not make sense. The third variant, *chiao* (fortunate) in the Li Yüeh text, is interchangeable with *chiao* (outcome). But this *chiao* itself can be understood variously and has led to different translations—as "manifest forms" (Lin Yutang), "the manifest" (Au-young Sum Nung), "outer manifestations" (Mei), "outer fringe" (Giles [p. 19], and Legge), "outer aspects" (John Wu), "limitations" (Hughes), "bounds" (Cheng Lin, p. 2, sec. 7), "borders"

(Bodde; see Fung, I, 178), and "mere shells" (Carus). Some of these translations have the support of Lu Te-ming, who takes *chiao* to mean "limit" or "border," although Lu says it also means "subtle" and "a small path." I do not know the basis for Ch'u Ta-kao's "apparent distinction" and Blakney's "outward container." I follow both Wang Pi and Ho-shang Kung, who both understand *chiao* as *kuei*, that is, "end" or "outcome." It is not "to return" as Erkes (p. 14) has it, but "to end up." Waley is correct in following this interpretation.

7. Ch'en Ching-yüan punctuates the sentence after *t'ung* (the same), instead of *t'ung-ch'u* (produced from the same). This punctuation preserves the ancient rhyme of the verse, and has been followed by Wu Ch'eng and by Yen Fu.

8. The word *hsüan* (deep and profound) has a very wide range of meanings; it means "dark," "abstruse," "deep," "profound," "secret," etc. In Taoist religion the aspect of mystery should be stressed, but in Taoist philosophy the profound or metaphysical aspect is paramount. The word simply has to be understood in its context.

9. Professor Boodberg has written an extremely provocative article on the translation of this chapter ("Philosophical Notes on Chapter One of the *Lao Tzu*," *Harvard Journal of Asiatic Studies*, XX [1957], 598-618). He says that "the philologist should protest with the utmost vigor the common translation of Chinese *yu* and *wu* as 'Being' and 'Non-being' respectively. . . . these two Chinese terms, even in Taoist environment, remained securely within the semantic and philosophical category of habit of possession, being both essentially transitive verbs, 'to have (something)' and 'not to have (something),' with objects following them in the normal course of grammatical and philosophical events" (p. 607). Evidently he overlooks the fact that in the *Lao Tzu* (chapters 2, 40, etc.), and in many places in the *Chuang Tzu* (especially chapters 2, 6, 12; *SPTK*, 1:33b-34a, 3:15a, 5:9a [cf. Giles (tr.), *Chuang Tzu*, pp. 41, 79, and 122, respectively]), to mention only a few instances, *yu* and *wu* are not transitive verbs and do not mean "having" or "not having" anything.

10. See chapters 37, 41, and 32, respectively.

2

WHEN THE *people of the world all know beauty as beauty,*
There arises the recognition of ugliness.
When they all know the good as good,
There arises the recognition of evil.
Therefore:
Being and non-being produce each other;
Difficult and easy complete each other;
Long and short contrast [1] *each other;*
High and low distinguish each other;
Sound and voice harmonize each other;
Front and behind accompany each other.

Therefore the sage manages affairs without action
And spreads doctrines without words.
All things arise, and he does not turn away [2] *from them.*
He produces them but does not take possession of them.
He acts but does not rely on his own ability. [3]
He accomplishes his task but does not claim credit for it. [4]
It is precisely because he does not claim credit that his
accomplishment remains with him.

COMMENT

That everything has its opposite, and that these opposites are
the mutual causations of each other, form a basic part of
Chuang Tzu's philosophy and later Chinese philosophy. It is
important to note that opposites are here presented not as
irreconcilable conflicts but as complements. The traditional
Chinese ideal that opposites are to be synthesized and har-
monized can be said to have originated with Lao Tzu.

The idea of teaching without words anticipated the Buddhist tradition of silent transmission of the mystic doctrine,
especially in the Zen (Ch'an) school. This is diametrically
opposed to the Confucian ideal, according to which a superior
man acts and thus "becomes the model of the world," and

speaks and thus "becomes the pattern for the world." [5] It is true that Confucianists say that a superior man "is truthful without any words," [6] but they would never regard silence itself as a virtue.[7]

Notes

1. The Wang Pi text has *chiao* (to contrast) instead of *hsing* (to contrast). Evidently Waley (p. 257) has followed Wang Pi, but the Ho-shang Kung and, according to Chiang Hsi-ch'ang, 46 other texts, have *hsing*. As Pi Yüan has pointed out, the word *chiao* is not found in ancient books, and, according to Ma Hsü-lun, whenever the long and the short are contrasted in ancient literature the word *hsing* is used. Above all, *chiao* does not rhyme in the verse but *hsing* does. Although both words mean the same, the Chinese character should be *hsing*.

2. The Tun-huang manuscript, the Fu I and Fan Ying-yüan texts, and the *Tao-te chen-ching tz'u-chieh* (*Pure Classic of the Way and Its Virtue* Explained) all have *wei-shih* (to be the beginning or to be in the front) instead of *tz'u* (to turn away). I Shun-ting says that Wang Pi's commentary on chapter 17 quotes from chapter 2 and uses *wei-shih* instead of *tz'u*; therefore, Wang's text must originally have *wei-shih*. But as Yü Yüeh has pointed out, in chapter 34 there is the passage, "All things depend on it for life, and it does not turn away from them." There is no need, therefore, to amend the text.

3. Ho-shang Kung's interpretation: "He does not expect any reward." These last two sentences also appear in chapters 10, 51, and 77.

4. This sentence, with the variation of one word, is also found in chapter 77.

5. *The Doctrine of the Mean*, ch. 29.

6. *Ibid.*, ch. 33.

7. For similar teachings on speaking few words, see below, chapters 5, 17, and 23.

3

DO NOT *exalt* [1] *the worthy, so that the people shall not compete.*

Do not value rare treasures, [2] *so that the people shall not steal.* [3]

Do not display objects of desire, so that the people's [4] *hearts shall not be disturbed.*

Therefore in the government of the sage,
> *He keeps their hearts vacuous,* [5]
> *Fills their bellies,*
> *Weakens their ambitions,*
> *And strengthens their bones,*

He always causes his people to be without knowledge (cunning) or desire,

And the crafty to be afraid to act.

By acting without action, all things will be in order.

COMMENT

The doctrine of not exalting the worthy or men of superior talent and virtue is directly opposed to that of the Confucianists, who honor them. [6] According to the Taoist view, honor leads to greed, discrimination, and strife. On the surface, the Taoist doctrine seems to agree with that of the Legalists, who would not have the worthy in high governmental positions. [7] But their reasons for doing so are utterly different. The totalitarian Legalists would avoid the worthy because it would be difficult for the ruler to control him. To the Taoists, however, when the ideal state is achieved, there will be no need of raising the worthy to high positions. This is made very clear in the *Chuang Tzu*. [8] Nevertheless, the ideal ruler of the Taoists is the sage, who is the ultimate of worthies. Until the ideal state is reached, the Taoists, like the Confucianists, would raise the worthy to high positions after all, although they frown on the idea of personal honor.

NOTES

1. Some texts have *shang* (above) instead of *shang* (to exalt), thus making the sentence mean putting the worthy in high office. This is the interpretation followed by Hughes (p. 146) and Waley.

2. These words also appear in chapter 64.

3. As Lü Hui-ch'ing reminds us, Confucius said, "If you [the ruler], sir, were not covetous, although you should reward them [the people] to do it, they would not steal" (*Analects*, 12:18).

4. This word appears in the Wang Pi text but does not appear in the Ho-shang Kung and 47 other texts. Its presence is necessary to maintain the parallelism of the three sentences.

5. *Hsü* (vacuous) is a Taoist term. It is not to be taken in its literal sense of being empty and is not to be equated with the Buddhist *k'ung*, which means emptiness or freedom from specific characteristics. Rather, as a description of a state of mind, it means absolute peacefulness and purity of mind, freedom from worry and selfish desires, not to be disturbed by incoming impressions or to allow what is already in the mind to disturb what is coming into the mind. As a feature of reality, it means a profound and deep continuum in which there is no obstruction. See comment on chapter 5.

6. See *Analects*, 19:3, and *Book of Mencius*, 2A:5.

7. See Shang Yang (d. 338 B.C.), *Shang-chün shu* (Book of Lord Shang), 2:10b. Cf. Duyvendak (tr.), *The Book of Lord Shang*, p. 226.

8. *Chuang Tzu*, ch. 12, *SPTK*, 5:17b. Cf. Giles (tr.), *Chuang Tzu*, p. 128.

4

Tao is *empty (like a bowl).*
It may be used but its capacity is never [1] *exhausted.*
It is bottomless, perhaps the ancestor of all things.
It blunts its sharpness,
It unties its tangles.
It softens its light.
It becomes one with the dusty world. [2]
Deep and still, it appears to exist forever. [3]
I do not know whose son it is.
It seems [4] *to have existed before the Lord.* [5]

COMMENT

This chapter, on the substance and function of Tao, shows clearly that in Taoism function is no less important than substance. Substance is further described in chapters 14 and 21, but here, as in chapters 11 and 45, function (*yung*, also meaning "use") is regarded with equal respect. There is no deprecation of phenomena, as is the case with certain Buddhist schools. To describe the world as dusty may suggest a lack of enthusiasm for it; indeed both Buddhism and later Taoism employ the word "dust" to symbolize the dirty world from which we should escape. It is significant to note, however, that Taoism in its true sense calls for identification with, not escape from, such a world.

NOTES

1. There is no need to read *huo* (perhaps) as *chiu* (long) as Duyvendak has; according to Ho-shang Kung, *huo* here means a long time.
2. These last four lines also appear in chapter 56.
3. Some texts have *ch'ang-ts'un* or *jo-ts'un* instead of *huo-ts'un*, but they all mean "remaining forever." That *huo* means "forever" has the authority of Ho-shang Kung. Again Duyvendak has

substituted *chiu* for *huo* and *jo,* but since they all mean the same, the substitution is unnecessary.

4. The word *hsiang* here means "seems" and repeats the feeling expressed in the word "appear" two lines before. To interpret it to mean "image," as do Arthur Waley and Duyvendak, or "form," as does Mears, would be to make the *Lao Tzu* more metaphysical than it really is.

5. All commentators agree that "the Lord" means the Lord of Heaven.

Heaven and *Earth are not humane.*[1]
   They regard all things as straw dogs.[2]
The sage is not humane.
   He regards all people as straw dogs.
How Heaven and Earth are like a bellows!
While vacuous, it is never exhausted.
When active, it produces even more.
Much talk will of course [3] *come to a dead end.*
It is better to keep to the center.[4]

COMMENT

The term "not humane" is, of course, extremely provocative. It may be suggested that this is Lao Tzu's emphatic way of opposing the Confucian doctrine of humanity and righteousness. Actually, the Taoist idea here is not negative but positive, for it means that Heaven and Earth are impartial, have no favorites, and are not humane in a deliberate or artificial way. This is the understanding of practically all commentators and is abundantly supported by the *Chuang Tzu.*[5] To translate it as "non-benevolent" [6] is grossly to misunderstand Taoist philosophy.

The two Taoist ideas, vacuity (*hsü*) and nothingness (*wu*), later employed and elaborated by the Buddhists, were completely unacceptable to Confucianists. To them, these ideas are charged with a great danger of nihilism, even if Taoism itself is not. The Neo-Confucianist Chang Tsai calls reality "Great Vacuity" (*t'ai-hsü*),[7] Chu Hsi characterizes man's nature as vacuous and intelligent,[8] and Wang Yang-ming (1472-1529) describes the original mind of man in the same terms.[9] But Chang's "Vacuity" is equivalent to material force (*ch'i*),[10] which is real and active. To Chu and Wang, as to other Neo-Confucianists, vacuity means purity, impartiality, being devoid of selfish desires, and so forth, instead of anything nihilistic. Even then, they used the term sparingly and with great care.

1. *Jen* (humane) has been variously translated as "love," "benevolence," "human-heartedness," "true manhood," etc. For a discussion of the translation of this term, see Wing-tsit Chan, *A Source Book in Chinese Philosophy* (Princeton, 1963), Appendix, "On Translating Certain Chinese Philosophical Terms."

2. Straw dogs were used for sacrifices in ancient China. After they had been used, they were thrown away and there was no more sentimental attachment to them.

3. Practically all translators, including Waley and Duyvendak, take *shu* to mean "quick," "soon," or "much," except Lin Yutang, who renders it as "wit." They find little support among Chinese commentators. According to Wang Pi, it means the principle (*li*) of things, and Ho-shang Kung has followed him. Lu Te-ming quotes Wang and adds the meaning of *shih* (tendency). In either case it means the course of things, or their history. This is the meaning to Wei Yüan. In Emperor Ming-huang's commentary, the word is pronounced to mean "frequently." I have found few commentators and no translators who have adopted that pronunciation. Chou Kan-t'ing's modern work, primarily devoted to phonetic explanation of the *Lao Tzu*, does not read *shu* as "frequently."

4. *Chung* (center) also means the mean or moderation, but here it means the center.

5. *Chuang Tzu*, ch. 2, *SPTK*, 1:36b. Cf. Giles tr.), *Chuang Tzu*, p. 42.

6. This is the translation by Carus, Ch'u Tao-kao, Heysinger, Giles, and Medhurst. Blakney's and Lin Yutang's "unkind," Bahm's "not sympathetic," Waley's "not ruthful," Wilhelm's "nicht Liebe nach Menschenart," Wai Tao and Goddard's "unjust like humans," and Welch's "not moral, not 'our kind,' not kind the way the Rites requires" (*The Parting of the Way* p. 45) are equally unacceptable.

7. *Cheng-meng* (Correcting Youthful Ignorance), ch. 1. In *Chang Heng-ch'ü chi* (Collected Works of Chang Tsai), 2:3a-7b.

8. In his *Ta-hsüeh chang-chü* (Commentary on the *Great Learning*), comment on the text.

9. *Ch'uan-hsi lu* (Instructions for Practical Living), sec. 32. See Wing-tsit Chan (tr.), *Instructions for Practical Living, and*

Other Neo-Confucian Writings by Wang Yang-ming (New York: Columbia University Press, 1963).

10. Variously translated as "matter," "matter-energy," "vital force," "breath," etc.

6

T HE SPIRIT *of the valley* [1] *never dies.*
   It is called the subtle and profound female.
The gate of the subtle and profound female [2]
   Is the root of Heaven and Earth.
It is continuous, and seems to be always existing.
Use it and you will never wear it out. [3]

COMMENT

The valley and the female, like the infant and water,[4] are Lao
Tzu's favorite symbols for Tao. The symbol of the valley is
employed again and again.[5] There is nothing mysterious about
it or its spirit; it simply stands for vacuity, vastness, openness,
all-inclusiveness, and lowliness or humility, all of which are
outstanding characteristics of Tao. This is the interpretation
of Wang Pi, and commentators, with only a few exceptions,
have followed him. To understand the "continuous" operation
as breathing, or the valley as the belly or the Void, and then
to interpret the whole passage as one on the yoga technique of
breathing,[6] or to single out the characteristic of stillness of
the valley and then to present it as an evidence of Taoist
quietism,[7] is to fail to interpret the passages in the context of
the whole. These interpretations are not supported by the
symbolic meaning of the valley elsewhere in the book.

The spirit of the chapter is far from quietism. Instead, it involves the idea of natural transformation and continuous creation. As Chu Hsi has said, "The valley is vacuous. As sound
reaches it, it echoes. This is the spontaneity of spiritual transformation. To be subtle and profound means to be wonderful. The female is one who receives something and produces
things. This is a most wonderful principle and it has the
meaning of production and reproduction." [8]

1. Yü Yüeh equates *ku* (valley) with *ku* (grain) so that the valley means nourishment of life, or, according to Takeuchi, the production and transformation of the myriad things. Hung I-hsüan equates *ku* with *yü* (desires). Neither improves the understanding of the text. Many Japanese translators have understood *ku* in the sense of vacuity or emptiness. Thus, to Hattori Unokichi, the spirit of *ku* means the condition of vacuity and nothingness; to Koyanagi, it is the view of emptiness; and to both Taoka and Yamamoto, it is pure intelligence or the spirit of vacuity.

2. The "Hsiang-erh" commentary interprets *ku* as "passion" and the gate of the female as the female reproductive organ. Significantly, this sexual interpretation has received no support. See below, chapter 10, notes 2 and 8.

3. This chapter is quoted in the *Lieh Tzu* as from the *Book of the Yellow Emperor*. (See *Lieh Tzu*, 1:1b. Cf. Graham [tr.], *The Book of Lieh Tzu*, p. 17.) The *Lieh Tzu*, however, freely attributes words to people and is therefore unreliable. *The Book of the Yellow Emperor*, if it ever existed, has long been lost.

4. See below, chapter 10, and comment on chapter 8.

5. In chapters 15, 28, 32, 39, and 41.

6. As Wu Ch'eng, Yang Tseng-hsin, Chiang Hsi-ch'ang, and Chang Chung-yüan (p. 169) have done. See comment on chapter 10.

7. This has been done by Waley (p. 57).

8. *Chu Tzu yü-lei* (Classified Conversations of Chu Hsi), 125:9a.

HEAVEN IS *eternal and Earth everlasting.*
  They can be eternal and everlasting because they
  do not exist for themselves,
And for this reason can exist forever.

Therefore the sage places himself in the background
  but finds himself in the foreground.
He puts himself away, and yet he always remains.
Is it not because he has no personal interests?
This is the reason why his personal interests
  are fulfilled.

COMMENT

This Taoist doctrine of self-denial expresses the same spirit as do the Christian doctrine of self-sacrifice and the Buddhist doctrine of non-ego. Although Buddhism puts its idea in the metaphysical term "non-ego" and Taoism in the ethical term "having no personal interest," their import is the same. In Taoism, however, unlike Buddhism, personal interests are to be fulfilled after all. He who loses his life will find it.

THE BEST *(man)* [1] *is like water.*
Water is good; it benefits all things and does not
compete with them.
It dwells in (lowly) places that all disdain.
This is why it is so near to Tao.

(The best man) in his dwelling loves the earth.
In his heart, he loves what is profound.
In his associations, he loves humanity.
In his words, he loves faithfulness.
In government, he loves order.
In handling affairs, he loves competence.
In his activities, he loves timeliness.
It is because he does not compete that he is
without reproach.

COMMENT

Water is perhaps the most outstanding among Lao Tzu's symbols for Tao. The emphasis of the symbolism is ethical rather than metaphysical or religious. It is interesting to note that, while early Indian philosophers associated water with creation [2] and the Greek philosophers looked upon it as a natural phenomenon, ancient Chinese philosophers, whether Lao Tzu or Confucius,[3] preferred to learn moral lessons from it. Broadly speaking, Western thought, derived chiefly from the Greeks, has been largely interested in metaphysical and scientific problems, Indian thought largely interested in religious problems, and Chinese thought largely interested in moral problems. It is not too much to say that these different approaches to water characterize the Western, the Indian, and the Chinese systems of thought.

1. Most commentators and translators have understood the Chinese phrase literally as the highest good, but some commentators and translators, including Lin Yutang, Cheng Lin (p. 15, sec. 78), and Bynner, have followed Wang Pi and taken the phrase to mean the best man. Both interpretations are possible. The former interpretation has a parallel in chapter 38, which talks about the highest virtue, while the latter has a parallel in chapter 17, where both Wang Pi and Ho-shang Kung interpret "the best" to mean the best ruler. I have followed Wang Pi, not only because his commentary on the text is the oldest and most reliable, but also because the *Lao Tzu* deals with man's way of life more than abstract ideas.

2. See *Rig Veda,* 10:129. See also comment on chapter 66.

3. See *Analects,* 9:16.

9

To hold *and fill a cup to overflowing* [1]
   Is not as good as to stop in time.
Sharpen a sword-edge to its very sharpest,
   And the (edge) will not last long.
When gold and jade fill your hall,
   You will not be able to keep them.
To be proud with honor and wealth
   Is to cause one's own downfall.
Withdraw as soon as your work is done. [2]
Such is Heaven's Way.

COMMENT

Note that one should withdraw only *after* his work is done. The Taoist way of life is not that of a hermit, although hermits have taken its name. The idea of withdrawal is not entirely absent even in Confucianism. Mencius said that it was the way of Confucius "to withdraw quickly from office when it was proper to do so." [3]

NOTES

1. Practically all Chinese commentators have accepted Ho-shang Kung's interpretation of this phrase as referring to filling a vessel. Although Waley is correct in saying that the expression also applies to stretching a bow, and this makes a better parallel to sharpening a sword, understanding it as filling a vessel expresses better the central Taoist concept of vacuity. As Yen Fu has pointed out, the idea of vacuity is behind it.
2. The Ho-shang Kung and some 50 other texts, according to Chiang Hsi-ch'ang, have *kung-ch'eng ming-sui* (work done and fame accomplished). Since this stress on fame does not agree with Taoist philosophy, I have preferred *kung-sui* (work accomplished) in the Wang Pi text.
3. *Book of Mencius*, 2A:2.

10

C AN YOU *keep* [1] *the spirit* [2] *and embrace the One without departing from them?*

Can you concentrate [3] *your vital force and achieve the highest degree of weakness like* [4] *an infant?*

Can you clean and purify your profound insight [5] *so it will be spotless?*

Can you love the people and govern the state without knowledge (cunning)? [6]

Can you play [7] *the role of the female in the opening and closing of the gates of Heaven?* [8]

Can you understand all and penetrate all without taking any action? [9]

> To produce things and to rear them,
> To produce, but not to take possession of them,
> To act, but not to rely on one's own ability,[10]
> To lead them, but not to master them—
> This is called profound and secret virtue.[11]

COMMENT

It is interesting that Taoism wants the concentration of *ch'i* (vital force, breath) to be weak, whereas Confucianism wants the vital force to be strong. The aim in Confucianism is what Mencius calls the "strong moving power" (*hao-jan chih ch'i*).[12] Such is the contrast between Confucianism and Taoism.

The concentration of *ch'i* is not yoga, as Waley thinks it is. Yoga aims at transcending the self and external environment. Nothing of the sort is intended here. It is true that in the *Huai-nan Tzu* the story of Yen Hui "sitting down and forgetting everything" [13] is recited to explain Lao Tzu's saying. But note that the concentration is followed by "loving the people" and "governing the state." Because the yoga breathing technique was later promoted by the religious Taoists, some scholars have unjustifiably read it into earlier texts.

1. Emperor Ming-huang thinks that *tsai* (to keep) is interchangeable with *tsai* (a particle for exclamation) and should be the last word of the preceding chapter. Commentators like Ch'u Po-hsiu, Sun I-jang, and Ma Hsü-lun have followed him. Futhermore, they contend, since all lines of this chapter contain four words except this first line, the word *tsai* must be superfluous to it. However, it is found in both the Wang Pi and Ho-shang Kung texts as well as in their commentaries, and is also found in the passage quoted in the *Huai-nan tzu*, 12:14a (Morgan [tr.], *Tao, The Great Luminant*, p. 129). The phrase *tsai ying-p'o* appears in a work by Ch'ü Yüan (343-277 B.C.). (See *Ch'u tz'u* [Elegies of Ch'u], 5:6a.) According to Takeuchi, Nakai Riken (1732-1817) thought the word *ying* was superfluous. In view of the *Ch'u tz'u*, his contention is untenable. Furthermore, the two words *ying-p'o* (the spirit) represent one concept, forming a parallel with the One. Without the word *tsai*, there would be no verb for "the spirit."

2. *Ying-p'o* means *hun-p'o*, the heavenly and earthly aspects of the soul. As generally understood, *hun* is the spirit of man's vital force, expressed in man's intelligence and power of breathing, whereas *p'o* is the spirit of man's physical nature, expressed in bodily movement. The "Hsiang-erh" commentary interprets *p'o* as semen, on the ground that *po* (white) forms a part of the character *p'o* and is pronounced like it. Since the "Hsiang-erh" commentary is a Taoist religious text, chiefly concerned with the conservation of human energy in order to prolong life, it has gone so far as to interpret "white" in chapter 28 as semen and "black" as the inside of the female organ, where, it says, it is dark.

3. *Chuan* means neither "to preserve," as Wang Pi thinks, nor "to employ," as Ho-shang Kung thinks, but "to concentrate," according to Chu Hsi. See *Chu Tzu yü-lei*, 125:10a.

4. The Fu I and many other texts, including the Wang Pi text, quoted by Liu Wei-yung, have the word *ju* (like). It is also present in the Wang Pi, Ho-shang Kung, and other commentaries.

5. Chang Chung-yüan (p. 169) reads *hsüan-lan* (profound insight) as "Dark Mirror"; Duyvendak reads it as "secret mirror." Their only reason is that the word *lan* and the word for mirror, *chien*, look alike.

6. In 49 texts, *chih* (knowledge) here and *wei* (action) two sentences below are transposed. Some modern scholars, notably

Yü Yüeh and Liu Shih-p'ei, think that the transposition is
logical because government involves action, whereas understanding involves knowledge. Duyvendak has followed Yü
Yüeh.

7. Read *wu* (no) as *wei* (action), according to the Fu I and 34 other
texts listed by Chiang Hsi-ch'ang.

8. Ho-shang Kung says the heavenly gates refer to the place in the
Polar Star where the Lord of Heaven is. He is definitely confusing Taoist philosophy with later Taoist religion. Modern
writers have explained it in terms of the senses, or specifically
the ears, mouth, and nose, or the alternation of activity and
tranquility in the operation of Nature, or the spiritual and
mental activities of man. Most writers, however, are satisfied
with Wang Pi's explanation that it means the way of Nature.
In the *Chuang Tzu*, ch. 23, *SPTK*, 8:13b (Giles [tr.], *Chuang
Tzu*, p. 227), it means "non-being." In his commentary on the
passage in the *Chuang Tzu*, Kuo Hsiang says that the gate of
Heaven is a general name for all things and that it is the same
as "the door of all subtleties" in chapter 1 of the *Lao Tzu*.
Ch'ien Chi-po (p. 36) reminds us that in the *I-wei ch'ien-tso
tu* (Penetration of the Law of Heaven in the Apocryphal
Treatise on the *Book of Changes*), the *ch'ien* or Heaven, that
is, the male principle of creation, is called the gate of Heaven.
But there the reference is only to its opening and not to both
opening and closing. Ch'ien has to punctuate the sentence
after "opening" to agree with the *I-wei ch'ien-tso tu*, but such
punctuation is most ungrammatical. Waley thinks *p'o* is literally "semen" and that "opening and closing" alludes to a
sexual technique.

9. According to Lo Chen-yü, the Lung-hsing tablet and several
Tun-huang manuscripts do not have the final interrogative
article *hu*.

10. These last two sentences also appear in chapters 2 and 51. Cf.
also chapter 34.

11. These last two sentences also appear in chapter 51. The term
hsüan-te (profound and secret virtue), which appears in chapter 65, is found also in the *Chuang Tzu*, ch. 12, *SPTK*, 5:9b
(Giles, p. 122).

12. See *Book of Mencius*, 2A:2.

13. *Huai-nan tzu*, ch. 12, *SPPY*, 12:14a. Cf. Morgan (tr.), *Tao, The
Great Luminant*, pp. 128-29.

11

THIRTY SPOKES *are united around the hub to make a wheel,*
   But it is on its non-being that the utility of the
     carriage depends.
Clay is molded to form a utensil,
  But it is on its non-being that the utility of the
    utensil depends.
Doors and windows are cut out to make a room,
  But it is on its non-being that the utility of the
    room depends.
Therefore turn being into advantage, and turn non-being
  into utility.

COMMENT

Nowhere else in Chinese philosophy is the concept of non-being more strongly emphasized. This chapter alone should dispel any idea that Taoism is negativistic, for non-being—the hole in the hub, the hollowness of a utensil, the empty space in the room—is here conceived not as nothingness but as something useful and advantageous.

The Taoist interest in non-being has counteracted the positivistic tendency in certain Chinese philosophical schools, especially the Legalist and Confucian, which often overlook what seems to be nonexistent. It has prepared the Chinese mind for the acceptance of the Buddhist doctrine of Emptiness, although neither the Taoist concept of non-being nor that of vacuity is identical with that of the Buddhist Void. In addition, it was because of the Taoist insistence on the positive value of non-being that empty space has been utilized as a constructive factor in Chinese landscape painting. In this greatest art of China, space is used to combine the various elements into an organic whole and to provide a setting in which the onlooker's imagination may work. By the same token, much is left unsaid in Chinese poetry, for the reader must play a creative role to bring the poetic idea into full realization. The Zen Buddhists have developed to the fullest the themes that real existence is found in the nonexistent and that true words are spoken in silence, but the origin of these themes must be traced to early Taoism.

12

THE FIVE *colors cause one's eyes to be blind.*
The five tones cause one's ears to be deaf.
The five flavors cause one's palate to be spoiled.[1]
Racing and hunting cause one's mind to be mad.
Goods that are hard to get [2] *injure one's activities.*[3]

For this reason the sage is concerned with the belly
and not the eyes.
Therefore he rejects the one but accepts the other.[4]

COMMENT

If this chapter is taken literally, it would mean the rejection of all sensations, withdrawing into oneself with one's eyes closed. But nothing of the sort is intended here. All commentators agree that the belly refers to the central or fundamental things of life and the eyes refer to the superficial things of life. Not a single commentator has suggested that this chapter teaches renunciation. What is demanded here is not an escape from the external world but the rejection of superficialities in favor of what is basic and central.

NOTES

1. The five colors are green, yellow, red, white, and black; the five sounds, the five full tones in the Chinese musical scale; the five tastes, salt, bitter, sour, acrid, and sweet. These fivefold classifications have resulted from the theory of Five Agents or Elements, which conceives things to be results of the interactions of the Five Agents, namely, Water, Fire, Wood, Metal, and Earth. Many things have been formed in sets of five to correspond to them.
2. This expression is also found in chapters 3 and 64.
3. Alternate interpretation by Ho-shang Kung: "Impede one's movements."
4. This sentence is also found in chapters 38 and 72.

13

B<small>E</small> <small>APPREHENSIVE</small> *when receiving favor or disgrace.*[1]
  Regard great trouble as seriously [2] *as you regard your
    body.*

*What is meant by being apprehensive when receiving favor
  or disgrace?*
Favor is considered inferior.[3]
*Be apprehensive when you receive them and also be
  apprehensive when you lose them.*
*This is what is meant by being apprehensive when receiving
  favor or disgrace.*
*What does it mean to regard great trouble as seriously as
  you regard the body?*
The reason why I have great trouble is that I have a body.
If [4] *I have no body,*
What trouble could I have?

*Therefore he who values the world as his body may be
  entrusted with the empire.*
*He who loves the world as his body may be entrusted with
  the empire.*[5]

COMMENT

While Taoism does not regard the body as an evil, it does regard it with extreme apprehension lest it lead to selfishness.
This attitude is quite different from that of Yang Chu, who
would preserve his body under any circumstances. It is therefore difficult to agree with Fung Yu-lan that Yang Chu was an
early Taoist.[6]

NOTES

1. Probably an old saying. The word *jo* can mean "then," "to be,"
   or "to be like." In the last meaning, the sentence would read,
   "Receive favor or disgrace like a shock."

2. Liu Shih-p'ei thinks that *kuei ta-huan* does not mean "to regard great trouble seriously" but "honor" and "great trouble," which parallel favor and disgrace. Few writers have followed him.

3. Wang Pi's text has "favor is inferior" and the expression can be understood as favor received by those in inferior positions. Wang Pi has commented on it in this sense. Ho-shang Kung, on the other hand, has "disgrace is inferior." According to Chiang Hsi-ch'ang, 9 other texts agree with Ho-shang Kung, 32 have "favor is inferior" and 6 have "favor is superior and disgrace inferior."

4. According to Wang Yin-chih, in ancient times *chi* (when) was interchangeable with *jo* (if). The Fu I and Fan Ying-yüan texts have *jo* instead of *chi*.

5. Chiang Hsi-ch'ang has listed 26 variations in 30 texts, but they do not affect the meaning.

6. See Fung Yu-lan, *A History of Chinese Philosophy*, I, 137.

14

W̱ᴇ ʟᴏᴏᴋ *at it and do not see it;*
  Its name is The Invisible.[1]
We listen to it and do not hear it;
  Its name is The Inaudible.
We touch it and do not find it;
  Its name is The Subtle (formless).

These three cannot be further inquired into,
And hence merge into one.
Going up high, it is not bright, and coming down
    low, it is not dark.
Infinite and boundless, it cannot be given any name;
It reverts to nothingness.
This is called shape without shape,
Form without objects.[2]
It is The Vague and Elusive.[3]
Meet it and you will not see its head.
Follow it and you will not see its back.
Hold on to the Tao of old in order to master the
    things [4] *of the present.*
From this one may know the primeval beginning
    (of the universe).
This is called the bond [5] *of Tao.*

Cᴏᴍᴍᴇɴᴛ

Subtlety is an important characteristic of Tao and is more important than its manifestations.[6] The Confucianists, on the other hand, emphasize manifestation. There is nothing more manifest than the hidden (subtle), they say, and "a man who knows that the subtle will be manifested can enter into virtue." [7] The Buddhists and Neo-Confucianists eventually achieved a synthesis, saying that "there is no distinction between the manifest and the hidden." [8]

To describe reality in terms of the invisible, the inaudible, and the subtle is an attempt to describe it in terms of non-being. Because the three Chinese words are pronounced *i, hsi,* and *wei,* respectively, they have been likened to *Jod, Heh, Vav,* indicating the name Jehovah, and to the Hindu god Ishvara,[9] but any similarity is purely accidental. The threefold description does not suggest any idea of trinity either. Basically, Taoist philosophy is naturalistic, if not atheistic, and any idea of a god is alien to it.

NOTES

1. According to Fan Ying-yüan, the old texts of Sun Teng, Wang Pi, and Fu I all had *chi* instead of *i,* but they both mean "invisible."

2. The Su Ch'e, Wu Ch'eng, Lin Hsi-i, and 9 other texts have "form" instead of "objects." Kao Heng thinks this is better because it forms a perfect parallel with the preceding phrase and does not repeat the term "without object" or "nothingness" in the preceding sentence. However, in chapter 21 both form and objects (things) are mentioned.

3. According to Chiao Hung and Wang Ch'ang, this sentence does not appear in the text inscribed on the Lung-hsing Temple tablet.

4. Liu Shih-p'ei suggests that *yu* (things) is interchangeable with *yü* (region), making the passage read, "Control the region of the present."

5. *Chi,* literally, "a thread," denotes tradition, discipline, principle, order, essence, etc. Generally it means the system, principle, or continuity that binds things together.

6. See also chapters 1 and 15.

7. *The Doctrine of the Mean,* chs. 1 and 33.

8. Ch'eng I, Preface to the *I chuan* (Commentary on the *Book of Changes*).

9. See Carus, Medhurst, and Old. For Legge's comments on early Western scholars' interpretations, see *The Texts of Taoism,* pp. 94 and 105-6.

15

O<small>F OLD</small> *those who were the best rulers* [1] *were subtly*
mysterious and profoundly penetrating; [2]
Too deep to comprehend.
And because they cannot be comprehended,
I can only describe them arbitrarily:

Cautious, like crossing a frozen stream in the winter,
Being at a loss, like one fearing danger on all sides,
Reserved, like one visiting, [3]
Supple and pliant, like ice about to melt.
Genuine, like a piece of uncarved wood,
Open and broad, like a valley,
Merged and undifferentiated, [4] *like muddy water.*

Who can make muddy water gradually clear through
tranquility?
Who can make the still gradually come to life
through activity?
He who embraces this Tao does not want to fill
himself to overflowing.
It is precisely because there is no overflowing that he
is beyond wearing out and renewal.

COMMENT

Here is another well known symbol used in the *Lao Tzu,*
namely the uncarved wood (*p'u*).[5] It connotes simplicity, plainness, genuineness in spirit and heart, and similar qualities.
Metaphysically it means the One, which is simple and undifferentiated. Ethically and psychologically it means a pure
heart and a simple mind.[6] Significantly, simplicity does not
mean blankness. As a state of mind it is characterized by care,
openness, the balance of tranquility and activity, and other
positive qualities.

1. Both the Wang Pi and Ho-shang Kung texts have *shih* (ruler), but the Fu I text has *tao*. Many modern scholars, including Ma Hsü-lun and many translators, have followed Fu I and taken the phrase to mean the most skillful in the practice of Tao. Ho-shang Kung's commentary says as much, but Ma is wrong in saying that the Ho-shang Kung text has the word *tao*. Yü Yüeh proposes to replace *shih* with *shang* (above). Since *shih* means "rulers above," the emendation is quite unnecessary.

2. *Hsüan-t'ung* (profound penetration) is also interchangeable with *hsüan-t'ung* (profound identification). See chapter 56, note 6. Ho-shang Kung interprets the term here in this second sense, as does Shih Yung. This understanding of *t'ung* as identification is supported by the *Chuang Tzu* (ch. 2, *SPTK*, 1:30a [Giles (tr.), *Chuang Tzu*, p. 39]), where all opposites and distinctions are identified as one.

3. *Jung* (appearance, attitude) in the Wang Pi text, but *k'o* (guest) in the Ho-shang Kung, Fu I, and 51 other texts mentioned by Chiang Hsi-ch'ang. *K'o* rhymes with the four following lines; *jung* does not. It is interesting that Waley has written a long commentary on *jung* (for this chapter), but chooses *k'o* here instead of *jung*.

4. The sevenfold description may suggest a progression (according to Medhurst), or seven categories of moral cultivation (according to Wu Ching-yü), but there is no need to treat the *Lao Tzu* so systematically.

5. See also chapters 19, 28, 32, 37, and 57.

6. It is not necessary to translate *p'u* literally as "uncarved wood" or "uncarved block," as Waley has done almost consistently. If any consistent translation is desired, it should be "simplicity."

16

A TTAIN *complete vacuity.*
Maintain steadfast quietude.

All things come into being,
And I see thereby their return.
All things flourish,
But each one returns [1] *to its root.*
This return to its root means tranquility.
It is called returning to its destiny.
To return to destiny is called the eternal (Tao).
To know the eternal is called enlightenment.
Not to know the eternal is to act blindly to
result in disaster.
He who knows the eternal is all-embracing.
Being all-embracing, he is impartial.
Being impartial, he is kingly (universal). [2]
Being kingly, he is one with Nature. [3]
Being one with Nature, he is in accord with Tao.
Being in accord with Tao, he is everlasting
And is free from danger throughout his lifetime.

COMMENT

The central idea here is returning to the root, which is to be achieved through tranquility. Generally speaking, in Taoist philosophy Tao is revealed most fully through tranquility rather than activity. Under its influence, Wang Pi has commented on the hexagram *fu* (to return) in the *Book of Changes* in the same light. He says, "Although Heaven and Earth are vast, possessing the myriad things in abundance, where thunder moves and winds circulate, and while there is an infinite variety of changes and transformations, yet its original [substance] is absolutely quiet and perfect non-being. Therefore only with the cessation of activities within Earth can the mind of Heaven and Earth be revealed." [4]

This Taoistic position is directly opposed by the Neo-Confucianists, who insist that the mind of Heaven and Earth is to be seen in a state of activity. As Ch'eng I says, "Former scholars all said that only in a state of tranquility can the mind of Heaven and Earth be seen. They did not realize that the mind of Heaven and Earth is found in the beginning of activity." [5]

NOTES

1. According to Chiang Hsi-ch'ang, the word *fu* in *fu-kuei* is omitted in 24 texts. The two words, both meaning "to return," are not redundant, for together they mean specifically "returning to the source." The combined term appears in chapters 28 and 52. The word *fu* is a key term in this chapter.

2. The Lung-hsing Temple tablet (according to Chiao Hung), and the Hsing-chou text (according to Yen K'o-chün), have *sheng* (to produce) instead of *wang* (kingly). This is also true in a Tun-huang manuscript, according to Jao Tsung-i. Ma Hsü-lun thinks that *sheng* is a corruption of *wang*, which in turn is a corruption of *chou* (universal). Duyvendak has followed him.

3. Ma thinks that *t'ien* (nature) should have been *ta* (great). In their translations, Ch'u Ta-kao and Duyvendak have followed Ma in using *chou* and *ta*.

4. See *Chou-i cheng-i* (Correct Meanings of the *Book of Changes*), chapter 3, hexagram *fu*.

5. *I chuan*, 2:33a.

T HE BEST [1] *(rulers) are those whose existence is (merely) known by the people.*[2]

The next best are those who are loved and praised.

The next are those who are feared.

And the next [3] *are those who are despised.*

It is only when one does not have enough faith in others that others will have no faith in him.[4]

(The great rulers) value their words highly.

They accomplish their task; they complete their work.

Nevertheless their people say that they simply follow Nature.[5]

COMMENT

Whether the people in idealized antiquity were not aware or barely aware of their government, the point is that the best way to govern is to leave the people alone and to follow the course of taking no action (*wu-wei*). This ideal of laissez faire is present in Confucianism, but it originated in Taoism.

NOTES

1. *T'ai-shang* is understood by Ho-shang Kung as the highest in time, that is, antiquity, but by most others as the highest in virtue.

2. The Wu Ch'eng and *Yung-lo ta-tien* (Great Library of the Yung-lo Period) texts have *pu* (not) instead of *hsia* (people). The Japanese *Koitsu sōsho* (Collection of Missing Ancient Texts) text has *hsia-pu.* In these cases the meaning is that the people did not know of the existence of their government. This version has been accepted by some modern scholars, including Hu Shih (*The Development of the Logical Method in Ancient China*, p. 16), and translators (Legge, Carus, Ch'u Ta-kao).

3. This phrase is not found in the 35 texts listed by Chiang Hsi-ch'ang.

4. This sentence is also found in chapter 23.

5. *Tzu-jan* (Nature), literally "self-so," means being natural or spontaneous.

W̱HEN THE *great Tao declined,*
The doctrine of humanity and righteousness arose.
When knowledge and wisdom appeared,
There emerged great hypocrisy.
When the six family relationships [1] *are not in harmony,*
There will be the advocacy of filial piety
and deep love to children. [2]
When a country is in disorder,
There will be the praise of loyal ministers.

COMMENT

This is, of course, a severe attack on conventional and superficial morality, the type of convention strongly promoted by hypocritical Confucianists. But more than that, this is a keen observation that moral professions are often unmistakable signs of a bad situation. It is undeniable that patriotism is most strongly demanded when loyalty to the country is questioned, and that the voice for peace is raised to the highest pitch at times of war.

NOTES

1. Father, son, elder brother, younger brother, husband, and wife.
2. Some texts, including the *Yung-lo ta-tien,* have *hsiao-tzu* (filial sons) instead of *hsiao-tz'u* (filial piety and deep love). Ma Hsülun maintains that this matches "loyal ministers" below, and Duyvendak has followed him. But the substitution does not enhance the understanding of the passage. Besides, deep love and filial piety are mentioned together in the next chapter. On the translation "deep love," see chapter 67, note 3.

ABANDON *sageliness and discard wisdom;*
   Then the people will benefit a hundredfold.
Abandon humanity and discard righteousness;
   Then the people will return to filial piety and
    deep love.[1]
Abandon skill and discard profit;
   Then there will be no thieves or robbers.
However, these three things are ornaments (wen) [2] *and are*
   not adequate.
Therefore let people hold on to these:
   Manifest plainness,
   Embrace simplicity,
   Reduce selfishness,
   Have few desires.

COMMENT

The sage as the ideal human being and the ideal ruler is mentioned thirty times in the book, yet here sageliness is condemned. There is no contradiction, for sageliness here means
the conscious "sageliness" of the Confucianists, and is therefore
mentioned along with wisdom, humanity, and righteousness.
With regard to the true sage, it is curious that while ancient
kings were regarded as models by most ancient schools, and
even by Chuang Tzu, they are ignored by Lao Tzu. It is not
that Lao Tzu does not look to the past, but rather that to him
the sage transcends time.

NOTES

1. In the Wu Ch'eng, Emperor T'ai-tsu, and *Yung-lo ta-tien* texts,
   this sentence precedes the first.
2. The word *wen* has many meanings—adornment, culture, literature, social systems, education, words, argument, superficiality,
   artificiality, grain, pattern, etc.—and has led to various transla-

tions, perhaps more diverse than any other word, as "externals" (Lin Yutang), "civilization" (Hughes), "adornment" (Waley and Mei), "outward show" (Giles, p. 44), "aesthetic" (Medhurst), "artifice" (Cheng Lin, sec. 148, p. 28), "culture" (Carus, Ch'u Ta-kao), "decorating" (Heysinger). John Wu's "criss-cross of Tao," Wilhelm's "Schein," Legge's "methods [of government]," Bynner's "methods of life," Bahm's "clear," and Erkes' "knowledge" are obviously interpretations. Among modern Asian writers, Kao Heng is unique in proposing to understand *wei-wen* (to be *wen*) as *wei-wen* (artificial *wen*). Kimura Eiichi is equally unique in interpreting the passage to mean that the three sentences are not adequate expressions and should be made to be related to the rest of the chapter. Takeuchi's interpretation of *wen* as "laws" lacks a sound basis. Chang Shun-i's understanding of *wen* as *wen-chiao* (cultural education) seems reasonable.

Among traditional commentators Wei Yüan seems to represent the majority in understanding *wen* as ornament, or what is on the surface, as against reality or substance. This is the meaning of *wen* in *Analects*, 16:6. Of all possible meanings, this is the most suitable here. Chang Chung-yüan's "external refinement" is equally good. According to Ho-shang Kung, ornament is inadequate as an instrument for teaching the people.

20

Abandon *learning and there will be no sorrow.*[1]

How much difference is there between "Yes, sir," and "Of course not"?
How much difference is there between "good" and "evil"?
What people dread, do not fail to dread.
But, alas, how confused, and the end is not yet.[2]
The multitude are merry, as though feasting on a day of sacrifice.
Or like ascending a tower in the springtime.[3]
I alone am inert, showing no sign (of desires),
Like an infant that has not yet smiled.
Wearied, indeed, I seem to be without a home.
The multitude all possess more than enough.
I alone seem to have lost all.
Mine is indeed the mind of an ignorant man,
Indiscriminate and dull!
Common folks are indeed brilliant;
I alone seem to be in the dark.
Common folks see differences and are clear-cut;
I alone make no distinctions.
I seem drifting as the sea; [4]
Like the wind blowing about, seemingly without destination.
The multitude all have a purpose;
I alone seem to be stubborn and rustic.
I alone differ from others,
And value drawing sustenance from Mother (Tao).[5]

COMMENT

A Confucianist would never say, "Abandon learning." Further, he would distinguish sharply between good and evil. The Neo-Confucianist, Ch'eng Hao, has been severely criticized for his saying, "Good and evil in the world are both the Principles of

Nature," [6] and Wang Yang-ming was likewise widely attacked for teaching that "in the original substance of the mind there is no distinction between good and evil." [7]

NOTES

1. This line is definitely out of place here. Because it rhymed in ancient times with the last two lines of the preceding chapter, because like them it contains four words, and because it expresses a similar idea, many scholars, notably Kuei Yu-kuang, Yao Nai, Ma Hsü-lun, Hu Shih (*Chung-kuo che-hsüeh shih ta-kang,* or Outline of the History of Chinese Philosophy, p. 66), Kao Heng, and Chiang Hsi-ch'ang, have shifted it to the end of the last chapter. Cheng Lin (sec. 129, p. 28), has followed them in his translation. Others, like I Shun-ting, Ch'en Chu, and Chang Mo-sheng have transferred it to the beginning of the preceding chapter, for the reason that like the first three sentences it begins with "abandon"; I Shun-ting has support from the *Wen Tzu* (ch. 1, *SPPY,* Pt. I, p. 3b), which quotes the passage in this arrangement. Ch'u Ta-kao and Chang Chung-yüan (p. 167) have followed them in their English versions. Interestingly enough, Duyvendak, who has shifted a good deal, insists that the opening line is the key to the chapter.

2. *Yang* literally means "dawn," but it also means "the end," "limit," "to stop," etc. I don't know the reason for Waley's rendering of "superficial."

3. Waley reads "spring terrace" instead of "tower in the spring-time." He could have added that, according to Chiang Hsi-ch'ang, this is the reading in 33 texts. But as Yü Yüeh has pointed out, "ascending a tower in the springtime" is in the same construction as "crossing a frozen stream in the winter" in chapter 15. Besides, he adds, neither the Wang Pi nor the Ho-shang Kung commentary groups "spring" and "tower" together. In any case the order of the words makes no practical difference. From one instance in Chinese literature Waley concludes that "spring terrace" means a carnival (pp. 248-49), but there seems to be no justification for this generalization.

4. Duyvendak has emended this line to read "wan like the waning moon."

5. Literally, "sucking from mother's breast." The term "Mother" occurs also in chapters 1, 25, 52, and 59. According to the earliest commentary on the *Lao Tzu* (*Han Fei Tzu,* ch. 20,

SPTK, 6:5a), "Mother" means Tao (cf. Liao [tr.], *Han Fei Tzu*, I, 183). Liu Shih-p'ei thinks that *shih* (sustenance) should be *te* (to obtain), referring to the phrase "keep to [or obtain] its mother" and citing instances in ancient texts where *te* has been corrupted to be *shih*.

6. *I-shu* (Surviving Works), 2A:1b. In defense of Ch'eng, Chu Hsi says that what Ch'eng means is that the contrast of good and evil results not from the original nature of man but from his deviation from his original good nature (*Chu Tzu yü-lei*, 97:8b). Yang Tseng-hsin thinks that in this sense, Ch'eng Hao agrees with Lao Tzu.

7. *Ch'uan-hsi lu*, sec. 315. See Chan (tr.), *Instructions for Practical Living, and Other Neo-Confucian Writings by Wang Yang-ming.*

21

THE ALL-EMBRACING *quality of the great virtue follows alone from the Tao.*
The thing that is called Tao is eluding and vague.
    Vague and eluding,[1] *there is in it the form.*[2]
    Eluding and vague, in it are things.[3]
Deep and obscure, in it is the essence.[4]
The essence is very real; in it are evidences.

From the time of old until now, its name (manifestations)[5]
    ever remains.
By which we may see[6] *the beginning of all things.*[7]
How do I know that the beginnings of all things are so?
Through this (Tao).[8]

COMMENT

From the philosophical standpoint, this is an extremely important chapter. The sentence, "The essence (*ching*) is very real (*chen*)," virtually forms the backbone of Chou Tun-i's *T'ai-chi-t'u shuo* (Explanation of the Diagram of the Great Ultimate), which centers on the "reality of the Non-ultimate and the essence of yin and yang."[9] And Chou's work laid the foundation of the entire Neo-Confucian metaphysics. It is remarkable how two basic Taoist terms were assimilated into Neo-Confucianism and assumed a central position. Of course, Neo-Confucian metaphysics is more directly derived from the *Book of Changes*, but the concepts of reality in the *Book of Changes* and in this chapter are strikingly similar.

NOTES

1. This description also appears in chapter 14.
2. See chapter 35, note 1.
3. Yü Yüeh contends that these two lines should be transposed, so that the third line rhymes with the second and the fourth with

the fifth, and so that the expressions "eluding and vague" can be repeated immediately. This is the order in the *Tao-tsang* (Taoist Canon) version of the Ho-shang Kung text, but there seems to be no logical necessity for the transposition. From the literary point of view, one order would seem to be as good as the other.

4. The word *ching* (essence) also means "intelligence," "spirit," "life force."

5. There seems to be no justification for Waley's translation of *ming* (name) as "to charge" the troops (p. 249). His translation stems from his interpretation of the word *yüeh* (to see) as "to cheer" and *chung-hu* (beginning of all things) as "many warriors"; both translations seem equally baseless.

6. *Yüeh* means "to inspect" or "to see," but Hu Shih (*Chung-kuo che-hsüeh shih ta-kang*, p. 60) and Ma Hsü-lun say that the original text of Wang Pi had *shuo* (to explain). On this basis Hu interprets this passage as one on the origin of names and terms.

7. Virtually all commentators have understand the word *fu* in its sense of "beginning." Yü Yüeh equates it with *fu* (father), but the implied meaning is still "origin" or "beginning." It also means "men." Waley probably got the idea of warriors from this meaning.

8. Wang Pi says that "this" refers to the aforesaid, but most commentators and modern writers take it to mean Tao, except Waley, who interprets it to mean "inward knowledge" and "intuition."

9. See his *T'ai-chi-t'u shuo*. Yin is the passive, female cosmic principle or force, while yang is the active, male cosmic principle.

22

To yield *is to be preserved whole.*
To be bent is to become straight.
To be empty is to be full.
To be worn out is to be renewed.
To have little is to possess.
To have plenty is to be perplexed.
Therefore the sage embraces the One
And becomes the model of the world.
He does not show himself; therefore he is luminous.
He does not justify himself; therefore he becomes
*   prominent.*
He does not boast of himself; therefore he is
*   given credit.*
He does not brag; therefore he can endure for long.[1]

It is precisely because he does not compete that the
*   world cannot compete with him.*[2]
Is the ancient saying, "To yield is to be preserved whole,"
*   empty words?*
Truly he will be preserved and (prominence and credit)
*   will come to him.*

Comment

Taoism seems to be advocating a negative morality. In this respect, it is not much different from the Christian doctrine taught in the Sermon on the Mount, which extols meekness, poverty, and so forth. Whatever negativism there may seem to be, it pertains to method only; the objective is entirely positive.[3]

NOTES

1. This and the preceding three lines are repeated with slight modification in chapter 24 (lines 3-6). Ma Hsü-lun thinks they ought to be shifted there to follow the sixth line.
2. This sentence is also found in chapter 66. Ma thinks it ought to become the fourth line in chapter 68.
3. The same spirit is expressed in chapter 45.

23

NATURE [1] SAYS *few words.*
    For the same reason [2] *a whirlwind does not last a
    whole morning.*
Nor does a rainstorm last a whole day.
What causes them?
It is Heaven and Earth (Nature).
If even Heaven and Earth cannot make them last long,
How much less can man?

Therefore he who follows Tao [3] *is identified with Tao.*
He who follows virtue [4] *is identified with virtue.*
*He who abandons (Tao) is identified with the abandonment
    (of Tao).*
*He who is identified with Tao—Tao is also happy to
    have him.*
*He who is identified with virtue—virtue is also happy
    to have him.*
*And he who is identified with the abandonment (of Tao)—
    the abandonment (of Tao) is also happy to abandon him.*
*It is only when one does not have enough faith in others
    that others will have no faith in him.* [5]

COMMENT

We have already encountered the Taoist teaching of the value
of saying little.[6] Here it is Nature that does not say much. On
this point Taoism and Confucianism agree. In fact, Confucius
has gone further, saying, "Does Heaven (Nature) say anything?
The four seasons run their course and all things are produced.
Does Heaven say anything?" [7]

NOTES

1. Nature is *tzu-jan* in Chinese; Yao Nai, on the assumption that
    the word *ku* (therefore) in the next sentence is an interpola-
    tion, thinks that this sentence stands by itself and should there-

fore be shifted to the preceding chapter. Kao Heng and Miu Er-shu agree. Apparently, they fail to see that the next sentence follows very naturally even without the word *ku.*

2. The word *ku* is not found in the Ho-shang Kung and 56 other texts listed by Chiang Hsi-ch'ang.

3. Following Yü Yüeh, the repetition of "he who follows Tao" has been dropped.

4. The Fu I text has *te* (to obtain) in place of *te* (virtue). Duyvendak has adopted the former.

5. This sentence is repeated in chapter 17. For this reason Hsi T'ung and Ma Hsü-lun think it should be deleted.

6. See chapters 2, 5, and 17.

7. *Analects,* 17:19.

24

HE WHO *stands on tiptoe is not steady.*
   He who strides forward does not go.
He who shows himself is not luminous.
He who justifies himself is not prominent.
He who boasts of himself is not given credit.
He who brags does not endure for long.[1]

From the point of view of Tao, these are like remnants
   of food and tumors of action,
Which all creatures detest.
Therefore those who possess Tao turn away from them.[2]

COMMENT

The Confucian *Doctrine of the Mean* says of absolute sincerity, "Such being its nature, it becomes prominent without any display, produces changes without motion, and accomplishes its ends without action." [3] It also says, "The way of the superior man is hidden but becomes more prominent every day, whereas the way of the inferior man is conspicuous but gradually disappears." [4]

NOTES

1. Lines 3-6 appear in chapter 22 in slightly different form.
2. These two lines are repeated in chapter 31.
3. *Doctrine of the Mean*, ch. 26.
4. *Ibid.*, ch. 33.

25

THERE WAS *something undifferentiated and yet complete,*
 Which existed before heaven and earth.
Soundless and formless, it depends on nothing
 and does not change.
It operates everywhere and is free from danger.
It may be considered the mother of the universe.
I do not know its name; I call it Tao.
If forced to give it a name, I shall call it Great.
Now being great means functioning everywhere.
Functioning everywhere means far-reaching.
Being far-reaching means returning to the original point.

Therefore Tao is great.
Heaven is great.
Earth is great.
And the king [1] *is also great.*
There are four great things in the universe, [2] *and the king is*
 one of them.
Man models himself after Earth.
Earth models itself after Heaven.
Heaven models itself after Tao.
And Tao models itself after Nature.

COMMENT

Taoist cosmology is outlined here simply but clearly. In the
beginning there is something undifferentiated, which is forever operating; it produces heaven and earth and then all
things. In essence this cosmology is strikingly similar to that of
the *Book of Changes.* In the system of Change, the Great Ultimate produces the Two Modes (yin and yang), which in turn
produce all things. We don't know to what extent Taoist
thought has influenced the *Book of Changes,* which the Confucianists have attributed to their ancient sages, chiefly Confucius. At any rate, this naturalistic philosophy has always
been prominent in Chinese thought, and later contributed

substantially to the naturalistic pattern of Neo-Confucian cosmology, especially through Chou Tun-i. As will be noted,[3] he has added the concept of the Non-ultimate to the philosophy of the *Book of Changes* in order better to explain the originally undifferentiated. It is to be noted that the term "Non-ultimate" comes from the *Lao Tzu*.[4]

NOTES

1. The Fu I and Fan Ying-yüan texts have "man" in place of "king." This substitution has been accepted by Hsi T'ung, Ma Hsü-lun, Ch'en Chu, Jen Chi-yü, and Ch'u Ta-kao. They have been influenced, undoubtedly, by the concept of the trinity of Heaven, Earth, and man, without realizing that the king is considered here as representative of men. Moreover, in chapters 16 and 39, Heaven, Earth, and the king are spoken of together.

2. *Yü,* ordinarily meaning "region," is explained by both Wang Pi and Ho-shang Kung as "that which is without name," or unlimited space, that is, the universe.

3. See comment on chapter 28.

4. See chapter 28.

THE HEAVY *is the root of the light.*
The tranquil is the ruler [1] *of the hasty.*
Therefore the sage [2] *travels all day*
Without leaving his baggage.[3]
Even at the sight of magnificent scenes,
He remains leisurely and indifferent.
How is it that a lord with ten thousand chariots
Should behave lightheartedly in his empire?
If he is lighthearted, the minister [4] *will be destroyed.*
If he is hasty, the ruler is lost.

COMMENT

As the Neo-Taoists of the fourth and fifth centuries repeatedly emphasized, the sage is not one who sits in the forest with folded arms and closed mouth. He is not a hermit. Instead, he travels all day, so to speak. What makes him a sage is that he never loses sight of the fundamental or the essential.

NOTES

1. As quoted by Wang Pi (in his commentary on the hexagram *heng* [constancy] in the *Book of Changes*), the sentence has "root" instead of "ruler."
2. According to Chiang Hsi-ch'ang, 42 texts, including the Fu I text and a T'ang dynasty manuscript in the British Museum, have "superior man" in place of "sage." The Wei Yüan text should be added to the list. Some commentators think "superior man" is correct because the sage, being the ideal man for taking no action, should not travel all day.
3. The Chinese term for "baggage" means something heavy.
4. The word "root," rather than "minister," appears in the Wang Pi and Ho-shang Kung and many other texts. Many texts have "minister," which rhymed with the word for ruler.

A GOOD *traveler leaves no track or trace.*
A good speech leaves no flaws.
A good reckoner uses no counters.
A well-shut door needs no bolts, and yet it cannot
be opened.
A well-tied knot needs no rope and yet none can untie it.

Therefore the sage is always good in saving men and
consequently no man is rejected.[1]
He is always good in saving things and consequently
nothing is rejected.[2]
This is called following[3] *the light (of Nature).*

Therefore the good man is the teacher of the bad,
And the bad is the material from which the good
may learn.
He who does not value the teacher,
Or greatly care for the material,
Is greatly deluded although he may be learned.
Such is the essential mystery.

COMMENT

Although this chapter is concerned with the way of life, it involves an idea that eventually became an important element in Taoist philosophy, namely, that of having no trace (*chi*). In Neo-Taoism this prominent idea has developed to mean that true reality lies in noumena and shows no traces. The whole history of Taoism shows a tendency to undermine traces, although its philosophy is not nihilistic. The idea of traces, like other Taoist ideas,[4] eventually entered into Neo-Confucianism. But unlike the Taoists, the Neo-Confucianists look upon traces as expressions of reality. As Ch'eng I says, "Heaven and Earth are the Way (Tao). Positive and negative spiritual forces are traces of creation."[5]

The Way of Lao Tzu / 147

NOTES

1. Ma Hsü-lun thinks this is originally the fifth line of chapter 62 transposed here by mistake. However, although the two lines are similar in thought, they are quite different in literary construction.
2. According to Fu I, these two lines did not appear in any ancient text, including Wang Pi's, but was found only in the Ho-shang Kung text.
3. The word *hsi*, here rendered as "following," is open to various interpretations: "To cover," "to penetrate," "to practice," "to secure by devious means," "double," etc. According to Ma Hsü-lun's commentary on chapter 52, this *hsi* and the *hsi* meaning "practice" were interchangeable in ancient times, but it is most often understood as "following."
4. Such as being and non-being (ch. 1), vacuity (ch. 5), and essence and reality (ch. 21).
5. *I chuan*, 1:7b-8a.

28

H<small>E</small> WHO *knows the male and keeps to the female*
 Becomes the ravine of the world.
Being the ravine of the world,
He will never depart from eternal virtue,
But returns to the state of infancy.
He who knows the white and yet keeps to the black [1]
Becomes the model for the world.
Being the model for the world,
He will never deviate from eternal virtue,
But returns to the state of the non-ultimate.
He who knows glory [2] *but keeps to humility*
Becomes the valley of the world.
Being the valley of the world,
He will be proficient in eternal virtue,
And returns to the state of simplicity (uncarved wood).
When the uncarved wood is broken up, it is turned into
 concrete things. [3]
But when the sage uses it, he becomes the leading official.
Therefore the great ruler does not cut up.

COMMENT

The important Taoist symbols of the female, the infant, and
the uncarved block are encountered once more. The basic
Taoist virtues of lowliness, meekness, simplicity, and unity are
again stressed. The concept of the Non-ultimate seems to be
incidental, but as already noted,[4] Chou Tun-i, often called the
founder of Neo-Confucianism, borrowed this concept from the
Lao Tzu and added it to that of the Great Ultimate of the
Book of Changes. He has been severely criticized, especially by
Lu Hsiang-shan (1139-93) for distinguishing the two and thus
bifurcating reality into two.[5] In defense of him, Chu Hsi says
that Chou never means that there is a Non-ultimate outside of
the Great Ultimate. What Chou means, Chu says, is that the
Non-ultimate is the state of reality before the appearance of
forms, whereas the Great Ultimate is the state after the ap-

pearance of forms, and that the two form a unity.[6] Chu Hsi's words are a good explanation of the philosophy behind the concepts of the Non-ultimate, the uncarved block, and concrete objects in this chapter.

NOTES

1. See above, chapter 10, note 2. White and black here symbolize glory and humility, respectively.

2. I Shun-ting contends that the words following "knows the white" up to this point are interpolations, on the grounds that the passage is quoted without these words in the *Chuang Tzu* (ch. 33, *SPTK*, 10:35b [Giles, tr., *Chuang Tzu*, p. 320]); without them the parallelism from the first to the fifteenth line would be perfect. Ma Hsü-lun, Kao Heng, and Chiang Hsi-ch'ang have supported him. But quotations in Chinese works are not always exact, especially in ancient works. With these words, the 15 lines form a threefold parallelism.

3. As Tao is transformed into the myriad things. The word *ch'i*, translated as "utensils" in chapter 11, should be understood here in its more general sense of concrete things. In later philosophy, especially in Neo-Confucianism, *ch'i* is contrasted with Tao, which has neither physical restriction nor physical form, but its meaning is not as general as matter, substance, or material entity.

4. See comment on chapter 25.

5. *Hsiang-shan ch'üan-chi* (Complete Works of Lu Hsiang-shan), 2:6a, 9a.

6. *Chu Tzu yü-lei*, 94:20b; *Chu Tzu wen-chi* (Collection of Literary Works by Chu Hsi), 36:8a-12a.

29

WHEN ONE *desires to take over the empire and act on it*
    (interfere with it),
I see that he will not succeed.
The empire is a spiritual thing,[1] and should not be acted on.
He who acts on it harms it.
He who holds on to it loses it.[2]

Among creatures some lead and some follow.
Some blow hot and some blow cold.
Some are strong and some are weak.
Some may break and some may fall.
Therefore the sage discards the extremes, the extravagant,
    and the excessive.

COMMENT

Wang Pi says in his commentary: "Spirit has no physical form
and has no spatial restriction, whereas concrete things (*ch'i*)
are produced through an integration of elements. When there
is an integration without form, it is therefore called a spiritual
thing. The nature of the myriad things is spontaneity. It should
be followed but not interfered with. . . . The sage understands
Nature perfectly and knows clearly the conditions of all things.
Therefore he goes along with them but takes no action. He is
in harmony with them, but does not impose anything on them.
He removes their delusions and eliminates their doubts. Hence
the people's minds are not confused and things are contented
with their own nature."

NOTES

1. The Chinese character for "thing" here is the same for "concrete
   thing." Duyvendak's suggestion that this "spiritual thing," or
   literally, "spiritual vessel," may be the nine sacred bronze
   vessels in ancient China is interesting, but proof is needed to
   establish it as fact.
2. These two sentences also appear in chapter 64.

30

H E WHO *assists the ruler with Tao does not dominate the world with force.*
The use of force usually brings requital.
Wherever armies are stationed, briers and thorns grow.
Great wars are always followed by famines.[1]

A good (general)[2] *achieves his purpose and stops,*
But dares not seek to dominate the world.
He achieves his purpose but does not brag about it.
He achieves his purpose but does not boast about it.
He achieves his purpose but is not proud of it.
He achieves his purpose but only as an unavoidable step.
He achieves his purpose but does not aim to dominate.
(For) after things reach their prime, they begin to grow old,
Which means being contrary to Tao.
Whatever is contrary to Tao will soon perish.[3]

COMMENT

Mencius says, "Those who nowadays serve their rulers say, 'We can extend our territories for our ruler and fill his treasuries and arsenals. . . . We can form alliances for him with other states and ensure our victory in battles.' Such so-called good ministers today are what the ancients called 'robbers of the people.' " [4] He also says, "Those who are skillful to fight should suffer the highest punishment." [5] How remarkably similar are these sayings to the two opening sentences!

NOTES

1. According to Lo Chen-yü, this sentence does not appear in the Lung-hsing tablet and a Tun-huang manuscript.
2. The *che* (person, he who) in the Ho-shang Kung and 53 other texts makes better sense than the *yu* (to have) in the Wang Pi text.

3. These last two sentences also appear in chapter 55. Yao Nai thinks that they should be deleted here but Ma Hsü-lun thinks they should be deleted from chapter 55.
4. *Book of Mencius*, 6B:9.
5. *Ibid.*, 4A:14.

31

F<small>INE</small> [1] WEAPONS *are instruments of evil.*
    They are hated by men.[2]
Therefore those who possess Tao turn away from them.
The good ruler when at home honors the left.[3]
When at war he honors the right.[4]
Weapons are instruments of evil, not the instruments of a good
    ruler.
When he uses them unavoidably, he regards calm restraint as
    the best principle.
Even when he is victorious, he does not regard it as
    praiseworthy,
For to praise victory is to delight in the slaughter of men.
He who delights in the slaughter of men will not succeed in
    the empire.

In auspicious affairs, the left is honored.
In inauspicious affairs, the right is honored.
The lieutenant general [5] *stands on the left.*
The senior general stands on the right.
This is to say that the arrangement follows that of funeral
    ceremonies.[6]
For the slaughter of the multitude, let us weep with sorrow
    and grief.
For a victory, let us observe the occasion with funeral
    ceremonies.[7]

COMMENT

Mencius says, "He who does not like to slaughter men can unite the empire" [8]—another saying strikingly similar to the one by Lao Tzu. Like the Confucianists, the Moists also condemn war.[9] The Buddhists are, of course, pacifists. But none has condemned war more strongly than Lao Tzu. Weapons of force are here labeled as instruments of evil. This universal condemnation of war has led the Chinese people to look down upon the soldier, putting him lower in the social scale than the farmer or the artisan. Until recent decades the general was always considered inferior to the scholar-official, and the war hero was not glorified. There are very few memorials to them in China.

NOTES

1. Wang Nien-sun says that *chia* (fine) should have been the ancient script for *wei* (only), on the assumption that since the two characters look alike, *chia* was used by mistake. But, as Lu Wen-ch'ao has pointed out, the use of *wei* as Wang suggested does not fit into the pattern of usage in the *Lao Tzu;* there is no reason why, here alone, the ancient script is used. Koyanagi interprets *chia* as "skillful" or "clever," meaning those skillful in using military weapons. Such use of the word is unidiomatic.

2. The word *wu*, ordinarily meaning "things" or "creatures," is used here to mean "men."

3. Symbolic of good omens.

4. Symbolic of evil omens.

5. Japanese translators like Yamamoto, Taoka, and Koyanagi have interpreted *p'ien chiang-chün* (lieutenant general) as "general in a certain area" and *shang chiang-chün* (senior general) as "general of the whole army." Such undertsanding of *p'ien* (partial) and *shang* (high) is unusual.

6. Most commentators agree that these last twelve lines, if not the entire chapter, are a mixture of commentary and text. The sixth line, particularly, sounds like a commentary on the first line. These last five sentences interrupt the preceding and following passages. They contain the terms "lieutenant general" and "senior general," which did not appear until Han times. Moreover, this chapter and chapter 66 are the only two in the present Wang Pi text which contain no comments. These five sentences may possibly have been his commentary, although his commentaries in other chapters are more philosophical and more plentiful. But both Tung Ssu-ching and Chao Ping-wen say Wang added a note to this chapter, saying, "I suspect it was not written by Lao Tzu." This note is not found in the present text but still appears in a manuscript (A.D. 1235) in Japan. Kanō Naoki saw this note in the Bibliothèque Nationale at Paris, in a fragment discovered in a Tun-huang cave.

See his *Chūgoku tetsugaku shi,* p. 181. It may be an explanation of Wang's failure to comment on this chapter.

7. While writers like Yao Nai, I Shun-ting, and Liu Shih-p'ei are content with pointing out the interpolations, Ma Hsü-lun, Kao Heng, and others propose to transpose them or delete them from the text, and Yang Liu-ch'iao has actually rearranged his text according to Kao Heng's proposal.

8. *Book of Mencius,* 1A:6.

9. *Mo Tzu,* chs. 17-19. See Y. P. Mei (tr.), *The Ethical and Political Works of Motse.*

32

Tao is *eternal and has no name.*

Though its simplicity [1] *seems insignificant, none in the world can* [2] *master it.*

If kings and barons would hold on to it, all things would submit to them spontaneously.

Heaven and earth unite to drip sweet dew.

Without the command of men, it drips evenly over all. [3]

As soon as there were regulations and institutions, there were names.

As soon as there are names, know that it is time to stop. [4]

It is by knowing when to stop that one can be free from danger. [5]

Analogically, Tao in the world may be compared to rivers and streams running into the sea. [6]

COMMENT

Lao Tzu persistently idealizes the nameless [7] and wants to preserve the simplicity that has no name.[8] To him names are given reluctantly; [9] nevertheless, they are not to be discarded,[10] and the nameless and the named seem to be of equal importance.[11] The conclusion is, however, inescapable: in the philosophy of Lao Tzu, names, whether in the sense of analytical concepts or in the sense of fame and titles,[12] break up original unity and simplicity and give rise to intellectual cunning and social discrimination. In this respect Taoism is diametrically opposed to Confucianism, Legalism, and the School of Logicians, who regard names as necessary for human progress and social organization. It should be noted, however, that Taoism has not gone as far as Buddhism, which rejects all names and characterizations as falsifying reality. What Taoism wants is to handle names carefully, to use them sparingly, and never to destroy the original unity and simplicity of Tao.

1. Hu Shih (*Chung-kuo che-hsüeh shih ta-kang*, p. 61) is unique in reading *ch'ang* (eternal) as *shang* (to exalt) and in ending the first sentence here, giving the sentence as: "Tao exalts the nameless and simplicity." Although this appears perfectly reasonable, it does not preserve the idea of the simplicity which has no name (in chapter 37) and the idea that simplicity is broken up to become concrete objects (in chapter 28).

2. The Ho-shang Kung text and 43 others listed by Chiang Hsi-ch'ang have "dare" instead of "can."

3. Hu (*op. cit.*) convincingly asserts that these two lines are interpolations because they do not rhyme with the rest or fit in with the ideas of the chapter. Chih Wei-ch'eng has followed him.

4. Hu (*ibid.*) reads *chih* (to stop) as *chih* (it); this agrees with the Ho-shang Kung and four other texts. If this reading is adopted, the idea becomes to know the names rather than to know the time to stop.

5. Hu (*ibid.*) contends that *pu-tai* (free from danger) should be read *pu-chih* (not well governed), but the term "free from danger" also appears in chapters 16, 25, 44, and 52.

6. Undoubtedly there are interpolations in this chapter. Aside from Hu, Ma Hsü-lun thinks the last six lines come from chapter 37. Ch'en Chu (*Chang-chü*) thinks lines 2-5 should be shifted to chapter 37 and the last line to chapter 66.

7. See chs. 1, 37, and 41.

8. Chs. 15, 19, 28, and 37.

9. Ch. 25.

10. Ch. 21.

11. Ch. 1.

12. As used in ch. 44.

33

H̲E WHO *knows others is wise;*
He who knows himself is enlightened.
He who conquers others has physical strength.
He who conquers himself is strong.
He who is contented is rich.
He who acts with vigor has will.
He who does not lose his place (with Tao) will endure.
He who dies but does not really perish enjoys long life.

COMMENT

What is it that dies but does not perish? Wang Pi says it is Tao on which human life depends and Wu Ch'eng (1249-1333) says it is the human mind. Other commentators have given different answers; most of them, however, believe that Lao Tzu means the immortality of virtue. Thus the Taoists conform to the traditional belief, already expressed in the *Tso chuan* (Tso's Commentary on the *Spring and Autumn Annals*), namely, the immortality of virtue, achievement, and words,[1] which has continued to be the typical Chinese idea of immortality.[2]

NOTES

1. *Tso chuan* (Duke Hsiang, 24th year). See Legge (tr.), *The Ch'un Ts'ew, with the Tso Chuen.*
2. Erkes thinks that *death* means that a dead man still possesses power to influence the living, and that *perishing* means that this power is gone, since the body has been dissolved. Dubs rejects this interpretation and insists that Lao Tzu means immortality of influence. (See Edward Erkes, "Ssu erh pu-wang" [dead but has not perished], *Asia Major*, III [1952], 156-59; note by Homer H. Dubs, *ibid.*, 159-61; Erkes' reply, *ibid.*, IV [1954], 149-50.) Most Chinese scholars would support Dubs.

34

THE GREAT *Tao flows everywhere.*
    It may go left or right.
All things depend [1] *on it for life, and it does*
    not turn away from them. [2]
It accomplishes its task, but does not claim
    credit for it.
It clothes [3] *and feeds* [4] *all things but does not claim*
    to be master over them.
Always without [5] *desires,* [6] *it may be called The Small.*
All things come to it and it does not master them;
    it may be called The Great.
Therefore (the sage) never strives himself for the
    great, and thereby the great is achieved. [7]

COMMENT

In commenting on this chapter, Yen Fu says that the left and
the right, the small and the great, are relative terms, and that
Tao in its original substance transcends all these relative qualities. Of greater significance, however, is the paradoxical character of Tao. This character is affirmed more than once in the
Lao Tzu. [8] In Neo-Confucianism, principle is both immanent
and transcendent, as is the Christian God. Ultimate being or
reality is by nature paradoxical.

NOTES

1. I Shun-ting reads *shih* (to depend) as *te* (to have) because the
   two characters look alike and Wang Pi's commentary has *te.*
   Ma Hsü-lun supports him. However, the reasons given appear
   to be insufficient to support the emendation.
2. Liu Shih-p'ei says *tz'u* (to turn away) should be read *wei-shih*
   (to be the beginning) as in chapter 2. See ch. 2, note 2.
3. The Ho-shang Kung and, according to Chiang Hsi-ch'ang, 32
   other texts have *ai* (to love) instead of *i* (to clothe).

4. The Fu I and, according to Chiang, 23 other texts have *pei* (to cover) instead of *yang* (to feed). The Fu I text has both *i* and *pei*. As Yü Yüeh has pointed out, *pei-yang* and *i-yang* are interchangeable.

5. Ch'en Chu (*Chang-chü*) punctuates the sentence here to read: "Let there always be non-being so that it may be called The Small."

6. Kao Heng changes "without desires" to "without action" and Chang Shun-i changes it to "without form." Duyvendak omits the phrase altogether in order to restore the parallelism between lines 5-6 and line 7.

7. This sentence also appears in chapter 63, with some variation.

8. See chs. 37, 38, 41, 48, and 63.

35

H OLD FAST *to the great form (Tao),*[1]
And *all the world will come.*
They come and will encounter no harm;
But enjoy comfort, peace, and health.
When there are music and dainties,
Passing strangers will stay.
But the words [2] *uttered by Tao,*
How insipid and tasteless!
We look at it; it is imperceptible.
We listen to it; it is inaudible.
We use it; it is inexhaustible.[3]

COMMENT

The reader is reminded that much of the *Lao Tzu* is devoted
to the art of government and many of its chapters are meant
for the ruler, as this chapter is. Because the book is a product
of an age of conflicting moral and political doctrines, social
chaos, wars, and the emergence of new social and political patterns, it is more concerned with world peace than the serene
and mystical life of an individual.

NOTES

1. The word *hsiang* (form) may be rendered as "symbol" (Hughes,
   John Wu, Lin Yutang), "image" (Legge), "idea" or "image"
   (Hu Shih, *The Development of the Logical Method in Ancient
   China,* p. 19), and "form" (Waley, Carus, Ch'u Ta-kao). There
   is no doubt that it is used here, and throughout the *Lao Tzu*
   (see chs. 14, 21, and 41), as an equivalent to Tao; therefore
   the translation "form" seems to be the best, for it is Tao itself
   and not something representing it. This is especially true of
   chapter 41, where the term "great form" appears.
2. The Fu I and many other texts have *yen* (words) instead of
   "mouth" as in the Wang Pi and Ho-shang Kung texts. Accord-

ing to Fan Ying-yüan, the original text of Wang Pi had *yen*, as does his commentary. *Yen* rhymes with the rest of the chapter, whereas the word for "mouth" does not.

3. Compare these lines with the first lines of chapter 14.

36

IN ORDER *to contract,*
It is necessary [1] *first to expand.*
In order to weaken,
It is necessary first to strengthen.
In order to destroy,
It is necessary first to promote.
In order to grasp,
It is necessary first to give.[2]
This is called subtle light.
The weak and the tender overcome the hard and the strong.
Fish should not be taken away from water.
And sharp weapons of the state should not be
     displayed to the people.

COMMENT

These are obviously Legalist techniques. In basic issues, Taoism and Legalism are incompatible, but they possess common elements—for example, the use of these techniques, and the doctrine of taking no action in government (in the Legalist case, after the ruler has achieved perfect control).

The Neo-Confucianists have criticized Lao Tzu severely for advocating these techniques. Ch'eng I condemns these methods as outright deceit, citing the fourth saying as an example, and says that it was Lao Tzu's doctrine that encouraged the Legalists, whom the Neo-Confucianists, like all Confucianists before them, denounced as immoral.[3] Chu Hsi, citing the same saying, attacks Lao Tzu as irresponsible and taking advantage of others.[4] To think that Taoism teaches treachery is nearly impossible. The intention is to promote naturalism, that is, following natural tendencies. However, although the motivation was not evil, the way the ideas are presented exposes the chapter to criticism on moral grounds.[5]

1. Ma Hsü-lun thinks *ku* (necessary) should be read *ku* (for the time being).

2. In the *Chan-kuo ts'e* (The Strategy of the Warring States), 22:1b, and the *Han Fei Tzu*, ch. 22, *SPTK*, 7:6a (Liao [tr.], *The Complete Works of Han Fei Tzu*, I, 230), there are two sayings remarkably similar to these two, but the two books refer to the *Chou shu* (Book of Chou) as the source. It is not clear if the two books are quoting from the *Lao Tzu*, or if all three draw from a common source.

3. *I-shu*, 18:39b.

4. *Chu Tzu yü-lei*, 125:1b.

5. See comment on chapter 43.

T AO INVARIABLY [1] *takes no action, and yet there is nothing left undone.*[2]
If kings and barons can keep it, all things will transform spontaneously.
If, after transformation, they should desire to be active,
I would restrain them with simplicity, which has no name.
Simplicity, which has no name, is free of desires.
Being free of desires, it is tranquil.
And the world will be at peace [3] *of its own accord.*

COMMENT

"Transform spontaneously" seems to be a passing remark here, but the idea became a key concept in the *Chuang Tzu* and later formed a key tenet in the Neo-Taoism of Kuo Hsiang. In the *Lao Tzu*, things transform themselves because Tao takes no action or leaves things alone. Chuang Tzu goes a step further, saying that everything is in incessant change and that is self-transformation.[4] In his commentary on the *Chuang Tzu*, Kuo Hsiang goes even further, stressing that things transform themselves spontaneously because they are self-sufficient, and there is no Nature behind or outside of them. Nature, he says, is but a general name for things.[5]

NOTES

1. Chiang Hsi-ch'ang reads the first two words as "Tao eternal," and Yang Liu-ch'iao has followed him.
2. Cf. ch. 48, line 4.
3. Chiang has named 44 texts, including that of Fu I, which have *cheng* (correct) instead of *ting* (peace, calm).
4. *Chuang Tzu*, ch. 17, *SPTK*, 6:20b. Cf. Giles (tr.), *Chuang Tzu*, p. 165.
5. *Ibid.*, ch. 2, *SPTK*, 1:21a.

THE MAN *of superior virtue is not (conscious of) his virtue,*
  And in this way he really possesses virtue.
The man of inferior virtue never loses (sight of) his virtue,
  And in this way he loses his virtue.
The man of superior virtue takes no action, but has no ulterior
  motive to do so.[1]
The man of inferior virtue takes action, and has an ulterior
  motive to do so.[2]
The man of superior humanity takes action, but has no
  ulterior motive to do so.
The man of superior righteousness takes action, and has an
  ulterior motive to do so.
The man of superior propriety [3] *takes action,*
And when people do not respond to it, he will stretch his arms
  and force it on them.
Therefore when Tao is lost, only then does the doctrine of
  virtue arise.
When virtue is lost, only then does the doctrine of humanity
  arise.
When humanity is lost, only then does the doctrine of
  righteousness arise.
When righteousness is lost, only then does the doctrine of
  propriety arise.
Now, propriety is a superficial expression of loyalty and
  faithfulness, and the beginning of disorder.
Those who are the first to know have the flowers of
  Tao but are the beginning of ignorance.

For this reason the great man dwells in the thick, and
  does not rest with the thin.
He dwells in the fruit, and does not rest with the flower.
Therefore he rejects the one, and accepts the other.[4]

COMMENT

Wang Pi, who wrote the best and most philosophical commentary on the *Lao Tzu*, has written the longest of his comments on this chapter. It says in part:

> How is virtue to be attained? It is to be attained through Tao. How is virtue to be completely fulfilled? It is through non-being as its function. As non-being is its function, all things will be embraced. Therefore in regard to things, if they are understood as non-being, all things will be in order, whereas if they are understood as being, it is impossible to avoid the fact that they are products [phenomena]. Although Heaven and Earth are extensive, non-being is their mind, and although sages and kings are great, vacuity is their foundation. . . . Although it is valuable to have non-being as its function, nevertheless there cannot be substance without non-being.

The concepts of substance and function, first mentioned here, were to play a very great role in Neo-Taoism, Buddhism, and Neo-Confucianism. In Chinese philosophy, whether Confucian, Taoist, or Buddhist, reality and manifestations, noumena and phenomena, the one and multiplicity are clearly distinguished as substance and function, but one involves the other. They are interpenetrated and virtually identical. In fact, the Chinese have conceived everything to be in the relationship of substance (the nature of a thing), and function (its various applications). For example, love (or humanity) is substance, since it constitutes the moral nature of all human relations. As it functions, in different human relations, it becomes faithfulness among friends, brotherly respect between brothers, and so forth. In all cases, substance and function depend upon each other.

NOTES

1. The Fu I, Yen Tsun, and Fan Ying-yüan texts have *pu wei* (not done) instead of *i-wei* (ulterior motive to do). The sentence would then read: "The man of superior virtue takes no action

but there is nothing left undone." Yü Yüeh, T'ao Hung-ch'ing, Hsi T'ung, and Ma Hsü-lun all agree, and Ch'u Ta-kao has followed this reading in his translation.

2. T'ao Hung-ch'ing thinks this sentence should be similarly emended to read: ". . . and there is something he will not do."

3. In a narrow sense, li (propriety) means rites, ritual, ceremonies, etc., but in a broad sense it means rules of behavior or principles of conduct.

4. This sentence is also found in chapters 12 and 72.

39

OF OLD *those that obtained the One:*
Heaven obtained the One and became clear.
Earth obtained the One and became tranquil.
The spiritual beings obtained the One and became divine.
The valley obtained the One and became full.
The myriad things obtained the One and lived and grew.
Kings and barons obtained the One and became rulers [1] *of the*
empire.
What made them so is the One. [2]
If heaven had not thus become clear,
It would soon crack.
If the earth had not thus become tranquil,
It would soon be shaken.
If the spiritual beings had not thus become divine,
They would soon wither away.
If the valley had not thus become full,
It would soon become exhausted.
If the myriad things had not thus lived and grown,
They would soon become extinct.
If kings and barons had not thus become honorable and high
in position, [3]
They would soon fall.
Therefore humble station is the basis of honor.
The low is the foundation of the high.

For this reason kings and barons call themselves children
without parents, lonely people without spouses, and men
without food to eat. [4]
Is this not regarding humble station as the basis of honor?
Is it not?
Therefore enumerate all the parts of a chariot as you may,
and you still have no chariot. [5]
Rather than jingle like the jade,
Rumble like the rocks.

The *Chuang Tzu* says that Lao Tzu built his doctrines "on the principle of eternal non-being and held the idea of the Great One (*T'ai-i*) as fundamental." [6] What is this Great One? It is equivalent to Tao but has different connotations. Tao denotes the Way, the principle, especially that of *wu-wei*, taking no unnatural action. The One, on the other hand, denotes unity and simplicity, the uncarved block before it is split up into individual things, and the number that is not relative to other numbers. It is things "merged into one." [7] It also denotes the beginning and the origin of things.[8] Chuang Tzu used it in still another sense, although it is implicit in the *Lao Tzu*, that is, the synthesis of all opposites. He says, "The universe and I exist together, and all things and I are one." [9] According to him, all distinctions and contraries are combined by Tao into one.[10] In religious Taoism, one of the major sects is named "Great One" or "Great Unity." [11]

NOTES

1. The word *cheng*, ordinarily meaning "upright," "firm," or "to rectify," here denotes a ruler.
2. Neither the Wang Pi nor the Ho-shang Kung text has the word "One," but the Fu I and 24 other texts have it, according to Chiang Hsi-ch'ang.
3. I Shun-ting, Hsi T'ung, and Liu Shih-p'ei read *kuei-kao* (honorable and high in position) as *chen* (ruler) in order to preserve the parallelism. But the parallelism is probably not intended here, since both honor and high position are discussed in the following sentences.
4. Compare a similar saying in chapter 42.
5. The Wu Ch'eng text reads: "Therefore supreme praise is no praise."
6. *Chuang Tzu*, ch. 33, *SPTK*, 10:35a. Cf. Giles (tr.), *Chuang Tzu*, p. 319.
7. Chapter 14. This is also the sense used in chapters 10 and 22.

8. This is the sense used in chapter 42.
9. Ch. 2, *SPTK*, 1:34a. Cf. Giles, p. 41.
10. *Ibid.*, *SPTK*, 1:30a. Cf. Giles, p. 39.
11. See comment on chapter 42.

40

R EVERSION *is the action of Tao.*
Weakness is the function of Tao.
All things in the world come from being.
And being comes from non-being.[1]

COMMENT

The doctrine of returning to the original is a prominent one
in the *Lao Tzu*.[2] It has contributed in no small degree to the
common Chinese cyclical concept, according to which the
Chinese believe that both history and reality operate in cycles.

NOTES

1. Cf. chapter 1. This seems to contradict the saying, "Being and
   non-being produce each other," in chapter 2. But to produce
   means not to originate but to bring about.
2. The doctrine is also encountered in one sense or another in
   chapters 14, 16, 25, 28, 30, and 52. To D. C. Lau, returning
   to the root is not a cyclical process. According to him, the
   main doctrine of the *Lao Tzu* is the preservation of life, which
   is to be achieved through "abiding by softness." Softness is
   real strength, because when strength is allowed to reach its
   limit, it falls, whereas softness preserves itself. Thus opposites
   are neither relative nor paradoxical, and their process is not
   circular but a gradual development to the limit and then an
   inevitable and sudden decline. This idea may be implied in
   the *Lao Tzu* but there is no explicit passage to support Lau's
   theory. See his "The Treatment of Opposites in Lao Tzu,"
   Bulletin of the School of Oriental and African Studies, XXI
   (1958), 349-50, 352-7.

41

WHEN THE *highest type of men hear Tao,*
They diligently practice it.
When the average type of men hear Tao,
They half believe in it.
When the lowest type of men hear Tao,
They laugh heartily at it.
If they did not laugh at it, it would not be Tao.

Therefore there is the established saying: [1]
The Tao which is bright appears to be dark.
The Tao which goes forward appears to fall backward.
The Tao which is level appears uneven.
Great virtue appears like a valley (hollow).
Great purity appears like disgrace.
Far-reaching virtue appears as if insufficient.
Solid virtue appears as if unsteady.
True substance appears to be changeable.
The great square has no corners.
The great implement (or talent) is slow to finish (or mature).
Great music sounds faint.
Great form has no shape.
Tao is hidden and nameless.
Yet it is Tao alone that skillfully provides for all and brings
them to perfection.

COMMENT

One must note that Tao is not for contemplation but for dili-
gent practice. The goal of Tao is not simply peace of mind or
purity of heart but the full realization of all things.

1. Hsi T'ung suggests that *chien-yen* (established saying) is the title of an ancient book, but he offers no evidence. The Fu I text has the additional word "says." Fan Ying-yüan says that the Ho-shang Kung text does not have the word "says," thus implying that the original Wang Pi text contained it.

42

Tao produced *the One.*
The One produced the two.
The two produced the three.
And the three produced the ten thousand things.
The ten thousand things carry the yin and embrace the yang,
and through the blending of the material force they
achieve harmony.

People hate to be children without parents, lonely people
without spouses, or men without food to eat,
And yet kings and lords call themselves by these names.
Therefore it is often the case that things gain by losing
and lose by gaining.

What others have taught, I teach also:
"Violent and fierce people do not die a natural death." [1]
I shall make this the father [2] of my teaching.

COMMENT

It is often understood that the One is the original material
force or the Great Ultimate, the two are yin and yang, the
three are their blending with the original material force, and
the ten thousand things are things carrying yin and embracing
yang. The similarity of this process to that of the *Book of
Changes,* in which the Great Ultimate produces the Two
Forces (yin and yang) and then the myriad things, is amazing.
The important point, however, is not the specific similarities,
but the evolution from the simple to the complex. This theory
is common to nearly all Chinese philosophical schools.

It should be noted that the evolution here, as in the *Book of
Changes,* is natural. Production (*sheng*) is not personal creation or purposeful origination, but natural causation.

NOTES

1. The same saying appears in the inscription on a metal statue in the imperial ancestral temple that Confucius visited. The story and the inscription appear in the *Shuo-yüan* (Collection of Discourses) compiled by Liu Hsiang (77-6 B.C.), 10:16b-17a. Commentators say the *Lao Tzu* quotes from the inscription, but both may have quoted from a common source.
2. Meaning the basis or the starting point.

43

THE SOFTEST *things in the world overcome* [1] *the hardest
    things in the world.* [2]
Non-being penetrates that in which there is no space.
Through this I know the advantage of taking no action.
*Few in the world can understand the teaching without words
    and the advantage of taking no action.* [3]

COMMENT

This is a reiteration of the doctrine, already set forth in chapter 36, that weakness overcomes strength, but instead of teaching weakness purely as a technique, it is here taught as the true principle. Since Taoism emphasizes non-being, this unorthodox idea is to be expected. Chu Hsi, commenting on Lao Tzu's doctrine, says Lao Tzu emphasizes the weak because it brings a pragmatic advantage, whereas in Confucianism both the weak and the strong are valuable in themselves, [4] but it is unfair to accuse Lao Tzu of ulterior motive. An important difference between Taoism and Confucianism is that the former, being radical, tends to the left and therefore stresses the unconventional, while the latter, being conservative, keeps to the center, that is, the norm.

NOTES

1. *Ch'ih-ch'eng,* literally, "galloping on horseback." The metaphor here means to capture a prey.
2. Ch'en Chu (*Chang-chü*) thinks this sentence should be shifted to the beginning of chapter 78.
3. Compare a similar saying in chapter 2. Ma Hsü-lun believes the last two sentences came from chapter 37.
4. *Chu Tzu yü-lei,* 125:11a.

44

WHICH DOES *one love more, fame or one's own life?*
Which is more valuable, one's own life or wealth?
Which is worse, gain or loss?
Therefore he who has lavish desires will spend extravagantly.
He who hoards most will lose heavily.
He who is contented suffers no disgrace.
He who knows when to stop is free from danger.
Therefore he can long endure.[1]

COMMENT

The teaching of contentment is a natural outcome of the doctrine of taking no action, but it was no less a reaction against the political and social situation in which struggle for fame, wealth, and personal gain was the order of the day.

NOTE

1. Compare a similar saying in chapter 32.

WHAT IS *most perfect seems to be incomplete;*
But its utility is unimpaired.
What is most full seems to be empty;
But its usefulness is inexhaustible.
What is most straight seems to be crooked.
The greatest skill seems to be clumsy.
The greatest eloquence seems to stutter.
Hasty movement overcomes cold,
(But) tranquility overcomes heat.[1]
By being greatly tranquil,
One is qualified to be the ruler of the world.

COMMENT

In no small degree these sayings have taught the Chinese people to respect the poor, the stupid, the weak, the lowly, for
they may be possessors of great wisdom and virtue. According
to one popular story, a sage-king sought advice from a fisher-
man, and similar tales abound in Chinese folk literature. Under the influence of Taoism, the lowly has been glorified in
Chinese folk literature and art. A key figure in many folk
stories is an immortal disguised as a poor or weak man; in fact,
one of the Eight Immortals in the Taoist religion is poor,
illiterate, and deformed.

NOTE

1. Chiang Hsi-ch'ang thinks that this sentence should read, "Tranquility overcomes hasty movement and cold overcomes heat,"
   since, in chapter 26, it is said, "The tranquil is the ruler of the
   hasty." However, the idea here is to emphasize the power of
   tranquility, which overcomes not only cold but even heat.

WHEN TAO *prevails in the world, galloping horses are turned back to fertilize (the fields with their dung).* [1]
When Tao does not prevail in the world, war horses thrive in the suburbs. [2]
There is no calamity [3] *greater than lavish desires.* [4]
There is no greater guilt [5] *than discontentment.*
And there is no greater disaster than greed.
He who is contented with contentment is always contented.

COMMENT

Contentment is a major tenet in Lao Tzu's teaching, [6] and this teaching has exerted a tremendous influence on the Chinese people. It reinforces the Confucian doctrine of moderation. Many people look upon contentment as negative. One cannot deny that this Taoist teaching had a negative effect, for it has somehow discouraged progress and advancement, but one must realize that contentment is entirely different from renunciation. There is no idea of total self-denial. The main point is to know where to stop. [7]

NOTES

1. As quoted by Chu Hsi, the sentence has an additional word, "cart," thus meaning that the horses are used to draw manure carts (*Chu Tzu yü-lei*, 125:12a). But no one, not even his pupil who recorded the saying, knew on what textual authority he added the word. Probably Chu Hsi was paraphrasing, as many Chinese writers often do when they quote.
2. Koyanagi understands *chiao* (suburb) as borderland between states. This interpretation is possible. But if the sentence refers to war, as he suggests, some word other than "thrive" would have been used.
3. The Ho-shang Kung text has "sin" instead of "calamity."
4. This sentence does not appear in the Wang Pi text but appears in 51 other texts, including the Ho-shang Kung and Fu I texts.

Its presence is supported by its quotation in the *Han Fei Tzu*, ch. 20, *SPTK*, 6:6b. Cf. Liao (tr.), *Han Fei Tzu*, I, 189.

5. The Ho-shang Kung text has "calamity" instead of "guilt."
6. See also chapters 32 and 44.
7. See comment on chapter 64.

O NE MAY *know the world without going out of doors.*
One may see the Way of Heaven without looking through
the windows.
The further one goes, the less one knows.
Therefore the sage knows without going about,
Understands [1] *without seeing,*
And accomplishes without any action.

COMMENT

"There is a basis for all affairs and a foundation for all things,"
says Wang Pi. "There may be many roads but their destination is the same, and there may be a hundred deliberations but
the result is the same.[2] There is a great tendency in Tao and
there is a generality in principle. By holding on to the Tao of
old, we can master the present.[3] Although we live in the present, we can know the past. This is why it is said that one may
know [the world] without going out of doors or looking
through the windows. . . . If we know the general principle of
things, we can know through thinking even if we do not travel.
If we know the basis of things, even if we do not see them, we
can point to the principle of right and wrong [which governs
them]."

NOTES

1. The word *ming* ordinarily means "name," but is interchangeable
   with *ming* meaning "to understand."
2. Paraphrasing the *Book of Changes*, "Appended Remarks," Pt. II,
   ch. 5. Cf. Legge (tr.), *The Yi King*, p. 389.
3. Paraphrasing *Lao Tzu*, chapter 14.

THE PURSUIT *of learning is to increase day after day.*
The pursuit of Tao is to decrease day after day.
It is to decrease and further decrease until one reaches the
point of taking no action.
No action is undertaken, and yet nothing is left undone.
An empire is often brought to order by having no activity.
If one (likes to)[1] *undertake activity, he is not qualified to*
govern the empire.[2]

COMMENT

Lao Tzu seems to be advocating a twofold method of cultivation—extension, or daily increase, for intellectual pursuit, and
intension, or daily decrease, for spiritual cultivation. If so, the
method bears an interesting similarity to that taught by Confucius, who says, "The superior man extensively studies literature and restrains himself [intensively] with the rules of propriety. Thus he will not violate the Way." [3] It is unlikely,
however, that Taoism, being basically anti-intellectual, encourages extensive learning. More probably, by daily increase
in learning is meant a meaningless and purposeless accumulation of facts and details. The statement is therefore a critical
one, intended to show the contrast with the pursuit of Tao.

The Confucianists have always been careful to maintain a
balance between intellectual pursuit and moral cultivation.
The Confucian doctrine of extensive learning and discipline
by rules of propriety has remained a fundamental one throughout the history of the Confucian school and has been stressed
by Wang Yang-ming especially.[4] The *Doctrine of the Mean*
urges the balance of "honoring the moral nature" and "following the path of study and inquiry." [5] A most famous dictum of
one of the leading Neo-Confucianists, Ch'eng I, is, "Self-culti-
vation requires seriousness and the pursuit of learning depends on the extension of knowledge." [6] Ch'eng I's chief fol-
lower, Chu Hsi, tends more to learning, while Chu's opponent,

Lu Hsiang-shan, tends more to moral cultivation. Referring to Lao Tzu's saying, Lu says, "Lao Tzu's theory about the pursuit of learning and pursuit of Tao is wrong. What I would say is merely to cling to the right and reject the wrong, and discard the depraved and go toward the correct." [7] Without realizing it, in emphasizing moral cultivation exclusively, he comes closer to Lao Tzu than he thought.

NOTES

1. This interpretation follows Ho-shang Kung's commentary.
2. Ch'en Chu (*Chang-chü*) thinks the last two sentences should be shifted to chapter 57.
3. *Analects*, 6:25.
4. *Ch'uan-hsi lu*, secs. 9, 25, 132, 140, and 220. See Chan (tr.), *Instructions for Practical Living, and Other Neo-Confucian Writings by Wang Yang-ming.*
5. *Doctrine of the Mean*, ch. 27.
6. *I-shu*, 18:5b.
7. *Hsiang-shan ch'üan-chi*, 35:18a.

49

THE SAGE *has no fixed (personal) ideas.*
He regards the people's ideas as his own.
I treat those who are good with goodness,
And I also treat those who are not good with goodness.
Thus goodness is attained.[1]
I am honest to those who are honest,
And I am also honest to those who are not honest.
Thus honesty is attained.
The sage, in the government of his empire, has no subjective
    viewpoint.[2]
His mind forms a harmonious whole with that of his people.[3]
They all lend their eyes and ears,[4] *and he treats them all*
    as infants.

COMMENT

In his famous statement on the calming of human nature, Ch'eng Hao says: "The constant (*ch'ang*, 'fixed') principle of Heaven and Earth is that their minds are in all things, and yet they have no minds of their own. The constant principle of the sage is that his feelings are in accord with all creations, and yet he has no feelings of his own. Therefore, for the training of the superior man there is nothing better than to become broad and extremely impartial and to respond spontaneously to all things as they come."[5] There is no better commentary on Lao Tzu's words.[6]

NOTES

1. Read *te* (to attain) instead of *te* (virtue), according to the Fu I and other texts. In ancient times the two words were interchangeable.
2. This is Wang Pi's interpretation.
3. Ma Hsü-lun proposes to read this line, "His mind is a harmoni-

ous whole," while Chu Ch'ien-chih proposes to read, "In the government of his empire, his mind is a harmonious whole."

4. The Wang Pi text does not have these words, but the Ho-shang Kung and Fu I texts do.

5. *Ming-tao wen-chi* (Collections of Literary Works by Ch'eng Hao), 3:1a.

6. On being honest to the dishonest, etc., see comment on chapter 63.

50

M AN COMES *in to life and goes out to death.*
  Three out of ten [1] *are companions of life.*
Three out of ten are companions of death. [2]
And three out of ten in their lives lead from activity to death. [3]
And for what reason?
Because of man's intensive striving after life.

I have heard that one who is a good preserver of his life will
  not meet tigers or wild buffaloes,
And in fighting will not try to escape from weapons of war.
The wild buffalo cannot butt its horns against him,
The tiger cannot fasten its claws in him,
And weapons of war cannot thrust their blades into him.
And for what reason?
Because in him there is no room for death.

COMMENT

The idea of the preservation of life is clearly apparent here.
Unfortunately, the obscurity of the first section of the chapter
has given rise to wild speculations. The second section of the
chapter, obviously composed of analogies (as are other parts
of the *Lao Tzu*), has been taken literally by many ignorant
followers of the Taoist religion, who confuse belief in magic
with Taoist philosophy. The most notorious example is that
of the Boxers, at the turn of this century. Being ardent followers of the Taoist religion, they actually believed that
through magic and superstitious practices they could make
their bodies immune to bullets.

NOTES

1. Han Fei Tzu understood "ten-three" not as three out of ten but
   thirteen and identified the four limbs and the nine external
   cavities as factors that sustain life, lead to death, or lead

through activity to death. See *Han Fei Tzu*, ch. 20, *SPTK*, 6:8a. Cf. Liao (tr.), *The Complete Works of Han Fei Tzu*, I, 196. Most commentators and Chinese writers prefer to follow Wang Pi, understanding "three-ten" to mean "three out of ten." Translators are about evenly divided.

2. See chapter 76 for similar expressions.

3. Some Chinese commentators have been highly imaginative in interpreting these enigmatic lines. Aside from Ho-shang Kung, Yeh Meng-te, Lin Tung, and others who have followed Han Fei Tzu, there have been Tu Kuang-t'ing, who identifies the thirteen as the Ten Evils and Three Karmas of Buddhism, and Fan Ying-yüan, who identifies the number as the rise and fall of the Five Agents. Others have suggested the sum of six for Water and seven for Fire, or of the Seven Feelings and Six Desires, or the twelve periods in the day plus one as their cycle (as pointed out by Ting Fu-pao and Chu Ch'ien-chih). Su Ch'e thinks Lao Tzu is referring to the nine ways of life and death. Among modern writers, Kao Heng believes the passage refers to the first thirty years in a hundred as that of man's growth, the next thirty (actually forty, but few can utilize them in full, Kao says) as a period of neither life nor death, that is, decline, and the remaining thirty years as a period of death. Chu Fei-huang says that the number ten refers to the ten directions and three to the periods of time (past, present, and future) as taught in Buddhism. According to Lu Shih-hung, three out of ten merely means a small number.

51

Tao produces *them.*
Virtue fosters them.
Matter gives them physical form.
The circumstances and tendencies complete them.
Therefore the ten thousand things esteem Tao and honor virtue.
Tao is esteemed and virtue is honored without anyone's order! [1]
They always come spontaneously.

Therefore Tao produces them and virtue fosters them.
They rear them and develop them.
They give them security and give them peace.
They nurture them and protect them.
(Tao) produces them but does not take possession of them.
It acts, but does not rely on its own ability.
It leads them but does not master them.
This is called profound and secret virtue. [2]

COMMENT

Significantly, the *Lao Tzu* is also called the *Tao-te ching*, or Classic of the Way and Its Virtue, the latter title meaning that the book deals with Tao and its characteristics. But of the 81 chapters only this one and chapter 21 mention Tao and *te* together as the two basic elements. [3] The relationship between Tao and *te* is not clearly stated, but it seems clear that *te* follows Tao (ch. 23) and that, while Tao produces all things, it is *te* that fosters them. Furthermore, in ancient Chinese classics, *te* (virtue or characteristic) is often equated with *te* (to obtain). It is generally understood that while Tao is the general principle by which all things come into being, *te* is Tao inherent in each individual thing; that is, *te* is what each thing has obtained from Tao. In this sense, *te* is its virtue or characteristic. When Ho-Shang Kung equated *te* with "one" in his commentary, he probably had this in mind.

NOTES

1. According to Chiang Hsi-ch'ang, the Fu I and 36 other texts have *chüeh* (rank of nobility) instead of *ming* (to order).
2. These last four sentences appear in chapter 10, where the subject is the sage, rather than Tao. The first two of these four sentences also appear in chapter 2. The second is repeated in chapter 77.
3. Chapters 23 and 41 also mention them, but not as the two basic elements.

52

THERE WAS *a beginning of the universe*
Which may be called the Mother of the universe.
He who has found [1] *the mother (Tao)*
And thereby understands her sons (things),
And having understood the sons,
Still keeps to its mother,
Will be free from danger throughout his lifetime.[2]

Close the mouth.
Shut the doors (of cunning and desires).[3]
And to the end of life there will be (peace) without toil.
Open the mouth.
Meddle with affairs.
And to the end of life there will be no salvation.
Seeing what is small is called enlightenment.[4]
Keeping to weakness is called strength.
Use the light.
Revert to enlightenment.
And thereby avoid danger to one's life—
This is called practicing [5] *the eternal.*

COMMENT

Ever since Han Fei, the first commentator on the *Lao Tzu*, equated "Mother" with Tao,[6] few commentators, if any, have disagreed with him. It is to be expected that with the development of modern psychology and sociology, modern ideas would be read into it. Erkes, for example, has regarded Tao as a mother-goddess,[7] but Duyvendak maintains that this attempt to personify the Way is mistaken.[8] Duyvendak also says that, while the image of the mother might suggest a matriarchal society, in the characteristically Chinese culture the patriarchal principle is predominant.[9] But he interprets "keeping to the mother" as "mystic union with the mother." However, it does not seem necessary to introduce mysticism here, and it is virtually impossible to do so in other chapters where "mother" is mentioned.[10]

NOTES

1. A number of texts have *chih* (to know) instead of *te* (to obtain).
2. This line is also found in chapter 16.
3. These two lines are also found in chapter 56.
4. Ma Hsü-lun says this line should go to chapter 55, but has given no reason for the change.
5. Forty-two texts, including the Fu I text, listed by Chiang Hsi-ch'ang, have *hsi* (to follow) instead of *hsi* (to practice), but the two words were interchangeable.
6. See *Han Fei Tzu*, ch. 20, *SPTK*, 6:5a (cf. Liao [tr.], *The Complete Works of Han Fei Tzu*, I, 183).
7. Erkes, "Arthur Waley's Laotse-Übersetzung," *Artibus Asiae*, V (1935), 300-1.
8. Duyvendak, *Tao Te Ching*, p. 56.
9. *Ibid.*, pp. 115-16.
10. Chs. 1, 20, 25, and 59.

I<small>F</small> I <small>HAD</small> *but little* [1] *knowledge*
  I should, in walking on a broad way,
Fear getting off [2] *the road.*
Broad ways are extremely even,
But people are fond of bypaths.
The courts are exceedingly splendid,
While the fields are exceedingly weedy,
And the granaries are exceedingly empty.
Elegant clothes are worn,
Sharp weapons are carried,
Foods and drinks are enjoyed beyond limit,
And wealth and treasures are accumulated in excess.
This is robbery and extravangance.
This is indeed not Tao (the Way). [3]

COMMENT

This is at once a bitter attack on corrupt government and a contrast between the government with Tao and that without Tao.

NOTES

1. The term *chieh-jan* can mean "firmly," "wisely," "especially," "hastily," etc., and support for each can be found in ancient literature. But in spite of Ho-shang Kung's understanding of it as "great," most commentators, from Ch'eng Hsüan-ying down, have preferred to follow Chang Chan's (*fl.* 310) commentaries on the *Lieh Tzu,* 4:2a (Graham, p. 77), where it is understood as "small" or "subtle." Koyanagi's interpretation of the term as "distinguishing the difference of things" has no linguistic support.
2. This is the meaning given by Wang Nien-sun.
3. Using the term *tao* both as an abstract noun and a concrete noun.

H<small>E WHO</small> *is well established (in Tao) cannot be pulled away.
He who has a firm grasp (of Tao) cannot be separated
from it.*

*Thus from generation to generation his ancestral sacrifice will
never be suspended.*

*When one cultivates virtue in his person, it becomes genuine
virtue.*

*When one cultivates virtue in his family, it becomes
overflowing virtue.*

*When one cultivates virtue in his community, it becomes
lasting virtue.*

*When one cultivates virtue in his country, it becomes abundant
virtue.*

When one cultivates virtue in the world, it becomes universal.

Therefore the person should be viewed as a person.
The family should be viewed as a family.
The community should be viewed as a community.
The country should be viewed as a country.
And the world should be viewed as the world.[1]
How do I know this to be the case in the world?
Through this.[2]

COMMENT

It was a common conviction in ancient China that the foundation of the empire lies in the state, that of the state in the family, and that of the family in the person.[3] Expressing this sentiment, Lao Tzu goes on to say that the person should be seen only through the person, and so forth—that is, with absolute objectivity and detachment. This viewpoint is characteristic of Shao Yung, the most Taoistic of the leading Neo-Confucianists. According to his famous theory of "viewing things from the viewpoint of things," one should view things as they are instead of subjectively and egoistically.[4] This is essentially the spirit of Taoism.

NOTES

1. The Chinese merely reads: "From person see person," etc. Wang Pi says: "The Tao in the person may be seen from the person's own state of mind," etc. Ho-shang Kung says: "From the person who cultivates the Tao, the person who does not cultivate Tao may be seen," etc. Wei Yüan says: "By one's own person, other persons may be seen," etc.
2. Most commentators agree that "this" refers to the cultivation of virtue in the person, in the family, and so forth.
3. According to Mencius, this was a common saying. See *Book of Mencius*, 4A:5. On what basis Waley says that the theory originated with Yang Chu is not clear. Neither Yang Chu nor the "Yang Chu" treatise says anything like this.
4. *Huang-chi ching-shih shu* (Supreme Principle Governing the World), 8B:16a.

55

H<small>E</small> WHO *possesses virtue in abundance*
May be compared to an infant.
Poisonous insects [1] *will not sting him.*
Fierce beasts will not seize him.
Birds of prey will not strike him.
His bones are weak, his sinews tender, but his grasp is firm.
He does not yet know the union of male and female,
But his organ [2] *is aroused,*
This means that his essence is at its height.
He may cry all day without becoming hoarse,
This means that his (natural) harmony is perfect.
To know harmony means to be in accord with the eternal.
To be in accord with the eternal means to be enlightened.
To force the growth of life means ill omen. [3]
For the mind to employ the vital force without restraint
    means violence. [4]
After things reach their prime, they begin to grow old,
Which means being contrary to Tao.
Whatever is contrary to Tao will soon perish. [5]

COMMENT

The infant is idealized in this book more than once.[6] Furthermore, Mencius says: "The great man is one who does not lose
his child's heart." [7] And Jesus taught that only as children
may we enter the kingdom of Heaven.[8] For Chuang Tzu, the
newborn calf, like the newborn child, is an ideal being.[9]

Su Ch'e has made the observation that Lao Tzu uses the infant as an analogy for Tao because he is talking about substance. Since the infant does not know how to respond to
things, Su says, it cannot act functionally. But as substance
it is perfect.

1. Following the Ho-shang Kung text. According to Lo Chen-yü, the Tun-huang and other texts, have "poisonous insects." Chiang Hsi-ch'ang mentions 50 texts that have "poisonous insects." In place of this expression, the Wang Pi text has "wasps, scorpions, and snakes." These words appear in Ho-shang Kung's commentary. Probably they got into the Wang Pi text by mistake.

2. Also following the Ho-shang Kung and 45 other texts (according to Chiang). Wang Pi's text has *ch'üan* (complete), which sounds like the word for the male organ but makes no sense here.

3. *Hsiang* (good omen) was occasionally used in ancient literature in the opposite sense. For example, see *Tso Chuan*, Duke Chao, 18th year.

4. Yü Yüeh says that the lines, "Use the light,/Revert to enlightenment," in chapter 52 were originally repeated here, for they are quoted along with this sentence in the *Huai-nan Tzu*, 12:7A. (Cf. Morgan [tr.], *Tao, The Great Luminant*, p. 114.) Since the quotation may have come from several sources, the argument is not conclusive.

5. These two sentences are also found in chapter 30. Ma Hsü-lun thinks they are misplaced here.

6. Chs. 10, 20, 28, and 49.

7. *Book of Mencius*, 4B:12.

8. Matthew 18:2-4.

9. *Chuang Tzu*, ch. 22, *SPTK*, 7:45a. Cf. Giles (tr.), *Chuang Tzu*, p. 212.

56

HE WHO *knows does not speak.*
  He who speaks does not know.[1]

Close the mouth.
Shut the doors.[2]
Blunt the sharpness.
Untie the tangles.
Soften the light.
Become one with the dusty world.[3]
This is called profound identification.[4]

Therefore it is impossible either to be intimate and
  close to him or to be distant and indifferent to him.
It is impossible either to benefit him or to harm him.
It is impossible either to honor him or to disgrace him.
For this reason he is honored by the world.[5]

COMMENT

The concept of profound identification (*hsüan-t'ung*) [6] has developed to be an important one in Taoist thought. It is found in both the *Chuang Tzu* [7] and the *Huai-nan Tzu*.[8] It means at once being merged with Tao in a harmonious state and removing all distinctions and differentiations. Commenting on the phrase in the *Chuang Tzu*, Ch'eng Hsüan-ying says: "When human beings do not lose their purity and are all at ease with themselves, follow their nature and preserve the principle underlying it, they will be merged with profound Tao." [9] Chuang Tzu means the same when he says: "The universe and I exist together, and all things and I are one." [10]

NOTES

1. Ma Hsü-lun thinks these two lines should be shifted to chapter 81. Ch'en Chu (*Chang-chü*) and Ch'u Ta-kao have followed him.

2. These last two sentences also appear in chapter 52.

3. These last four sentences also appear in chapter 4. I Shun-ting says all six sentences are interpolations. Ma Hsü-lun, Ch'en Chu (*Chang-chü*), and Ch'u Ta-kao have followed him.

4. Ch'en Meng-chia (p. 6) thinks *hsüan* (profound) is similar in pronunciation to *hun* (undifferentiated). *Hsüan* would then mean "merged as one."

5. This is repeated in chapter 62. Because the two characters look alike, Kao Heng proposes to change *kuei* (to honor) to *chen* (ruler) both here and in chapter 62.

6. Variously rendered as "mysterious leveling" (Waley), "mysterious equality" (Duyvendak), "mystic unity" (Lin Yutang, Blakney), "profound unity" (Au-young Sum Nung), "absolute equality" (Ch'u Ta-kao), "union with the dark one" (Erkes), "the Deep's identity" (Heysinger), "mystic whole" (John Wu), "mysterious agreement" (Legge), "conformity with the principle of Tao" (Giles, p. 27), "perfection of harmony" (Carus), "great harmony" (Cheng Lin, sec. 99, p. 19), etc.

7. *Chuang Tzu,* ch. 10, *SPTK,* 4:22b (Giles [tr.], *Chuang Tzu,* p. 103).

8. *Huai-nan Tzu,* 16:6a.

9. See Juan Yü-sung, *Chuang Tzu chi-chu* (Collected Commentaries of the *Chuang Tzu*), Pt. II, A, 11a.

10. *Chuang Tzu,* ch. 2, *SPTK,* 1:34a (Giles [tr.], *Chuang Tzu,* p. 41).

57

Govern the state with correctness.
Operate the army with surprise[1] tactics.
Administer the empire by engaging in no activity.
How do I know that this should be so?
Through this:[2]
 The more taboos and prohibitions there are in the world,
The poorer the people will be.
 The more sharp weapons the people have,
The more troubled the state will be.
 The more cunning and skill man possesses,
The more vicious things will appear.
 The more laws and orders[3] are made prominent,
The more thieves and robbers there will be.
Therefore the sage says:
 I take no action and the people of themselves are
  transformed.
 I love tranquility and the people of themselves become
  correct.
 I engage in no activity and the people of themselves
  become prosperous.
 I have no desires and the people of themselves become
  simple.

COMMENT

In advocating government through correctness (*cheng*, or rectification), Lao Tzu is essentially in agreement with Confucius,
who says: "To govern is to rectify. If you lead the people by
being rectified yourself, who will dare not be rectified?"[4] In
rejecting laws, he is also in agreement with Confucius in spirit,
if not in letter, for Confucius says that if people are regulated
by law and punishment, they will avoid wrongdoing but will
have no sense of honor and shame. He prefers to lead them by
rules of propriety so they will set themselves right.[5] Further,
Confucius shares the Taoist idea of government through taking

The Way of Lao Tzu / 201

no action.[6] But to advocate the use of surprise military tactics is entirely contrary to the spirit of both Taoism and Confucianism. As Chu Hsi has remarked, this is indeed a very strange sort of "engaging in no activity."[7]

NOTES

1. *Ch'i*, literally, "strange," connotes particularly the extraordinary that deviates from the correct and good. It is rendered "vicious" below and in chapter 74, and "perverse" in chapter 58.

2. Compare the last two lines of chapters 21 and 54. Yü Yüeh holds that since both of these two chapters end with "Through this," these five lines should be shifted to chapter 56 so it may also end with the same phrase. Ma Hsü-lun, however, proposes to shift them to the end of chapter 48.

3. The Ho-shang Kung and some other texts have "things" instead of "order."

4. *Analects*, 12:17.

5. *Ibid.*, 2:3.

6. *Ibid.*, 15:4.

7. *Chu Tzu yü-lei*, 125:11a.

58

WHEN THE *government is non-discriminative and dull,*
The people are contented and generous.
When the government is searching and discriminative,
The people are disappointed and contentious.
Calamity is that upon which happiness depends;
Happiness is that in which calamity is latent.
Who knows when the limit will be reached?
Is there no correctness (used to govern the world)? [1]
Then the correct again becomes the perverse.
And the good will again become evil. [2]
The people have been deluded for a long time.
Therefore the sage is as pointed as a square but does not pierce.
He is as acute as a knife but does not cut.
He is as straight as an unbent line but does not extend.
He is as bright as light but does not dazzle.

COMMENT

In pointing out that calamity and happiness are latent in each
other, Taoism is not advocating being indifferent to them but
rather seeing beyond the apparent and understanding the
reality which is not readily apparent. This approach is perhaps somewhat unconventional but it sharpens the imagination and broadens the vision. It has in no small degree taught
Chinese poets, artists, and philosophers to look under the surface of apparent reality. Chiefly because of the influence of
Taoism, they are seldom positivists who do not look beyond
natural phenomena.

NOTES

1. According to Chiang Hsi-ch'ang, 38 texts have the additional
   word *hsieh* (perversion). The sentence could then read: "Is
   there neither right nor wrong?"—as Waley has understood it.
   But *hsieh* is here used in the sense of a question and therefore

its addition does not alter the meaning of the sentence. Because Wang Pi did not comment on the sentence, Ch'en Chu (*Chang-chü*) proposes to delete it.
2. These three lines are very obscure.

59

To RULE *people and to serve Heaven there is nothing better
    than to be frugal.*
Only by being frugal can one recover quickly.
To recover quickly means to accumulate virtue heavily.
*By the heavy accumulation of virtue one can overcome
    everything.*
*If one can overcome everything, then he will acquire a capacity
    the limit of which is beyond anyone's knowledge.*
*When his capacity is beyond anyone's knowledge, he is fit to
    rule a state.*
He who possesses the Mother (Tao) [1] *of the state will last long.*
*This means that the roots are deep and the stalks are firm,
    which is the way of long life and everlasting vision.* [2]

COMMENT

The hope for everlasting life has been a major aspect of both
Taoist philosophy and religion. This hope has ultimately developed belief in a cult of immortals (*hsien*), in which Taoist
recluses are believed to enjoy an everlasting life which they
spend either in mystic contemplation or in helping others to
salvation. It should be made very clear, however, that this development took place centuries later in popular religion, and
was derived, indirectly, from Chuang Tzu rather than from
Lao Tzu. In the *Chuang Tzu* there are a number of phrases
and stories about the pure man living on morning dew, etc.,
which later Taoists used (or rather misused) to promote the
cult of immortals. Lao Tzu's contribution lies elsewhere, in
promoting the general Chinese desire for longevity.

NOTES

1. See comment on chapter 52.
2. "Long life and everlasting vision" simply means long life, as Kao
    Yu says, in his explanation of the phrase in the *Lü-shih ch'un-*

ch'iu (Mr. Lü's Spring and Autumn Annals). (See *Lü-shih ch'un-ch'iu*, ch. 1, sec. 3, *SPPY*, 1:7b; Richard Wilhelm [tr.], *Frühling und Herbst des Lü Bu We*, p. 7.) In the *Chuang Tzu*, the term "lasting vision" is used to mean "gazing for a long time." ("A child gazes all day without moving its eyes." See *Chuang Tzu*, ch. 23, *SPTK*, 8:8b. Cf. Giles [tr.], *Chuang Tzu*, p. 255.) However, as pointed out by Shih Yung in his commentary on this chapter of the *Lao Tzu*, the literal meaning does not apply here. Waley contends that "fixed staring" (his translation) was used by the Taoists as a method of inducing trances. This interpretation is accurate in regard to later religious Taoists, but errs in reading yoga into the *Lao Tzu*. Waley interprets frugality as "laying up a store," and goes on to say that "this 'laying of the new upon the old' is here used as a symbol for the reinforcing of one's stock of vital energy by quietist practice" (p. 213). He is here following Ho-shang Kung's commentary. This interpretation puts much yoga indeed into the *Lao Tzu*; many would join Duyvendak in rejecting Waley's interpretation.

60

R ULING A *big country is like cooking a small fish.*[1]
　 If Tao is employed to rule the empire,
　　Spiritual beings will lose their supernatural power.
Not that they lose their spiritual power,
　　But their spiritual power can no longer harm people.
Not only will their supernatural power not harm people,
　　But the sage also will not harm people.[2]
When both do not harm each other,
Virtue will be accumulated in both for the benefit (of
　　the people).[3]

COMMENT

At a time when people firmly believed that spiritual beings
had almost absolute power over men and punished or re-
warded them at their whim, Lao Tzu virtually said that spiritual beings are controlled by Tao and that punishment and
reward depend upon man's moral behavior. What a far cry
from the Taoist religion, which believes in demons and their
mysterious power! Lao Tzu's rational and moral approach is
in agreement with Confucius, who says: "He who commits a
sin against Heaven has no god to pray to." [4] As understood by
Chu Hsi [5] and other Neo-Confucianists, Heaven is identical
with principle, the Neo-Confucian equivalent to Tao.

NOTES

1. Too much handling will spoil it.
2. By interfering with them.
3. This sentence is not clear and commentators and translators have
   interpreted it in their own way. The interpretation here follows *Han Fei Tzu,* ch. 20, *SPTK,* 6:6a. Cf. Liao (tr.), *The
   Complete Works of Han Fei-Tzu,* I, 187.
4. *Analects,* 3:13.
5. *Lun-yü chi-chu* (Collected Commentaries on the *Analects*), ch. 2,
   comment on the passage.

61

A BIG COUNTRY *may be compared to the lower part of a river.*[1]
It is the converging point of the world;
  It is the female [2] *of the world.*
The female always overcomes the male by tranquility,
  And by tranquility she is underneath.[3]
A big state can take over a small state if it places itself below the small state;
And the small state can take over a big state if it places itself below the big state.
Thus some, by placing themselves below, take over (others),
And some, by being (naturally) low, take over (other states).[4]

After all, what a big state wants is but to annex and herd others,
And what a small state wants is merely to join and serve others.
Since both big and small states get what they want,
The big state should place itself low.

COMMENT

Although the idea of lowliness is typically Taoist, calculation and strategy are characteristic of the Legalists and Diplomatists, who specialized in clever schemes. The spirit of the whole chapter is definitely contrary to that of "taking no action," unless the strategist is considered as taking no "unnatural" action.[5]

NOTES

1. The Fu I and two other texts add "of the world" at the end of this sentence.
2. There are several variants for this word. The Wang Pi and Ho-shang Kung texts are followed here.
3. Ma Hsü-lun proposes that these three lines be moved to chapter

66. He also says that parts of chapters 32 and 66 should be placed here, for the reason that the passages express similar ideas.

4. Yü Yüeh prefers "take over small states" and "take over big states," but I Shun-ting favors "take over" and "being taken over."

5. Ch'en Chu (*Lao Tzu*) suggests that this chapter is a later addition to the book.

62

TAO IS *the storehouse* [1] *of all things.*
It is the good man's treasure and the bad man's refuge.
Fine words can buy honor,
And fine [2] *deeds can gain respect from others.*
Even if a man is bad, when has (Tao) rejected him? [3]
Therefore on the occasion of crowning an emperor or installing
the three ministers, [4]
Rather than present large pieces of jade preceded by teams
of four horses,
It is better to kneel [5] *and offer this Tao.*
Why did the ancients highly value this Tao?
Did they not say, "Those who seek shall have it and those who
sin shall be freed"?
For this reason it is valued by the world.

COMMENT

The point that not even the evil man is rejected, previously
expressed in chapter 27, is repeated here. Directly or indirectly,
it has prepared for the development in Buddhism of the doctrine of universal salvation, according to which all creatures,
including sinners, will be saved.

NOTES

1. Literally, the southwestern corner of the house, the most highly
   honored place in the house, where family worship was carried
   out, grains and treasures were stored, etc.
2. The texts have *shih-tsun-hsing* (buy honorable acts) and punctuate after *tsun,* making the sentence read: "Fine acts can sell,
   and honorable acts. . . ." Yü Yüeh, on the authority of the
   Huai-nan Tzu, 12:11b (omitted from Morgan [tr.], *Tao, The*
   Great Luminant), and 18:9a (not translated in Morgan), has
   added the second word "fine." The present translation follows
   him, as do Hsi T'ung, Ma Hsü-lun, and many others.

3. Cf. a similar saying in chapter 27. Ma Hsü-lun says the sentence should be placed there.
4. Grand tutor, grand preceptor, and grand protector.
5. As Chu Hsi has remarked, when the ancient Chinese sat down (*tso*), they bent their knees on the floor and sat on them. It is wrong, he says, to interpret *tso* here to mean sitting in meditation, as in Zen Buddhism (*Chu Tzu yü-lei*, 68:1a).

63

A CT WITHOUT *action.*
Do without ado.

Taste without tasting.
Whether it is big or small, many or few,[1] *repay*
   hatred with virtue.[2]
Prepare for the difficult while it is still easy.
Deal with the big while it is still small.
Difficult undertakings have always started with what
   is easy.
And great undertakings have always started with what
   is small.
Therefore the sage never strives for the great,
And thereby the great is achieved.[3]
He who makes rash promises surely lacks faith.
He who takes things too easily will surely encounter
   much difficulty.
For this reason even the sage regards things as difficult.
And therefore he encounters no difficulty.

COMMENT

When Confucius was asked, "What do you think of repaying hatred with virtue?" he answered, "In that case, what are you going to repay virtue with? Rather, repay hatred with uprightness (*chih*) and repay virtue with virtue." [4] Some writers think that the questioner was a Taoist. The saying was likely a common one that Lao Tzu appropriated because the idea fitted in well with his doctrine, stated in different words in chapter 49. A number of writers have contrasted the position of Lao Tzu with that of Confucius, maintaining that while Lao Tzu teaches turning the other cheek, Confucius teaches undeviating justice. Nothing is further from the truth. The word *chih* is not to be understood as severity or justice in the sense of "an eye for an eye" but uprightness, that is, absolute impartiality, using what is right as the standard of action.

Since what is virtuous is upright and what is upright is virtuous, Confucius and Lao Tzu are not so far apart as they may seem. Confucianists, however, think that the Taoist position is based on sentiment and personal preference. Perhaps this was in Confucius' mind when he made the reply. But it would be unfair to Lao Tzu to suppose that he was sentimental (as the commentator Wu Ch'eng thought). Lao Tzu's saying is not as emphatic as Christ's injunction, "Love your enemies," [5] but Carus holds that it is more logical and less paradoxical.[6] In any case, the spirit is the same.

NOTES

1. The text reads "big small, many few," and can therefore be open to many interpretations. Many commentators believe that some words are missing.
2. Ma Hsü-lun suggests that the second half be shifted to chapter 79, for the reason that it deals with the subject in that chapter.
3. Repeating the sentence in chapter 34. Ma has not suggested deleting the sentence here.
4. *Analects,* 14:36.
5. Matthew 5:44.
6. See his comment on this chapter (on p. 182 of his translation).

64

W̅HAT REMAINS *still is easy to hold.*
    What is not yet manifest is easy to plan for.
What is brittle is easy to crack.
What is minute is easy to scatter.
Deal with things before they appear.
Put things in order before disorder arises.
A tree as big as a man's embrace grows from a tiny shoot.
A tower of nine stories begins with a heap of earth.
The journey of a thousand li [1] *starts from where one stands.*
He who takes action fails.
He who grasps things loses them. [2]
For this reason the sage takes no action and
    therefore does not fail.
He grasps nothing and therefore he does not lose anything. [3]
People in their handling of affairs often fail when they
    are about to succeed.
If one remains as careful at the end as he was at the
    beginning, there will be no failure.

Therefore the sage desires to have no desire, [4]
He does not value rare treasures. [5]
He learns to be unlearned, [6] *and returns to what the multitude*
    has missed (Tao).
Thus he supports all things in their natural state but does
    not take any action.

COMMENT

The central theme of this chapter is *wu-wei* or taking no action, which, as stated in the concluding line, means supporting all things in their natural state.

    An important aspect of taking no action is having no desires. This is a recurrent theme in the *Lao Tzu.* [7] Here the sage only has desires to have *no desires.* Obviously, having no desires does not mean having no desires at all, but having no impure or selfish desires. Chapter 19 teaches having few desires and chapter 61 approves fulfilling desires.

It is interesting to note that ancient Confucianism never went so far as to teach having no desires. Mencius advocates only having few desires.[8] But, under the influence of Taoism, the Neo-Confucianist Chou Tun-i made having no desires a key idea in his philosophy.[9]

NOTES

1. A *li* is about a third of a mile.
2. These two sentences repeat those in chapter 29.
3. Hsi T'ung and Ma Hsü-lun think these four sentences should be returned to chapter 29.
4. Ho-shang Kung interprets "desire not desire" to mean that the sage desires what the multitude does not desire.
5. This sentence repeats one in chapter 3.
6. Wang Pi understands the expression "learn not learn" to mean that the sage learns without learning; Ho-shang Kung interprets it to mean that the sage learns what the multitude cannot learn.
7. Chs. 3, 19, 34, 37, 46, and 57.
8. *Book of Mencius*, 7B:35.
9. See his *T'ai-chi-t'u shuo* and *T'ung-shu* (Penetrating the *Book of Changes*), ch. 20. For English translations, see Chan, *A Source Book in Chinese Philosophy*, ch. 28, secs. 1-2.

65

I N ANCIENT *times those who practiced Tao well*
*Did not seek to enlighten the people, but to make them
ignorant.*
*People are difficult to govern because they have too much
knowledge.*
*Therefore he who rules the state through knowledge is a
robber of the state;*
*He who rules a state not through knowledge is a blessing to
the state.*
One who knows these two things also (knows) the standard.[1]
*Always to know the standard is called profound and secret
virtue.*[2]
Virtue becomes deep and far-reaching,
And with it all things return to their original state.
Then complete harmony [3] *will be reached.*

COMMENT

The doctrine of making people ignorant has been criticized
more than any other doctrine taught by Lao Tzu. However,
one must remember that his whole philosophy is against cunning, deliberation, and overdevelopment of knowledge. Moreover, the Taoist sage himself is expected to be ignorant.[4] Perhaps he means the same thing as the ancient poet who sang:

> Without awareness or knowledge,
> Follow the principle of the Lord.[5]

The outstanding Neo-Confucianist, Chang Tsai, says, "If one
does so (follows the principle of the Lord) deliberately or
consciously, one will lose the Principle of Nature." [6] But too
many rulers in Chinese history have adopted the policy of keeping the people ignorant, and, rightly or wrongly, critics have
held Lao Tzu responsible.

NOTES

1. Instead of *chi* (to scrutinize), as in the Wang Pi text, the Ho-shang Kung and, according to Chiang Hsi-ch'ang, 52 other texts have *chieh* (model). Commentators have agreed, however, that *chi* here is a borrowed word used in the same sense as *chieh*.

2. See chapter 10, note 11.

3. It is interesting to note that this term (*ta-shun*, complete harmony) and the term "profound and secret virtue" appear together in the *Chuang Tzu,* ch. 12, *SPTK,* 5:9b (Giles [tr.], *Chuang Tzu,* p. 122).

4. See chapter 20.

5. *Book of Odes,* Ode 241.

6. *Cheng-meng,* ch. 6, *Chang Heng-ch'ü chi,* 3:10a.

THE GREAT *rivers and seas are kings of all mountain streams*
Because they skillfully stay below them.
That is why they can be their kings.[1]
Therefore, in order to be the superior of the people,
One[2] *must, in the use of words, place himself below them.*
And in order to be ahead of the people,
One must, in one's own person, follow them.
Therefore the sage[3] *places himself above the people and they*
do not feel his weight.
He places himself in front of them and the people do not
harm him.
Therefore the world rejoices in praising him without getting
tired of it.

It is precisely because he does not compete that the world
cannot compete with him.[4]

COMMENT

A well-known Indian classic says: "These rivers, my dear, flow,
the eastern toward the east, the western toward the west. They
go just from ocean to ocean. They become the ocean itself." [5]

For the Indians, the analogy is employed to show that all
things are identified with Brahman, the Absolute. For the
Chinese, the analogy signifies an ideal human relation. Such
is the contrast between Indian and Chinese thought.[6]

NOTES

1. Sentences very similar to these are found in the inscription on
   a metal statue referred to in chapter 42, note 1.
2. The Ho-shang Kung and many other texts have "sage."
3. This word is present in both the Wang Pi and Ho-shang Kung
   texts but absent in many others.
4. Repeating chapter 22.
5. *Chāndogyo Upanishad*, 6:10, 1.
6. See comment on chapter 8.

ALL THE *world says that my Tao is great* [1] *and does not seem to resemble (the ordinary).* [2]

It is precisely because it is great that it does not resemble (the ordinary).

If it did resemble, it would have been small for a long time.

I have three treasures. Guard and keep them:
  The first is deep love, [3]
  The second is frugality,
  And the third is not to dare to be ahead of the world.
Because of deep love, one is courageous.
Because of frugality, one is generous.
Because of not daring to be ahead of the world, one becomes the leader of the world.
Now, to be courageous by forsaking deep love,
To be generous by forsaking frugality,
And to be ahead of the world by forsaking following behind— This is fatal.

For deep love helps one to win in the case of attack,
  And to be firm in the case of defense.
When Heaven is to save a person,
  Heaven will protect him through deep love.

COMMENT

This chapter, a key one in the *Lao Tzu*, concentrates on the three basic virtues cherished in Taoism, namely, deep love (*tz'u*), frugality or simplicity, and not being ahead, or humility. Of these, the first is the most important. In this respect, Taoism is not so different from Confucianism as it may appear to be. Lao Tzu repeatedly attacks the Confucian doctrine of humanity (*jen*, love),[4] which is practically a synonym for *tz'u*. In fact, he attacks *tz'u* itself,[5] but, as true virtues and not as conventional ornaments, humanity and deep love are highly treasured.[6] In their true sense, these Confucian and Taoist moral values are not different after all.

1. The second sentence clearly shows that the first should not be punctuated after the word "great" and should not be translated "greatly," as in some translations.

2. The term *pu-hsiao* (not to resemble) is open to many possible interpretations: "unworthy," "seems to be like folly," "indescribable," "cannot be distinguished," etc.

3. The word *tz'u* (deep love) has been variously translated as "pity" (Waley), "forbearance" (Duyvendak), "love" (Lin Yutang, Ch'u Ta-kao), "compassion" (Carus, Blakney, Wai-Tao and Goddard, Au-young Sum Nung, Heysinger, Cheng Lin, sec. 173, p. 33, etc.), "kindness" (Erkes, Hughes), "care" (Bynner), "mercy" (John Wu, Mei), "gentleness" (Legge, Giles, p. 354, Bahm), etc. It simply means great or deep love. In chapters 18 and 19 it is used with special reference to the love of parents for children. Here it is used with reference to all men.

4. See chs. 5, 18, 19, and 38.

5. In chs. 18 and 19.

6. See ch. 8.

68

A SKILLFUL *leader of troops is not oppressive with his*
    military strength.[1]
A skillful fighter does not become angry.
A skillful conqueror does not compete with people.
One who is skillful in using men puts himself below them.

This is called the virtue of non-competing.
This is called the strength to use men.
This is called matching Heaven, the highest principle of old.[2]

COMMENT

The Neo-Confucianist, Chou Tun-i, says, "As the world is
transformed and brought to completion, government reaches
its perfection. This is matching Heaven, the highest principle
of old." [3] For Lao Tzu, matching Heaven means humility and
vacuity. The difference between the two illustrates a fundamental difference between Taoism and Confucianism. Comparatively speaking, the former is more interested in the individual, and the latter, in society.

NOTES

1. The interpretation of this sentence follows Wang Pi.
2. Ma Ch'i-ch'ang, Hsi T'ung, and Ma Hsü-lun agree that "of old"
   are the first words of the next chapter, but Yü Yüeh calls them
   spurious.
3. *T'ung-shu,* ch. 17. See Chan, *A Source Book in Chinese Philosophy,* ch. 28, sec. 2.

69

THE STRATEGISTS *say:*
    "I dare not take the offensive but I take the defensive;
    I dare not advance an inch but I retreat a foot."
This means:
    To march without formation,
    To stretch one's arm without showing it,
    To confront enemies without seeming to meet them,
    To hold weapons without seeming to have them.
There is no greater disaster than to make light of the enemy.
Making light of the enemy will destroy my treasures.[1]
Therefore when armies are mobilized and issues joined,
The man who is sorry[2] *over the fact will win.*

COMMENT

It is surprising how much of the *Lao Tzu* is devoted to military strategy. Besides this chapter, chapters 36 and 68, and to some extent chapters 57, 67, and 76, deal with this subject, which is utterly uncharacteristic of Taoism. Do they not contradict the Taoists' strong opposition to the use of force?[3] Or are these chapters later interpolations? Did the School of Strategists grow out of Taoism? Was Lao Tzu a strategist? Or did he make use of military operations because they were the most exciting and critical events of his day and he could most strongly make his points with them? In any case, those who understand Lao Tzu in terms of quietism will surely find the presence of these chapters difficult to explain.

NOTES

1. One cannot be sure if "my treasures" refers to the three treasures in chapter 67. According to Ho-shang Kung, the latter part of the sentence does not mean "will destroy my treasures," but "will destroy my body right here."

2. Yü Yüeh says that the word *ai* (ordinarily meaning "sorrow") does not make sense here. He suspects that it is a corruption

of *hsiang*, which is an old form meaning "to yield." Liu Shih-p'ei thinks that *ai* refers to the idea of a funeral in chapter 31, and I Shun-ting says *ai* is interchangeable with *ai* (to love). In fact, Ho-shang Kung interprets *ai* here to mean *tz'u* (deep love), mentioned two chapters earlier. However, Yü Yüeh's emendation seems more suitable in this chapter.

3. See chs. 30, 31, and 53.

70

MY DOCTRINES *are very easy to understand and very easy to practice,*
But none in the world can understand or practice them.
My doctrines have a source (Nature); my deeds have a master (Tao).
It is because people do not understand this that they do not understand me.
Few people know me, and therefore I am highly valued.
Therefore the sage wears a coarse cloth on top and carries jade within his bosom.

COMMENT

Confucius also remarks that the world did not know him.[1] He had recourse to Heaven, declaring that "it is Heaven that knows me!" Lao Tzu, however, turned to no one, but took the situation in good humor.

NOTE

1. *Analects,* 14:37.

71

T̲o̲ ̲k̲n̲o̲w̲ *that you do not know is the best.*[1]
   To pretend to know when you do not know is a disease.
Only when one recognizes this disease as a disease can one
   be free from the disease.
The sage is free from the disease.
Because he recognizes this disease to be disease, he is free
   from it.

COMMENT

Lao Tzu here agrees with Confucius, who taught one to say
that he knows when he does know, and to say that he does not
know when he does not know.[2]

NOTES

1. Ho-shang Kung's interpretation: "To know Tao and say you do
   not know is the best. Not to know Tao and say you know is
   a disease."
2. *Analects,* 2:17.

72

WHEN THE *people do not fear what is dreadful,*[1]
Then what is greatly dreadful will descend on them.
Do not reduce [2] *the living space of their dwellings.*
Do not oppress their lives.
It is because you do not oppress them that they are not
oppressed.
Therefore the sage knows himself but does not show himself.
He loves himself but does not exalt himself.
Therefore he rejects the one but accepts the other.[3]

COMMENT

In the Ho-shang Kung text, the title for this chapter is "loving
oneself." It is because one loves oneself that one should dread
the dreadful. On the surface, this philosophy sounds very
much like that of Yang Chu, who valued his own life.[4] Referring to the *Lao Tzu,* chapters 13 and 44, where Lao Tzu
teaches valuing the body and loving one's own life, Fung Yu-
lan maintains that what Lao Tzu teaches here are "loose ends"
of Yang Chu's doctrine.[5] But the spirit of loving oneself is
here entirely different from that of Yang Chu. According to
Mencius, Yang Chu was an egoist—"Though he might benefit
the entire world by plucking out a single hair, he would not
do it." [6] Nothing could be more incompatible with Lao Tzu's
unselfishness.

NOTES

1. According to Chiao Hung, *wei,* ordinarily meaning "power," here
   means "to be dreadful." According to Ho-shang Kung, however, it means what is harmful. Ma Hsü-lun contends that the
   fourth line of chapter 28 should be at the beginning of this
   chapter, because it expresses a similar idea.
2. The Wang Pi text has *ya* (familiar) but the Ho-shang Kung and
   44 other texts listed by Chiang Hsi-ch'ang have *hsia* (narrow).

However, the two words are interchangeable, both meaning "narrow."

3. This sentence is also found in chapters 12 and 38. Ch'en Chu (*Lao Tzu*) thinks that the last three lines should go to chapter 70 because they do not seem to belong here.

4. *Lü Shih chun-ch'iu*, ch. 17, sec. 7, *SPPY*, 17:16a. See Richard Wilhelm (tr.), *Frühling und Herbst des Lü Bu We*, p. 285.

5. *A History of Chinese Philosophy*, I, 142.

6. *Book of Mencius*, 7A:26.

73

Hᴇ ᴡʜᴏ *is brave in daring will be killed.*
He who is brave in not daring will live.
Of these two,[1] *one is advantageous and one is harmful.*
Who knows why Heaven dislikes what it dislikes?
Even the sage considers it a difficult question.[2]
The Way of Heaven does not compete, and yet it skillfully
  achieves victory.
It does not speak, and yet it skillfully responds to things.
It comes to you without your invitation.
It is not anxious about things and yet it plans well.
Heaven's net is indeed vast.
Though its meshes are wide, it misses nothing.

Cᴏᴍᴍᴇɴᴛ

The last two lines have become a common proverb in China. Throughout history the Chinese people have had a strong belief that good deeds bring good fortune, and evil deeds, evil fortune. As the well-known saying has it, "All blessings will descend on the well-doer and all miseries will descend on the evil-doer." [3] Some understand this saying as assuring rewards and punishments from the Lord on High. Others take it as the natural result of a moral law. In either case, belief in retribution is firm. The analogy of Heaven's net has greatly strengthened this belief and has given the Chinese a vivid image to support it. Both the belief and the image have formed the basis of popular Taoist religious treatises such as the *T'ai-shang kan-ying p'ien* (Tract of the Most Exalted One on Influence and Response).[4]

Nᴏᴛᴇs

1. Some texts have "to know" or "always to know" before this phrase.
2. According to Lo Chen-yü, this sentence does not appear in the

Tun-huang text. Hsi T'ung and Ma Hsü-lun say it is a sentence from chapter 63 repeated here by mistake.

3. *Book of History,* "Book of Shang," ch. 4. Cf. Legge (tr.), *Shoo King,* p. 198.

4. See Teitaro Suzuki and Paul Carus (trs.), *T'ai-Shang Kan-Ying P'ien, Treatise of the Exalted One on Response and Retribution.*

74

THE PEOPLE [1] *are not afraid of death.*
  Why, then, threaten them with death?
Suppose the people are always afraid of death and we can
  seize those who are vicious [2] and kill them,
Who would dare to do so?
There is always the master executioner (Heaven) who kills.
To undertake executions for the master executioner is like
  hewing wood for the master carpenter.
Whoever undertakes to hew wood for the master carpenter
  rarely escapes injuring his own hands.

COMMENT

Emperor T'ai-tsu of the Ming dynasty wrote in the preface to
his commentary on the *Lao Tzu:*

> After I ascended the throne, for a long time I did not
> learn the ways of the wise kings of the past. I asked people
> about them, and they each had their own views. One day, as
> I casually looked over various books, I came across the
> *Tao-te ching.* I found its language simple and its thoughts
> profound. After some time I came upon the saying, "The
> people are not afraid of death. Why, then, threaten them
> with death?"
> At that time the empire was just getting settled. The
> people were unruly and officials corrupt. Even if ten men
> were executed in public in the morning, by the evening a
> hundred others would have committed the same crimes.
> Does this situation not show that what the classic says is
> eminently true? I therefore abolished capital punishment
> and imprisoned criminals or made them work instead. In
> less than a year I felt much better. Thereupon I realized
> that this classic is the ultimate root of all things, the greatest
> teacher of kings, and the best treasure of all ministers and
> the people. It has nothing to do with alchemy and pills of
> immortality. Alas!

When a ruler asked Confucius about government, saying,
"What do you think of killing the wicked and associating with
the good?" Confucius replied, "In your government what is

the need of killing? If you desire what is good, the people will be good. The character of the ruler is like wind and that of the people is like grass. In whatever direction the wind blows, the grass always bends." [3]

In addition to the opposition to capital punishment, there is always the thought implicit in this chapter that the natural law must be left to take its own course. Those who interfere with it do so only at their own peril. [4]

NOTES

1. Many texts have "always" here.
2. See ch. 57, note 1.
3. *Analects*, 12:19.
4. This is the point strongly emphasized by Hu Shih. See his *Chung-kuo che-hsüeh shih ta-kang*, p. 65.

75

T HE PEOPLE *starve because the ruler eats too much tax-grain.*
Therefore they starve.
They are difficult to rule because their ruler does too many
things.
Therefore they are difficult to rule.
The people take death lightly because their ruler strives for
life too vigorously.
Therefore they take death lightly.
It is only those who do not seek after life that excel in making
life valuable.[1]

COMMENT

This is easily the strongest protest against oppressive government in Chinese literature. It is so strong that it has led Hu
Shih to describe Lao Tzu as a rebel.[2] Lao Tzu's bitterness
reflects the unbearable situation at the time, but it is also a
natural consequence of the Taoist philosophy, which is essentially that of the lowly people and the oppressed.

NOTES

1. Ma Hsü-lun proposes to transfer this sentence to chapter 50.
2. *Chung-kuo che-hsüeh shih ta-kang,* pp. 50-51.

WHEN MAN *is born, he is tender and weak.*
At death, he is stiff and hard.
All things,[1] the grass as well as trees, are tender and
supple while alive.
When dead, they are withered and dried.

Therefore the stiff and the hard are companions of death.
The tender and the weak are companions of life.
Therefore if the army is strong, it will not win.
If a tree is stiff, it will break.[2]
The strong and the great are inferior, while the tender
and the weak are superior.

COMMENT

The superiority of weakness over strength is a constant theme of the *Lao Tzu*.[3] Here a new note is struck about that theme. Weakness is not only superior to strength; it is the very principle of life.

NOTES

1. Some texts omit these two words.
2. Fu I, Huang Mao-ts'ai, Yü Yüeh, I Shun-ting, Hsi T'ung, Liu Shih-p'ei, and Ma Hsü-lun are unanimous in saying that *ping* (soldier) in the Wang Pi text and *kung* (together) in the Ho-shang Kung text are corruptions of the word *che* (to break).
3. See especially chapters 43 and 78.

Heaven's Way *is indeed like the bending of a bow.*
When (the string) is high, bring it down.
When it is low, raise it up.
When it is excessive, reduce it.
When it is insufficient, supplement it.
The Way of Heaven reduces whatever is excessive and
supplements whatever is insufficient.
The way of man is different.
It reduces the insufficient to offer to the excessive.

Who is able to have excess to offer to the world?
Only the man of Tao.

Therefore the sage acts, but does not rely on his own ability.[1]
He accomplishes his task, but does not claim credit for it.[2]
He has no desire to display his excellence.

COMMENT

Lao Tzu is here teaching the doctrine of the equality of all things. In the *Chuang Tzu*, the doctrine has developed to be a central one. The second chapter of the *Chuang Tzu*, perhaps the most important in that book, is entitled "The Equality of All Things," or literally "leveling all things." Beauty and ugliness, right and wrong, construction and destruction, and the like, are all united by Tao to become one. This, says Chuang Tzu, is natural equalization.[3] As Wang Pi has commented on the *Lao Tzu* chapter, because of man's interest in his own person, he cannot equalize things. Only Heaven (Nature), or one who possesses the character of Heaven, can do so.

NOTES

1. This sentence is found also in chapters 2, 10, and 51.
2. Repeating the sentence in chapter 2 with the variation of one word. Ma Hsü-lun thinks that these two lines should be trans-

ferred to chapter 51, while Ch'en Chu (*Chang-chü*) wants them deleted because they repeat chapter 2.

3. *Chuang Tzu*, ch. 2, *SPTK*, 1:29b-31a. Cf. Giles (tr.), *Chuang Tzu*, pp. 38-39.

78

Tʜᴇʀᴇ ɪs *nothing softer and weaker than water,*
 And yet there is nothing better for attacking hard and
 strong things.[1]
For this reason there is no substitute for it.[2]
All the world knows that the weak overcomes the strong and
 the soft overcomes the hard.
But none can practice it.
Therefore the sage says:
 He who suffers disgrace for his country
 Is called the lord of the land.
 He who takes upon himself the country's misfortunes
 Becomes the king of the empire.
Straight words seem to be their opposite.[3]

Cᴏᴍᴍᴇɴᴛ

"How blest are those who have suffered persecution for the
cause of right; the kingdom of heaven is theirs." [4]

Nᴏᴛᴇs

1. Ma Hsü-lun thinks this sentence should be shifted to chapter 43
   to be its second sentence.
2. Ma says this sentence should be transferred to chapter 43 to
   follow its present second sentence.
3. Kao Heng believes this was originally a comment and should
   therefore be deleted. Some writers put it at the beginning of
   the next chapter.
4. Matthew 5:10.

To patch *up great hatred is surely to leave some hatred behind.*
How can this be regarded as good?
Therefore the sage keeps the left-hand portion (obligation) of a contract [1]
And does not blame the other party.
Virtuous people attend to their left-hand portions,
While those without virtue attend to other people's mistakes.

"The Way of Heaven has no favorites.
It is always with the good man." [2]

COMMENT

Confucius says, "He who requires much from himself and demands little from others will keep complaints away." [3] *The Doctrine of the Mean* also says, "He (the superior man) rectifies himself and seeks nothing from others. Hence he has no complaint to make." [4] Thus Confucianism and Taoism have combined to instill in the Chinese mind the wisdom of compliance.

NOTES

1. In ancient times, contracts were written on two bamboo slips which fitted together. The left one, being a symbol of inferiority, was given the debtor.
2. These sayings, probably an ancient proverb, are also found with slight variation in the inscription referred to in chapter 42, note 1.
3. *Analects*, 15:14.
4. *Doctrine of the Mean*, ch. 14.

Lᴇᴛ ᴛʜᴇʀᴇ *be a small country with few people.*
Let there be ten times and a hundred times [1] *as many
   utensils*
But let them not be used.
Let the people value their lives [2] *highly and not migrate far.*
Even if there are ships and carriages, none will ride in them.
Even if there are arrows and weapons, none will display them.
*Let the people again knot cords and use them (in place of
   writing).*
*Let them relish their food, beautify their clothing, be content
   with their homes, and delight in their customs.*
*Though neighboring communities overlook one another and
   the crowing of cocks and barking of dogs can be heard,*
*Yet the people there may grow old and die without ever
   visiting one another.*

Cᴏᴍᴍᴇɴᴛ

This may be a description of the simple, agricultural society
in which Lao Tzu lived, but, more likely, it is an idealized
state. Whether it is Lao Tzu's concept of *wu-wei* (taking no
action) in practice, as Su Ch'e contends in his commentary, or
an application of the doctrine of the nameless, as Hu Shih
thinks, [3] the ideal of a simple, stable, and contented society
is clear. To be sure, this is not primitivism, for there is satisfactory material enjoyment. But the whole concept is definitely
contrary to the values of a modern "civilized" society. Yen Fu
has observed that the description is one of an ordered small
society in ancient times, and is not applicable today.

Nᴏᴛᴇs

1. According to Yü Yüeh, *shih-po* (ten, hundred) means "military
   weapons." Yamamoto, Hattori, and Koyanagi understand
   shih-po and *ch'i* (utensils) to mean "people with talents ten

times or a hundred times more than the ordinary." In view of the following lines, *ch'i* is better understood as "utensils" than as "talents."

2. Literally, "taking death seriously."

3. *Chung-kuo che-hsüeh shih ta-kang,* p. 64.

81

Tᴿᴜᴇ ᴡᴏʀᴅs *are not beautiful;*
  Beautiful words are not true.
A good man does not argue;
  He who argues is not a good man.
A wise man has no extensive knowledge;
  He who has extensive knowledge is not a wise man.

The sage does not accumulate for himself.
The more he uses for others, the more he has himself.
The more he gives to others, the more he possesses
    of his own.
The Way of Heaven is to benefit others and not to injure.
The Way of the sage is to act but not to compete.[1]

COMMENT

As if this chapter were meant to be a general conclusion to
the book, the basic ideas of simplicity, the One,[2] the Way of
Heaven, and the Way of the sage are all reiterated.

NOTES

1. Ma Hsü-lun says the last sentence belongs to chapter 77.
2. As Wang Pi has said, the basis of beauty lies in simplicity, and
   that of knowledge, in unity.

Bibliography of Works
in Western Languages[1]

A. TRANSLATIONS

Chuang Tzu. Chuang Tzu, A New Selected Translation with an Exposition of the Philosophy of Kuo Hsiang. Translated by FUNG YU-LAN. Shanghai: Commercial Press, 1933.

———. *Chuang Tzu, Mystic, Moralist, and Social Reformer.* Translated by HERBERT A. GILES. 2nd edition, revised, 1926. London: Allen & Unwin, 1961.

Ch'un-ch'iu. The Ch'un Ts'ew, with the Tso Chuen. Translated by JAMES LEGGE. London: Henry Frowde, 1893.

CONFUCIUS. *The Wisdom of Confucius.* Edited and translated by LIN YUTANG. New York: Modern Library, 1938.

Han Fei Tzu. The Complete Works of Han Fei Tzu. Translated by W. K. LIAO. 2 vols. London: Probsthain, 1939, 1959.

HO-SHANG KUNG. *Ho-shang-kung's Commentary on Lao-tse.* Translated by EDUARD ERKES. Ascona, Switzerland: Artibus Asiae Publishers, 1950.

Hsün Tzu. The Works of Hsüntze. Translated by HOMER H. DUBS. London: Probsthain, 1928.

Huai-nan Tzu. Tao, The Great Luminant. Translated by EVAN MORGAN. Shanghai: Kelly and Walsh, 1935.

I ching. The Yi King. Translated by JAMES LEGGE. Oxford: Clarendon Press, 1882.

K'ung Tzu chia-yü. "Familiar Sayings of Kong-Fu-Tze," translated by C. de Harlez, *The Babylonian and Oriental Record,* VI-VII (1893-94), *passim.*

[1] This bibliography includes works referred to in the text, and should be useful in providing references for further reading. For a detailed and analytical bibliography for such reading, see Wing-tsit Chan, *An Outline and an Annotated Bibliography of Chinese Philosophy*, pp. 17-20. In most cases, well-known works are listed by their titles, since they are referred to in the text by their titles. Translations of the *Lao Tzu* are listed alphabetically by the names of translators.

Lao Tzu. AU-YOUNG SUM NUNG (tr.). *Lao Tzu's Tao Teh King.* New York: March and Greenwood, 1938.

———. BAHM, ARCHIE J. (tr.). *Tao Teh King by Lao Tzu.* New York: Ungar, 1958.

———. BLAKNEY, R. B. (tr.). *The Way of Life, Lao Tzu.* New York: American Library, 1955.

———. BYNNER, WITTER (tr.). *The Way of Life According to Laotzu.* New York: John Day, 1944.

———. CARUS, PAUL (tr.). *The Canon of Reason and Virtue.* Chicago: Open Court, 1945. First published, 1913.

———. CHENG LIN (tr.). *The Works of Lao Tzu, Truth and Nature.* Taipei: The World Book Co., 1953.

———. CH'U TA-KAO (tr.). *Tao Te Ching.* London: The Buddhist Society, 1945. First published, 1937.

———. DUYVENDAK, J. J. L. (tr.). *Tao Te Ching, The Book of the Way and Its Virtue.* London: Murray, 1954.

———. GILES, LIONEL (tr.). *The Sayings of Lao Tzu.* London: Murray, 1917. First published, 1904.

———. HEYSINGER, I. W. (tr.). *The Light of China. The Tao Teh King of Lao Tsze.* Philadelphia: Research Publishing Co., 1903.

———. HUGHES, E. (tr.). "Tao Te Ching," in his *Chinese Philosophy in Classical Times.* London: Dent, 1954.

———. LEGGE, JAMES (tr.). "The Tao Teh King; The Tao and Its Characteristics," in *The Texts of Taoism.* Translated by JAMES LEGGE. New York: The Julien Press, 1959. First published, 1891.

———. LIN YUTANG (tr.). *The Wisdom of Laotse.* New York: Modern Library, 1948.

———. MEARS, ISABELLA (tr.). *Tao Teh King.* London: Theosophical Publishing House, 1922.

———. MEDHURST, C. SPURGEON (tr.). *The Tao Teh King.* Chicago: Theosophical Book Concern, 1905.

———. MEI, Y. P. (tr.). "Selections from the *Lao Tzu* (or *Tao-te Ching*)," in *Sources of Chinese Tradition.* Compiled by WILLIAM THEODORE DE BARY, WING-TSIT CHAN, and BURTON WATSON. New York: Columbia University Press, 1960.

———. OLD, WALTER GORN (tr.). *The Simple Way, Laotze.* London: Rider, 1922.

———. WAI-TAO and DWIGHT GODDARD (trs.). *Laotzu's Tao and Wu-Wei.* Santa Barbara: Dwight Goddard, 1935.

————. WALEY, ARTHUR (tr.). *The Way and Its Power, A Study of the Tao Te Ching*. London: Allen & Unwin, 1934.

————. WILHELM, RICHARD (tr.). *Laotse Tao Te King*. Jena: Eugen Diederichs, 1921.

————. WU, JOHN C. H. (tr.). *Tao Teh Ching*. New York: St. John's University Press, 1961.

————. WU WU TZE and D. L. PHELPS (trs.). *The Philosophy of Lao-tzu*. Chengtu: Modern Industrial Society, 1926.

Li Chi. The Li Ki. Translated by JAMES LEGGE. Oxford: Clarendon Press, 1885.

LIANG CH'I-CH'AO. *History of Chinese Political Thought During the Early Tsin Period*. Translated by L. T. CHEN. New York: Harcourt, Brace, 1930.

Lieh Tzu. The Book of Lieh Tzu. Translated by A. C. GRAHAM. London: Murray, 1960.

Lü-shih ch'un-ch'iu. Frühling und Herbst der Lü Bu We. Translated by RICHARD WILHELM. Jena: Eugen Diederichs, 1928.

Mo Tzu. The Ethical and Political Works of Motse. Translated by Y. P. MEI. London: Probsthain, 1929.

SHANG YANG. *The Book of Lord Shang*. Translated by J. J. L. DUYVENDAK. London: Probsthain, 1928.

Shih chi. Les mémoires historiques de Se-Ma Ts'ien. Translated by EDOUARD CHAVANNES. Vol. V. Paris: Leroux, 1905.

Shu ching. The Shoo King. Translated by JAMES LEGGE. Oxford: Clarendon Press, 1879.

T'ai-shang kan-ying p'ien. T'ai-Shang Kan-Ying P'ien, Treatise of the Exalted One on Response and Retribution. Translated by TEITARO SUZUKI and PAUL CARUS. Chicago: Open Court, 1906.

WANG YANG-MING. *Instructions for Practical Living, and Other Neo-Confucian Writings by Wang Yang-ming*. Translated by WING-TSIT CHAN. New York: Columbia University Press, 1963.

B. OTHER WORKS

BODDE, DERK. "The New Identification of Lao Tzu Proposed by Professor Dubs," *Journal of the American Oriental Society*, LXII (1942), 8-13.

———. "Further Remarks on the Identification of Lao Tzu," *ibid.*, LXIV (1944), 24-27.

———. *See* FUNG YU-LAN.

BOODBERG, PETER A. "Philological Notes on Chapter One of the *Lao Tzu*," *Harvard Journal of Asiatic Studies*, XX (1957,) 598-618.

CHAN, WING-TSIT. "Neo-Confucianism and Chinese Scientific Thought," *Philosophy East and West*, VI (1957), 309-32.

———. *An Outline and an Annotated Bibliography of Chinese Philosophy*. New Haven: Yale University, Far Eastern Publications, reprinted with supplement, 1961.

———. *A Source Book in Chinese Philosophy*. Princeton: Princeton University Press, 1963.

———. *See above*, WANG YANG-MING.

———, WILLIAM THEODORE DE BARY, and BURTON WATSON (comps.). *Sources of Chinese Tradition*. New York: Columbia University Press, 1960.

CHANG CHUNG-YÜAN. "The Concept of Tao in Chinese Culture," *Review of Religion*, XVII (1953), 115-32.

———. "Selected Chapters from *Tao Te Ching*," *The Middle Way*, XXX (1956), 164-71.

———. "Tao and the Sympathy of All Things," *Eranos-Jahrbuch*, XXIV (1955), 407-32.

———. "An Introduction to Taoist Yoga," *Review of Religion*, XX (1956), 131-48.

CORDIER, HENRI. *Bibliotheca Sinica*. Paris: Libraire Orientale et Américaine, 1904.

CREEL, H. G. "On Two Aspects in Early Taoism," in KAIZUKA SHIGEKI (ed.), *Silver Jubilee Volume of the Zinbun-Kagaku-Kenkyusyo*. Kyoto University, 1954.

———. "What Is Taoism?" *Journal of the American Oriental Society*, LXXVI (1956), 139-52.

DUBS, HOMER H. "The Date and Circumstances of the Philosopher Lao-dz," *Journal of the American Oriental Society*, LXI (1941), 215-21.

———. "The Identification of the Lao-dz, a Reply to Professor Bodde," *ibid.*, LXII (1942), 300-4.

———. "Note on *Ssu erh pu-wang*," *Asia Major*, III (1952), 159-61.

———. "Taoism," in HARLEY FARNSWORTH MACNAIR (ed.), *China*. Berkeley: University of California Press, 1946.

ERKES, EDUARD. "Arthur Waley's Laotse-Übersetzung," *Artibus Asiae*, V (1935), 285-307.

——. "*Ssu erh pu-wang*," *Asia Major*, III (1952), 156-59, and IV (1954), 149-50.

FUNG YU-LAN. *A History of Chinese Philosophy*. Translated by DERK BODDE. 2 vols. Princeton: Princeton University Press, 1952-53.

——. *A Short History of Chinese Philosophy*. New York: Macmillan, 1948.

——. *The Spirit of Chinese Philosophy*. Translated by E. R. HUGHES. London: Kegan Paul, 1947.

HU SHIH. "A Criticism of Some Recent Methods Used in Dating Lao Tzu," *Harvard Journal of Asiatic Studies*, II (1937), 373-97.

——. *The Development of the Logical Method in Ancient China*. 3rd edition. Shanghai: Oriental Book Co., 1928.

HUGHES, E. R. *Chinese Philosophy in Classical Times*. London: Dent, 1954.

KARLGREN, B. "On the Authenticity and Nature of the *Tso chuan*," *Göteborgs Högskolas Årsskrift*, XXXII (1926), 1-65.

——. "The Poetical Parts in Lao-Tsi," *ibid.*, XXXVII (1932), 1-45.

LAU, D. C. "The Treatment of Opposites in Lao Tzu," *Bulletin of the School of Oriental and African Studies*, XXI (1958), 344-60.

LEGGE, JAMES. *The Texts of Taoism*. New York: The Julien Press, 1959. First published, 1891.

LIN TUNG-CHI. "The Chinese Mind: Its Taoist Substratum," *Journal of the History of Ideas*, VIII (1947), 259-73.

NEEDHAM, JOSEPH. *Science and Civilisation in China*. Vol. II, *History of Scientific Thought*. Cambridge: Cambridge University Press, 1956.

WELCH, HOLMES. *The Parting of the Way. Lao Tzu and the Taoist Movement*. Boston: Beacon Press, 1957.

Bibliography of Works
in Chinese and Japanese [1]

Chan-kuo ts'e. See LIU HSIANG.

CHANG CH'I-CHÜN. *Lao Tzu.* Taipei, 1958.　張起鈞　老子

CHANG MO-SHENG. *Lao Tzu pai-hua chü-chieh* (*Lao Tzu* Explained in the Colloquial). Hong Kong, 1956.
張默生　老子白話句解

CHANG PING-LIN (1868-1936). *Tao-han wei-yen* (Subtle Words of Chang Ping-lin). Hangchow, 1917.　章炳麟　菿漢微言

CHANG SHOU-CHIEH (*fl.* 1736). *Shih chi cheng-i* (Correct Meanings of the *Records of the Historian*).　張守節　史記正義

CHANG SHUN-I. *Lao Tzu t'ung-shih* (General Explanation of the *Lao Tzu*). Shanghai, 1946.　張純一　老子通釋

CHANG TSAI (1020-1077). *Chang Heng-ch'ü chi* (Collected Works of Chang Tsai). *Cheng-i-t'ang ch'üan-shu* (Complete Library of the Hall of Rectifying the Way) edition.
張載　張橫渠集　正誼堂全書

---

[1] This bibliography includes only works referred to in addition to the *Analects, Book of Mencius, Doctrine of the Mean, Book of Changes, Book of History,* and *Book of Filial Piety,* which are referred to by their English titles. With a few exceptions, dates of authors, but not years or places of publication, are given for works published before 1912. Where a specific edition has been used, it is mentioned. In most cases works referred to in the text by titles are here listed by their titles.

———. *Cheng-meng* (Correcting Youthful Ignorance), in the *Chang Heng-ch'ü chi*. 正蒙

CHAO PING-WEN (1159-1232). *Tao-te chen-ching chi-chieh* (Collected Explanations of the *Pure Classic of the Way and Its Virtue*). 趙秉文　道德眞經集解

CH'EN CHING-YÜAN (1025-1094). *Tao-te ching chu* (Commentary on the *Classic of the Way and Its Virtue*).
陳景元　道德經註

CH'EN CHU. *Lao-hsüeh pa-p'ien* (Eight Essays on the Study of Lao Tzu). Shanghai, 1928.　陳柱　老學八篇

———. *Lao Tzu*. Shanghai, 1934 edition.　老子

———. *Lao Tzu chang-chü* (New Annotation of the *Lao Tzu*), in the *Lao-hsüeh pa-p'ien*.　老子章句

———. *Lao Tzu chi-hsün* (Collected Explanations of the *Lao Tzu*). Shanghai, 1928.　老子集訓

CH'EN MENG-CHIA. *Lao Tzu fen-shih* (*Lao Tzu* Analytically Explained). Chungking, 1945.　陳夢家　老子分釋

CH'EN, SHIH-HSIANG. "Hsiang-erh Lao Tzu Tao-ching Tun-huang ts'an-chüan lun-cheng" (On the Historical and Religious Significance of the Tun-huang MS of *Lao-tzu*, Book I, with Commentaries by "Hsiang-erh"), *Tsing-hua Journal of Chinese Studies*, I, 2 (1957), 41-62.
陳世驤　想爾老子道經燉煌殘卷論證　　清華學報

CH'ENG HAO (1032-1085). *Ming-tao wen-chi* (Collection of Literary Works by Ch'eng Hao), in the *Erh-Ch'eng ch'üan-shu*.
程顥　明道文集

CH'ENG HAO and CH'ENG I (1033-1107). *Erh-Ch'eng ch'üan-shu* (Complete Works of the Two Ch'engs). *SPPY*.

二程全書

———. *I-shu* (Surviving Works), in the *Erh-Ch'eng ch'üan-shu*.

遺書

CH'ENG HSÜAN-YING (*fl.* 647-663). *Chuang Tzu su-chieh* (Commentary on the *Chuang Tzu*).　成玄英　莊子疏解

———. *Lao Tzu chu* (Commentary on the *Lao Tzu*). Fragments.

老子注

CH'ENG I. *I chuan* (Commentary on the *Book of Changes*), in the *Erh-Ch'eng ch'üan-shu*.　程頤　易傳

CHIANG HSI-CH'ANG. *Lao Tzu chiao-ku* (*Lao Tzu* Collated and Explained). Shanghai, 1937.　蔣錫昌　老子校詁

CHIAO HUNG (1541-1620). *Lao Tzu i* (Aid to the *Lao Tzu*). *Supplement to the Tao-tsang* edition.　焦竑　老子翼

———. *Lao Tzu k'ao-i* (Inquiry into the Variants in the *Lao Tzu*), in the *Lao Tzu i*.　老子攷異

CH'IEN CHI-PO. *Lao Tzu tao-te ching chieh-t'i chi ch'i tu-fa* (About the Text of the *Lao Tzu, the Classic of the Way and Its Virtue,* and How to Study It). Shanghai, 1934.

錢基博　老子道德經解題及其讀法

CH'IEN MU. *Chuang-Lao t'ung-pien* (General Discussions of Lao Tzu and Chuang Tzu). Hong Kong, 1957.

錢穆　莊老通辨

———. *Chung-kuo ssu-hsiang shih* (History of Chinese Thought). Taipei, 1952.　中國思想史

———. *Hsien-Ch'in chu-tzu hsi-nien* (Chronological Studies on the Pre-Ts'in Philosophers). Revised edition. Hong Kong, 1956.　先秦諸子繁年

CHIH WEI-CH'ENG. *Lao Tzu tao-te ching* (*Lao Tzu, the Classic of the Way and Its Virtue*). Shanghai, 1926 edition. 支偉成　老子道德經

Chiu T'ang shu (History of the T'ang Dynasty). *PNP.*　舊唐書

Chou-i cheng-i (Correct Meanings of the *Book of Changes*). *SPTK.*　周易正義

CHOU KAN-T'ING. *Lao Tzu yin-shih* (Pronunciations in the *Lao Tzu*). Chi-nan, 1939.　周幹庭　老子音釋

Chou shu (Book of Chou).　周書

CHOU TUN-I (1017-1073). *T'ai-chi-t'u shuo* (Explanation of the Diagram of the Great Ultimate).　周敦頤　太極圖說

———. *T'ung-shu* (Penetrating the *Book of Changes*).　通書

CHU CH'IEN-CHIH. *Lao Tzu chiao-shih* (*Lao Tzu* Collated and Explained). Shanghai, 1958.　朱謙之　老子校釋

CHU FEI-HUANG. *Lao Tzu shu-chi* (Notes on the *Lao Tzu*). Shanghai, 1936.　朱芾煌　老子述記

CHU HSI (1130-1200). *Chu Tzu wen-chi* (Collection of Literary Works by Chu Hsi)　朱熹　朱子文集，*SPPY*, entitled *Chu Tzu ta-ch'üan* (Complete Literary Works of Chu Hsi). 朱子大全

———. *Chu Tzu yü-lei* (Classified Conversations of Chu Hsi). 1880 edition.　朱子語類

———. *Lun-yü chi-chu* (Collected Commentaries on the *Analects*).　論語集註

———. *Ta-hsüeh chang-chü* (Commentary on the *Great Learning*). 大學章句

CH'U PO-HSIU (of the Sung Dynasty, 970-1279), quoted by Liu Wei-yung (*q.v.*). 褚伯秀

Ch'u tz'u (Elegies of Ch'u). *SPPY*. 楚辭

Chuang Tzu. SPTK, entitled *Nan-hua chen-ching* (Pure Classic of Nan-hua). 莊子 南華眞經

Ch'un-ch'iu (Spring and Autumn Annals). 春秋

Ch'un-Ts'ew. See Ch'un-ch'iu.

FAN YING-YÜAN (1240-1269). *Lao Tzu tao-te ching ku-pen chi-chu* (Collected Commentaries on the Ancient Text of the *Lao Tzu, the Classic of the Way and Its Virtue*). 范應元 老子道德經古本集註

FU I (555-639). *Chiao-ting ku-pen Lao Tzu* (Ancient Text of the *Lao Tzu* Collated). 傅奕 校定古本老子

Han Fei Tzu. SPTK. 韓非子

Han shu. See PAN KU.

HATTORI UNOKICHI (1867-1939) (compiler). *Rōshi (Lao Tzu), Kambun taikai* (Great Chinese Works) series, 1911. 服部宇之吉 老子 漢文大系

HO-SHANG KUNG (*fl.* 179-159 B.C.?). *Lao Tzu chu* (Commentary on the *Lao Tzu*). 河上公 老子注

HO SHIH-CH'I. *Ku-pen tao-te ching chiao-k'an* (Old Texts of the *Classic of the Way and Its Virtue* Collated). Peking, 1936. 何士驥 古本道德經校刊

HO TUN-WENG. *Lao Tzu hsin-i* (New Explanations of the *Lao Tzu*). Hong Kong, 1959. 何遁翁 老子新繹

Hou Wai-lu. *Chung-kuo ku-tai ssu-hsiang hsüeh-shuo shih* (History of Ancient Chinese Thought and Theories). Revised edition. Shanghai, 1950.
侯外廬　中國古代思想學說史

―――, *et al. Chung-kuo ssu-hsiang t'ung-shih* (General History of Chinese Thought). Vol. I. Peking, 1957.　中國思想通史

Hsi T'ung (1876-1936). *Lao Tzu chi-chieh* (Collected Explanations of the *Lao Tzu*). Shanghai, 1925.　奚侗　老子集解

Hsü Fu-kuan. *Chung-kuo ssu-hsiang shih lun-chi* (Collected Essays on the History of Chinese Thought). Taichung, 1949.
徐復觀　中國思想史論集

Hsü kao-seng chuan (Supplement to the *Biographies of Eminent Monks*).　續高僧傳

Hsü Ti-shan (1893-1941). *Tao-chiao shih* (History of the Taoist Religion). Shanghai, 1934.　許地山　道教史

Hsün Tzu. SPTK.　荀子

Hsüntze. See Hsün Tzu.

Hu Che-fu. *Lao-Chuang che-hsüeh* (Philosophy of Lao Tzu and Chuang Tzu). Shanghai, 1935.　胡哲敷　老莊哲學

Hu Shih (1891-1962). *Chung-kuo che-hsüeh shih ta-kang* (Outline of the History of Chinese Philosophy). Shanghai, 1938 edition.　胡適　中國哲學史大綱

―――. *Hu Shih lun-hsüeh chin-chu* (Recent Essays on Learned Subjects by Hu Shih). Shanghai, 1935.　胡適論學近著

―――. *Shuo ju* (On the Literati), in *Hu Shih lun-hsüeh chin-chu.*　說儒

Hu Yüan-chun. *Lao Tzu shu-i* (Explanations of the *Lao Tzu*). Nanking, 1933.　胡遠濬　老子述義

Huai-nan Tzu, by Liu An (d. 122 B.C.). *SPPY.*   淮南子　劉安

Huang K'an (445-545). *Lun-yü su* (Commentary on the *Analects*), in the *Thirteen Classics.*   皇侃　論語疏

Huang Mao-ts'ai (*fl.* 1174). *Lao Tzu chieh* (*Lao Tzu* Explained). Fragments quoted in Chiao Hung, *Lao Tzu i.*
黃茂材　老子解

Hung I-hsüan (b. 1765). *Tu-shu ts'ung-lu* (Notes from Reading).
洪頤煊　讀書叢錄

Hung-ming chi (Essays Elucidating the Doctrine). *SPTK.*
弘明集

I ching (Book of Changes).   易經

Inoue Shūten. *Rōshi no shinkenkyū* (New Study of the *Lao Tzu*). Tokyo, 1928.   井上秀天　老子ノ新研究

I Shun-ting (1858-1920). *Tu Lao cha-chi* (Notes from Reading the *Lao Tzu*).   易順鼎　讀老札記

I-wei ch'ien-tso tu (Penetration of the Law of Heaven in the Apocryphal Treatise on the *Book of Changes*). *Chü-chen ts'ung-shu* (Collected Precious Works Series) edition, 1899.
易緯乾鑿度　聚珍叢書

Jao Tsung-i. *Lao Tzu hsiang-erh chu chiao-chien* (A Study of Chang Tao-ling's Hsiang-erh Commentary of *Tao Te Ching*). Hong Kong, 1956.   饒宗頤　老子想爾注校箋

Jen Chi-yü. *Lao Tzu chin-i* (Colloquial Translation of the *Lao Tzu*). Peking, 1956.   任繼愈　老子今譯

Juan Yü-sung. *Chuang Tzu chi-chu* (Collected Commentaries on the *Chuang Tzu*). Shanghai, 1936.   阮毓崧　莊子集註

Kanō Naoki (1867-1947). *Chūgoku tetsugaku shi* (History of Chinese Philosophy). Tokyo, 1953.

狩野直喜　中國哲學史

Kao Heng. *Ch'ung-ting Lao Tzu cheng-ku* (Revised Collation of the *Lao Tzu*). Peking, 1956.　高亨　重訂老子正詁

Kao Yu (*fl.* 205). *Lü-shih ch'un-ch'iu chu* (Commentary on *Mr. Lü's Spring and Autumn Annals*).　高誘　呂氏春秋註

Kimura Eiichi. *Rōshi no shinkenkyū* (New Study of the *Lao Tzu*). Tokyo, 1959.　木村英一　老子9新研究

Ko Hung (253-333?). *Shen-hsien chuan* (Biographies of Immortals).　葛洪神仙傳

Koitsu sōsho (Collection of Missing Ancient Texts).　古逸叢書

Kojima Kenkichirō (1866-1931). *Shina shoshi hyakkakō* (Inquiry on the Hundred Schools of Ancient Chinese Philosophy). Tokyo, 1931.　兒島獻吉郎　支那諸子百家考

Koyanagi Shigeta (translator). *Rōshi* (*Lao Tzu*). Tokyo, 1929.

小柳司氣太　老子

Ku Chieh-kang. "Ts'ung Lü-shih ch'un-ch'iu t'ui-ts'e Lao Tzu chih ch'eng-shu shih-tai," (Inferring the Date of the *Lao Tzu* from *Mr. Lü's Spring and Autumn Annals*), in *Ku-shih pien*, Vol. IV.

顧頡剛　從呂氏春秋推測老子之成書時代

Ku-shih pien (Discussions on Ancient History). 7 vols. 1916-41. Vol. IV. Peking, 1933.　古史辨

Kuei Yu-kuang (1506-1571). *Lao Tzu hui-han* (Collection on the *Lao Tzu*).　歸有光　老子彙函

K'ung Tzu chia-yü (Schools Sayings of Confucius). *SPPY.*
孔子家語

K'UNG YING-TA (574-648). *Li chi cheng-i* (Correct Meanings of the *Book of Rites*).　孔穎達　禮記正義

KUO HSIANG (d. 132). *Chuang Tzu chu* (Commentary on the *Chuang Tzu*).　郭象　莊子註

KUO MO-JO. *Ch'ing-t'ung shih-tai* (Bronze Age). Shanghai, 1951 edition.　郭沫若　青銅時代

Kuo-yü (Conversations of the States). *SPPY.*　國語

Lao Tzu che-hsüeh t'ao-lun chi (Symposium on the Philosophy of Lao Tzu). Peking, 1959.　老子哲學討論集

LENG CH'ING-HSIAO. *Lao Tzu hsüeh-an* (Study of Lao Tzu). Shanghai, 1926.　郎擎霄　老子學案

Li chi (Book of Rites).　禮記

Li Ki. See Li chi.

LI YÜEH (651-683). *Tao-te ching hsin-chu* (New Commentary on the *Classic of the Way and Its Virtue*).
李約　道德經新注

LIANG CH'I-CH'AO (1873-1929). *Hsien-Ch'in cheng-chih ssu-hsiang shih* (History of Political Thought before the Ch'in Dynasty). Shanghai, 1923.　梁啓超　先秦政治思想史

———. *Ku-shu chen-wei chi ch'i nien-tai* (Authenticity of Ancient Texts and Their Dates), in LIANG CH'I-CH'AO, *Yin-ping-shih ho-chi.*　古書眞僞及其年代

———. *Lao Tzu che-hsüeh* (Philosophy of Lao Tzu), in *Yin-ping-shih ho-chi.*　老子哲學

———. *Liang Jen-kung hsüeh-shu yen-chiang chi* (Collection of Liang Ch'i-ch'ao's Lectures on Learned Subjects). Shanghai, 1923. 梁任公學術演講集

———. *Yin-ping-shih ho-chi* (Collection of Literary Works of Yin-ping Study). Shanghai, 1923. 欽冰室合集

LIANG YÜ-SHENG (1745-1819). *Shih chi chi-i* (Doubts on the *Records of the Historian*), in the *Kuang-ya ts'ung-shu* (The Extension of Correct Meanings Series). 1920 edition.
梁玉繩　史記志疑　廣雅叢書

Lieh Tzu. SPTK, entitled *Ch'ung-hsü chih-te chen-ching* (Pure Classic of the Perfect Virtues of Simplicity and Vacuity).
列子　冲虛至德眞經

LIN HSI-I (*fl.* 1235). *Lao Tzu k'ou-i* (Pronunciations and Meanings of the *Lao Tzu*).　林希逸　老子口義

LIN TUNG (*fl.* 1229). *Lao Tzu chu* (*Lao Tzu* Annotated).
林東　老子註

LIU HSIANG (77-6 B.C.) (compiler). *Chan-kuo ts'e* (Strategy of the Warring States). *SPPY.*　劉向　戰國策

———. *Ch'i-lüeh* (Bibliography in Seven Brief Sections).　七略

———. *Lieh-hsien chuan* (Biographies of the Many Immortals).
列仙傳

———. *Shuo-yüan* (Collection of Discourses). *SPTK.*　說苑

LIU SHIH-P'EI (1884-1919). *Lao Tzu chiao-pu* (Collation of the *Lao Tzu* Supplemented). Shanghai, 1910.
劉師培　老子斠補

LIU WEI-YUNG (*fl.* 1299). *Tao-te chen-ching chi-i* (Collected Commentaries on the *Pure Classic of the Way and Its Virtue*).
劉惟永　道德眞經集義

Lo Chen-yü. *Lao Tzu k'ao-i* (Inquiry into the Variants in the *Lao Tzu*). N.p., 1923.　羅振玉　老子考異

Lo Ken-tse. *Chu-tzu k'ao-so* (Inquiries on Ancient Philosophers). Peking, 1958.　羅根澤　諸子考索

Lu Hsiang-shan (1139-1193). *Hsiang-shan ch'üan-chi* (Complete Works of Lu Hsiang-shan). *SPPY*.
陸象山　象山全集

Lu Shih-hung. *Lao Tzu hsien-tai-yü chieh* (*Lao Tzu* Explained in Contemporary Colloquial). Chungking, 1944.
陸世鴻　老子現代語解

Lu Te-ming (556-627). *Ching-tien shih-wen* (Explanation of Words in the Classics).　陸德明　經典釋文

———. *Lao Tzu yin-i* (Pronunciations and Meanings of the *Lao Tzu*).　老子音義

Lu Wen-ch'ao (1717-1793). *Pao-ching-t'ang wen-chi* (Collection of Literary Works of the Hall of Embracing the Classics).
盧文弨　抱經堂文集

Lü Hui-ch'ing (*fl.* 1078). *Tao-te chen-ching chuan* (Commentary on the *Pure Classic of the Way and Its Virtue*).
呂惠卿　道德眞經傳

Lü-shih ch'un-ch'iu (Mr. Lü's Spring and Autumn Annals).
SPPY.　呂氏春秋

Ma Ch'i-ch'ang (1855-1929). *Lao Tzu ku* (Etymological Meanings of the *Lao Tzu*). Shanghai, 1920.　馬其昶　老子故

Ma Hsü-lun. *Lao Tzu chiao-ku* (*Lao Tzu* Collated and Explained). Peking, 1956. A revision of the *Lao Tzu ho-ku* (Critical Collation of the *Lao Tzu*) of 1924.
馬敍倫　老子校詁　老子覈故

MING-HUANG, EMPEROR (685-762). *Tao-te ching chu* (Commentary on the *Classic of the Way and Its Virtue*).
明皇　道德經註

MIU ERH-SHU. *Lao Tzu hsin-chu* (New Annotation of the *Lao Tzu*). Shanghai, 1934.　繆爾紓　老子新註

Mo Tzu.　墨子

Motse. See Mo Tzu.

PAN KU (32-92). *Han shu* (History of the Former Han Dynasty). *PNP.*　班固　漢書

PI YÜAN (1730-1797). *Lao Tzu tao-te ching k'ao-i* (Inquiry into the Variants in the *Lao Tzu, the Classic of the Way and Its Virtue*), in the *Hsün-ching-t'ang ts'ung-shu* (Collection of the Hall of the Explanation of the Classics).
畢沅　老子道德經攷異　訓經堂叢書

SAITŌ SETSUDŌ (1797-1865). *Rōshi ben* (An Examination on the *Lao Tzu*).　齋藤拙堂　老子辨

SHANG YANG (d. 338 B.C.). *Shang-chün shu* (Book of Lord Shang). *SPPY.*　商鞅　商君書

SHAO YUNG (1011-1077). *Huang-chi ching-shih shu* (Supreme Principles Governing the World). *SPPY.*
邵雍　皇極經世書

Shih chi. See SSU-MA CH'IEN.

SHIH YUNG (*fl.* 1159). *Tao-te ching ch'üan-chieh* (Complete Explanation of the *Classic of the Way and Its Virtue*).
時雍　道德經全解

Shoo King. See Shu ching.

Shu ching (Book of History).　書經

Ssu-k'u ch'üan-shu tsung-mu t'i-yao (Essentials of the Complete Catalogue of the Four Libraries). 1933 edition.
四庫全書總目提要

SSU-MA CHEN (*fl.* 727). *Shih chi so-yin* (Tracing the Hidden Meanings of the *Records of the Historian*). *PNP.*
司馬貞　史記索引

SSU-MA CH'IEN (145-86 B.C.). *Shih chi* (Records of the Historian). *PNP.*　司馬遷　史記

SSU-MA KUANG (1019-1086). *Tao-te ching shu-yao* (Essentials of the *Classic of the Way and Its Virtue*).
司馬光　道德經述要

SU CH'E (1039-1112). *Lao Tzu chu* (Commentary on the *Lao Tzu*).　蘇轍　老子注

Sui shu (History of the Sui Dynasty). *PNP.*　隋書

SUN I-JANG (1848-1908). *Cha-i* (Notes), section on Lao Tzu.
孫詒讓　札迻

SUN TENG (209-241). *Lao Tzu chu* (*Lao Tzu* Annotated). Fragments in the *Tao-tsang*.　孫登　老子注

Sung shih (History of the Sung Dynasty). *PNP.*　宋史

Ta-Tai li chi (Book of Rites by the Elder Tai). *SPTK.*
大戴禮記

Taishō daizōkyō (Taisho Edition of the Buddhist Canon).
大正大藏經

T'ai-p'ing yü-lan (Imperial Collection of the T'ai-p'ing Period). *SPTK.*　太平御覽

T'ai-shang kan-ying p'ien (Tract of the Most Exalted One on Influence and Response).　太上感應篇

T'AI-TSU (1328-1398). *Tao-te chen-ching chu* (Commentary on the *Pure Classic of the Way and Its Virtue*).
太祖　道德眞經注

T'AI-TSUNG. 太宗 See MING-HUANG.

TAKEUCHI YOSHIO. *Rōshi no kenkyū* (Study of the *Lao Tzu*). Tokyo, 1947.　武內義雄　老子の研究

T'AN CHENG-PI. *Lao Tzu tu-pen* (Lao Tzu Reader). Shanghai, 1949.　譚正璧　老子讀本

T'ang shu (History of the T'ang Dynasty). *PNP.*　唐書

TAOKA REIUN (1870-1912). *Wayaku rōshi* (Japanese Translation of the *Lao Tzu*). Tokyo, 1910.　田崗嶺雲　和譯老子

Tao-te chen-ching tz'u-chieh (*Pure Classic of the Way and Its Virtue* Explained).　道德眞經次解

Tao-te ching (Classic of the Way and Its Virtue).　道德經

Tao Teh King. See Tao-te ching.

Tao-tsang (Taoist Canon).　道藏

T'AO HUNG-CH'ING (1859-1917). *Tu Lao Tzu cha-chi* (Notes from Reading the *Lao Tzu*). Shanghai, 1919.
陶鴻慶　讀老子札記

TING FU-PAO. *Lao Tzu tao-te ching chien-chu* (Annotation of the *Lao Tzu, the Classic of the Way and Its Virtue*). Shanghai, 1927.　丁福保　老子道德經箋注

TS'AO JU-LIN. *Chou-Ch'in chu-tzu k'ao* (Inquiry on the Philosophers of the Chou and Ch'in Dynasties). Peking, 1929.
曹汝霖　周秦諸子考

Tso chuan (Tso's Commentary on the *Spring and Autumn Annals*).　左傳

Tso Tsüen. See Tso chuan.

Tsuda Sōkichi. *Dōke no shisō to sono tenkai* (Taoist Thought and Its Development). Tokyo, 1939.
津田左右吉　道家の思想て其展開

Ts'ui Shu (1740-1816). *Chu-Ssu k'ao-hsin lu* (Inquiry into the True Facts Concerning Confucius), in the *Ts'ui Tung-pi i-shu* (Surviving Works of Ts'ui Shu). 1924 edition.
崔述　洙泗考信錄　崔東壁遺書

Tu Kuang-t'ing (*fl.* 901). *Tao-te ching kuang-sheng-i su* (Commentary Elaborating on the Imperial Commentary on the *Classic of the Way and Its Virtue*).
杜光庭　道德經廣聖義疏

Tu Tao-chien (*fl.* 1306). *Tao-te hsüan-ching yüan-chih* (Original Meanings of the *Profound Classic of the Way and Its Virtue*).　杜道堅　道德玄經原旨

Tung Ssu-ching (of the Sung Dynasty, 960-1279). *Tao-te ching chi-chieh* (Collected Explanations of the *Classic of the Way and Its Virtue*).　董思靖　道德經集解

Wang An-shih (1021-1086). *Lao Tzu chu* (Commentary on the *Lao Tzu*). Fragments in the *Wen-hsien t'ung-k'ao* (General Collection of Literary Works and Documents).
王安石　老子注　文獻通考

Wang Ch'ang (1725-1806). *Chiao Lao Tzu* (*Lao Tzu* Collated).
王昶　校老子

Wang Chung (1744-1794). *Lao Tzu k'ao-i* (Inquiry into the Errors about Lao Tzu), in the supplement to the *Shu-hsüeh*.
汪中　老子考異

———. *Shu-hsüeh* (Notes from Studies). *SPTK.*　述學

Wang Chung-min. *Lao Tzu k'ao* (Bibliography of the *Lao Tzu*). Peking, 1927.　王重民　老子考

WANG FU-CHIH (1619-1692). *Lao Tzu yen* (Elucidation of the *Lao Tzu*), in the *Ch'uan-shan i-shu* (Surviving Works of Wang Fu-chih).　王夫之　老子衍　船山遺書

WANG HSIEN-CH'IEN (1842-1917). *Chuang Tzu chi-chieh* (Collected Explanations of the *Chuang Tzu*). 1935 edition.　王先謙　莊子集解

WANG NIEN-SUN (1744-1832). *Tu-shu tsa-chi* (Miscellaneous Notes from Reading). 1933 edition.　王念孫　讀書雜志

WANG PI (226-249). *Lao Tzu chu* (Commentary on the *Lao Tzu*).　王弼　老子註

WANG SHIH-P'ENG (1112-1171). *Mei-hsi Hsien-sheng wen-chi* (Collection of Literary Works by Wang Shih-p'eng).　王十朋　梅溪先生文集

WANG YANG-MING (1472-1529). *Ch'uan-hsi lu* (Instructions for Practical Living).　王陽明　傳習錄

WANG YIN-CHIH (1766-1834). *Ching-chuan shih-tz'u* (Explanations of Terms in the Classics and Commentaries).　王引之　經傳釋詞

WEI YÜAN (1794-1856). *Lao Tzu pen-i* (Original Meanings of the *Lao Tzu*).　魏源　老子本義

Wen Tzu. SPPY.　文子

WU CH'ENG (1249-1333). *Tao-te ching chu* (*Classic of the Way and Its Virtue* Annotated).　吳澄　道德經注

WU CHING-YÜ. *Lao Tzu i su-cheng* (Textual Commentary on the *Lao Tzu*). Hong Kong, 1957.　吳靜宇　老子義疏證

YAMADA SUMERU (translator). *Rōshi* (*Lao Tzu*). Tokyo, 1957.　山田統　老子

YAMAMOTO DŌUN (1636-c. 1687). *Rōshi (Lao Tzu). Kanseki kokuji kaitai zensho* (Complete Chinese Works with Japanese Annotation) series. Tokyo, 1910.
山本洞雲　老子　漢籍國學解題全書

YANG HSING-SHUN. *Chung-kuo ku-tai che-hsüeh-chia Lao Tzu chi ch'i hsüeh-shuo* (China's Ancient Philosopher, Lao Tzu, and His Doctrines). Peking, 1957.
楊興順　中國古代哲學家老子及其學說

YANG LIU-CH'IAO. *Lao Tzu i-huo (Lao Tzu* Rendered in the Colloquial). Peking, 1958.　楊柳橋　老子譯話

YANG TSENG-HSIN. *Tu Lao Tzu jih-chi* (Daily Notes from Reading the *Lao Tzu*). N.p., 1926.　楊增新　讀老子日記

YAO FAN (1701-1771). *Yüan-ch'un-t'ang pi-chi* (Notes from the Quails-aiding Hall). 1835 edition.　姚範　援鶉堂筆記

YAO NAI (1731-1815). *Lao Tzu chang-i* (Commentary on the *Lao Tzu*). SPPY.　姚鼐　老子章義

YEH MENG-TE (1077-1148). *Lao Tzu chieh (Lao Tzu* Explained).
葉夢得　老子解

YEH SHIH (1150-1223). *Hsi-hsüeh chi-yen* (Notes from Study and Recitations).　葉適　習學記言

YEN FU (1853-1921). *P'ing-tien Lao Tzu tao-te ching (Lao Tzu, the Classic of the Way and Its Virtue,* Commented on and Punctuated). Shanghai, 1931.　嚴復　評點老子道德經

YEN JO-CH'Ü (1636-1704). *Ssu-shu shih-ti* (Explanations of Geographical Terms in the *Four Books*). Supplement.
閻若璩　四書釋地

YEN K'O-CHÜN (1762-1843). *Lao Tzu T'ang-pen k'ao-i* (Inquiry into the Variants of the T'ang Dynasty Texts of the *Lao Tzu*). 嚴可均　老子唐本考異

YEN LING-FENG. *Chung-wai Lao Tzu chu-shu mu-lu* (Bibliography on the *Lao Tzu* in Chinese and Foreign Languages). Taipei, 1957.　嚴靈峯　中外老子著述目錄

———. *Lao-Chuang yen-chiu* (Studies on Lao Tzu and Chuang Tzu). Hong Kong, 1959.　老莊研究

———. *Lao Tzu chang-chü hsin-pien tsuan-chieh* (New Arrangement and Commentary on the *Lao Tzu*). Taipei, 1955. 老子章句新編纂解

YEN TSUN (*fl.* 53-24 B.C.). *Lao Tzu chih-kuei* (Essential Principles of the *Lao Tzu*). Fragments.　嚴遵　老子旨歸

Yi King. See I ching.

Yung-lo ta-tien (Great Library of the Yung-lo Period). 永樂大典

YÜ YÜEH (1821-1906). *Chu-tzu p'ing-i* (Textual Critique of the Various Philosophers). 1936 edition.　俞樾　諸子平議

A Glossary of Chinese Names and Terms [1]

ai

   (a) sorrow 哀

   (b) to love 愛

Au-young Sum Nung 歐陽心農

Chan Ho 詹何

Chan, Wing-tsit 陳榮捷

ch'an, meditation 禪

Chang Chan 張湛

Chang Chun-hsiang 張君枏

Chang Chung-yüan 張鍾元

Chang Hsü 張煦

Chang Lu 張魯

Chang Tao-ling 張道陵

ch'ang, eternal, fixed 常

ch'ang-ts'un, remaining forever 常存

Chao 昭

che

   (a) he who 者

   (b) to break 折

chen

   (a) true, real 眞

   (b) ruler 貞

Chen, L. T. 陳立奐

Ch'en 陳

cheng, correct, to rectify 正

Cheng Hsüan 鄭玄

Cheng Lin 鄭麐

Ch'eng Hao 程顥

Ch'eng I 程頤

chi

   (a) bond 紀

   (b) invisible 幾

   (c) to scrutinize 稽

   (d) trace 迹

   (e) when, if, and 及

Ch'i

ch'i

   (a) concrete thing, utensil 器

[1] Characters for dynasties and well-known places are not included here since they are not necessary for the purpose of identification.

Ch'ü Yüan	屈原	hsiang-erh, "think," "so"	想爾
Erh	耳	hsiao-tzu, filial sons	孝子
fa, method	法	hsiao-tz'u, filial piety and deep love	孝慈
fang-shih, priest-magician	方士	Hsiao-wen	孝文
fu		hsieh, perversion	邪
(a) beginning	甫	Hsien	獻
(b) father	父	hsien, immortal	仙
fu-kuei, to return	復歸	hsing	
Fung Yu-lan	馮友蘭	(a) nature	性
hao-jan chih ch'i, strong moving power	浩然之氣	(b) to contrast	形
heng, constancy	恒	Hsing-chou	邢州
Ho-shang Chang-jen	河上丈人	Hsing Ping	邢昺
Hsi	僖	hsü, vacuous	虛
hsi		hsüan, profound	玄
(a) exclamatory article	兮	hsüan-huang, heaven and earth	玄黃
(b) inaudible	希	hsüan-lan, profound insight	玄覽
(c) to follow	襲	hsüan-te, profound and secret virtue	玄德
(d) to practice	習	hsüan-t'ien, heaven	玄天
hsia		Hsüan-tsang	玄奘
(a) narrow	狹	hsüan-t'ung	
(b) people, below	下	(a) profound identification	玄同
hsiang		(b) profound penetration	玄通
(a) form, seems	象	hu, final interrogative article, preposition	乎
(b) good omen	祥		
(c) to yield	襄		

Huan	桓	Kong Fu-Tze	孔夫子
Huan Yüan	環淵	*ku*	
Huang Fang-kuang	黃方剛	(a) for the time being, therefore	故
Huang K'an	皇侃	(b) grain	穀
Hui Shih	惠施	(c) necessary	固
hun, undifferentiated	混	(d) valley	谷
hun-p'o, soul	魂魄	Ku Te-seng	顧鐵僧
huo, perhaps	或	K'u	苦
huo-ts'un, remaining forever	或存	Kuan Yin	關尹
i		Kuang-ho	光和
(a) invisible	夷	*kuei*	
(b) to clothe	衣	(a) to end	歸
I-chou	易州	(b) to honor	貴
i-wei, to do	以爲	*kuei-kao*, honorable and high	貴高
Itō Rangu	伊藤蘭嵎	*kuei-shen*, spiritual beings	鬼神
jen, humane	仁	*kuei-ta-huan*, to regard great trouble seriously	貴大患
jo, then, to be, to be like, if	若	Kung	宮
jo-ts'un, remaining forever	若存	*kung*	
ju		(a) impartial	公
(a) like, as	如	(b) together	共
(b) literati	儒	*kung-ch'eng ming-sui*, work done and fame accomplished	功成名遂
jung, appearance	容	Kung-sun Lung	公孫龍
Kaizuka Shegeki	貝塚茂樹	*k'ung*, emptiness	空
Kao Yu	高誘		
Ko Hsüan	葛玄		
k'o, guest	客		

Kuo Hsiang	郭象	*ming*	
Lao Lai Tzu	老萊子	(a) name	名
Lao P'eng	老彭	(b) to order	命
Lao Tzu, Lao dz, Lao Tze, Lao-tse, Lao Tzzy	老子	(c) to understand	明
		Mou Tzu	牟子
Lau, D. C.	劉殿爵	Nakai Riken	中井履軒
LI	里	Pan Piao	班彪
Li		*pei,* cover	被
(a) place name	厲	P'ei	沛
(b) surname	李	P'ei K'ai	裴楷
li		*pen-t'i,* original substance	本體
(a) a third of a mile	里	*pen-wu,* pure being, original non-being	本無
(b) principle, order	理	P'eng-tsu	彭祖
(c) propriety	禮	*p'ien chiang-chün,* lieutenant general	偏將軍
Liao, W. K.	廖文奎	*ping,* soldier	兵
Lin Tung-chi	林同濟	*po,* white	白
Lin Yutang	林語堂	*Po-na-pen,* Choice Works Edition	百衲本
Liu Hsin	劉歆	Po-yang	伯陽
Lo-yang	洛陽	*pu,* not	不
Lu	魯	*pu-chih,* not well-governed	不治
Lu-i	鹿邑	*pu-hsiao,* not to resemble, unworthy	不肖
Lung-hsing	龍興		
Lü Pu-wei	呂不韋	*pu-tai,* free from danger	不殆
Mei, Y. P.	梅貽寶	*pu-wei,* not done	不為
miao, mystery, subtlety	妙	*p'u,* plainness	樸
Min	閔		

sa, thirty	卅	*ta*, great	大
san-shih, thirty	三十	*ta-shun*, complete harmony	大順
Se-ma Ts'ien	司馬遷	*t'ai-hsü*, profound vacuity	太虛
shang		*t'ai-i*, great one	太一
(a) above	上	*t'ai-shang*, highest, antiquity	太上
(b) high, to exalt	尚	TAN	儋
shang chiang-chün, senior general	上將軍	Tan	聃
sheng, to produce	生	*tan*, long ear	耽
shih		*tao*, way	道
(a) ruler	士	Tao-chia	道家
(b) sustenance	食	Tao-chiao	道教
(c) tendency	勢	*tao-shih*, Taoist priest, practitioner of the Way	道士
(d) to depend	恃	*te*	
shih-po, ten, hundred	什伯	(a) to obtain, to have	得
shih-tsun-hsing, to bring honor and to act	市尊行	(b) virtue	德
Shoo King, Book of History	書經	*t'ien*, nature	天
shou-ts'ang shih, curator of archives	守藏史	Ting	定
shu, course	數	*ting*, peace, calm	定
Shu ching, Book of History	書經	*tsai*	
shuo, to explain	說	(a) exclamation	哉
ssu, then, thereupon, this	斯	(b) to keep	載
ssu erh pu-wang, die but not perish	死而不亡	Tseng Tzu	曾子
Sung	宋	Ts'in	秦
		tso, to sit	坐
		Ts'ui Hao	崔浩

Tsung	宗	(b) to be *wen*	爲文
Tuan-kan Mu	段干木	Wen	文
Tuan-kan P'eng	段干朋	*wen*	
Tun-huang	敦煌	(a) ornament	文
Tung Chung-shu	董仲舒	(b) to hear	聞
t'ung, same	同	*wen-chiao,* cultural education	文敎
t'ung-ch'u, produced from the same	同出	*wu*	
Tzu	子	(a) no	無
tzu-jan, nature	自然	(b) things	物
Tzu-kung	子貢	Wu, John C. H.	吳經熊
tz'u		*wu-ming,* nameless	無名
(a) deep love	慈	*wu-wei,* taking no action	無爲
(b) to turn away	辭	Wu Wu Tzu	悟無子
Wai-Tao	外道	*wu-yü,* having no desires	無欲
Wan-li	萬曆	*ya,* familiar	狎
wang, kingly.	王	*yang*	
Wei	魏	(a) active force	陽
wei		(b) dawn	央
(a) activity	爲	(c) to feed	養
(b) dreadful	威	Yang Chu	楊朱
(c) only (ancient script)	佳	Yang Hsiung	揚雄
(d) only (modern script)	唯	*yeh,* final interrogative particle	耶　邪
(e) subtle	微	*yen,* word	言
wei-shih, to be the beginning	爲始	Yen Hui	顏回
wei-wen		Yen Tsun	嚴遵
		yin, negative force	陰
(a) artificial *wen*	僞文	Yin Hsi	尹喜

ying-p'o, spirit	營魄	(b) interrogative article	與
yu, to be, to have, things	有	(c) preposition	于
yu-ming, named	有名	(d) region	域
yu-yü, having desires	有欲	*yüan,* origin	元
yung, function, use	用	*yüeh,* to see	閱
YÜ, preposition	於	Zen	禪
yü		Zinbun-Kagaku-Kenkyusyo	人文科學研究所
(a) desire	欲		

Index

Affection. *See* Deep love

Alchemy, 26

Analects: compilation of, 72; ideas of, 69, 71; not mentioning Lao Lai Tzu, 47; absence of reference to Lao Tzu, 63; compared with the *Lao Tzu,* 30; style of, 65; terminology of, 66-68, 69

Ancestors, 6

Ancient kings, 132

Art, 203. *See also* Painting, Poetry

Au-young Sum-nung: interpretations of terms, 99, 200, 220; as translator, 83, 90

Bahm, Archie J., 83, 133, 220

Beauty, 101

Being, 7, 18, 173. *See also* Nonbeing

Benevolence. *See jen*

Bhagavadgita, 17

Blakney, R. B., 100, 108, 200, 220

Bodde, Derk, 50, 100

Body, 122

Boodberg, Peter, 100

Book of Changes: cosmology of, 24, 25, 137, 144, 145, 149, 176; style and contents of, 65, 67, 68, 72

Book of Filial Piety, 64

Book of History, 49, 65

Book of Rites, 42, 45, 46

Book of the Yellow Emperor, 111

Bravery, 228

Breathing, 77, 80, 110. *See also* Yoga

Buddha-mind, 24

Buddha-nature, 24

Buddhism: in commentaries, 92; concepts of, 98; compared with Taoism, 101, 105, 107, 112, 124, 154, 157; Taoist influences on, 23-24, 210

Bynner, Witter, 83, 114, 133, 220

Calamity, 203, 222

Carus, Paul: comment of, 125; interpretations of terms, 100, 108, 130, 162, 200, 220; as translator, 83, 90

Center, 107

Ceremonies. *See* Propriety, rules of

Chalmers, John, 83

Chan Ho, 52, 73

Chan-kuo ts'e, 49, 63, 64, 66

Ch'an. *See* Zen

Chang Chan, 78, 194

Chang Chun-hsiang, 55

Chang Chung-yüan, 34, 111, 117, 133, 135

Chang Hsü, 57

Chang Hsüeh-ch'eng, 71

Chang Ling, 27

Chang Lu, 27, 91

Chang Mo-sheng, 135

Chang Ping-lin, 50

Chang Shou-chieh, 55

273

Chung-kuo che-hsüeh shih ta-kang, 35
Ch'ü Yüan, 117
Commentaries: early, 77; editions of, 81; of Han Fei Tzu, 7-8; "Hsiang-erh," 33-34; of Ho-shang Kung, 78-80; Japanese, 91; number of, 77, 91; philosophical, 78, 80-81; religious, 77-81; translation of, 83; of Wang Pi, 78, 80
Communal life, 14
Community, 71, 195, 238
Competition. See Non-competition
Compliance, 13
Concentration, 116
Concrete thing, 149, 151
Confucianism: compared with Buddhism, 101; contrasted with Taoism, 3, 103, 107, 116, 124, 134, 157, 221; similarities with Taoism, 115, 141, 143, 152, 154, 184, 197, 219, 237. See also Confucius
Confucianists: criticism of Taoism, 17, 164, 178; criticized, 68
Confucius: criticized, 43; compared with Lao Tzu, 17-19, 113, 141, 201, 207, 212, 224, 225; contemporary of Lao Tzu, 35; visit to Lao Tzu, 36-38, 42, 46, 48
Contention. See Non-competition
Contentment, 13, 159, 179, 181. See also Stop, knowing when to
Correctness, 201, 203
Cosmology, 137, 144
Creation, 176. See also Producing things, Production and reproduction
Credit, claiming no, 101, 115, 116, 130, 160, 190, 234

Creel, H. G., 21, 34

Darwin, 82
Death, 159, 230, 232, 233, 238. See also Life and death
Deep and profound, the. See Profound, the
Deep love, 68, 131, 132, 219
Desires: evil of, 103, 179, 181; having few, 132; having no, 13, 23, 25, 160, 166, 201, 214
Destiny, 23, 128
Disgrace, 13, 122, 149, 179, 199, 236
Doctrine of the Mean, 143, 184
Doctrine without words. See Words
Dubs, Homer H., 8, 40, 49, 52, 159
Dusty world, 13, 105, 199
Duyvendak, J. J. L.: emendation of text, 135, 142, 161; interpretations of terms, 98, 105, 106, 108, 117, 129, 131, 151, 192, 200, 206, 220; on the Lao Tzu, 62, 63; punctuation of passages, 99, 118; rearrangement of text, 83, 135

Einsteinian theory, 8
Empire: governing, 184, 201, 236; observing, 195; taking over, 67, 122, 151, 184, 201, 208. See also Government, Ruler
Emptiness, 116. See also Void
Enlightenment, 128, 159, 192, 197
Erh, 36, 38, 39. See also Li Erh
Erkes, Eduard: on Ho-shang Kung commentary, 66, 79, 80, 83, 87; interpretations of terms, 100, 133, 159, 192, 200, 220
Essence, 137
Eternal, the, 69, 197. See also

Heysinger, I. W., 90, 108, 133, 200, 220
History of the Former Han Dynasty, 49, 72, 74, 75, 77-79
Ho-shang Chang-jen, 78
Ho-shang Kung: comments on passages, 117, 133, 135, 206; about commentary, 75, 77-81; interpretations of terms, 99, 100, 102, 105, 108, 114, 115, 117, 118, 121, 130, 145, 189, 190, 194, 196, 215, 222, 223, 225, 226; punctuation of passages, 99; his text referred to, 74, 83, 87, 102, 104, 117, 123, 127, 142, 146, 148, 152, 158, 160, 162, 171, 175, 181, 182, 187, 198, 202, 208, 217, 218, 226, 233
Honor, 115
Hou Wai-lu: on Lao Tzu, 14, 53; on the *Lao Tzu*, 62, 89
hsi (exclamatory particle), 65
Hsi T'ung: collation and emendation of text, 142, 145, 169, 171, 210, 233; interpretation of term, 175; rearrangement of the text, 215, 221, 229
"Hsiang-erh" commentary, 33-34, 77, 91
Hsiao-wen, 37
Hsien, Duke, 36, 48, 50
Hsing-chou text, 129
Hsing Ping, 57
hsü (vacuity). *See* Vacuity
Hsü Ti-shan, 88
hsüan (deep and profound), 100. *See also* Profound, the
Hsüan-tsang, 82
Hsün Tzu, 41, 45, 63, 64, 65
Hsün Tzu, 51, 66, 68, 72
hu (exclamatory particle), 65, 66
Hu Shih: interpretations of terms, 130, 138, 158, 231; on Lao Tzu, 6, 35, 40, 44, 52; on the *Lao Tzu*, 63, 64, 68, 70, 71, 73; rearrangement of text, 135
Huai-nan Tzu, 22, 39, 63, 67, 79, 199
Huan Yüan, 73
Huang Fang-kuang, 44, 52, 56
Huang K'an, 80
Huang Mao-ts'ai, 99, 233
Hughes, E. R., 99, 104, 133, 162, 220
Hui Shih, 63, 68, 69
Humanity, 107, 143, 219
Humanity and righteousness, 62, 68, 88, 107, 131, 132, 167
Humility, 13, 149
Hung I-hsüan, 91, 111

I-chou, 74
I Shun-ting: emendation and collation of text, 150, 156, 160, 171, 200, 209, 223; on commentaries, 102; interpretation of terms, 223; rearrangement of text, 135
Ignorance, 13
Immortality: on earth, 26-28, 34, 77, 80, 91, 205, 230; of virtue, 159
Immortals, 34, 180, 205
Indian philosophy, 113, 218
Individual, 71, 195
Infant, 13, 110, 116, 134, 149, 186, 197
Investigation of principle, 82
Itō Rangu, 51, 53

Jao Tsung-i, 33, 129
Japan, commentaries in, 77, 91
Jehovah, 125
jen (humanity), 108. *See also* Humanity, Humanity and righteousness
Jen Chi-yü, 145

pared with Confucianism, *see* Confucianism *and* Neo-Confucianism; condemning force, *see* Force; influence on Buddhism, 23-24; influence on Neo-Confucianism, *see* Neo-Confucianism; influence on Neo-Taoism, 23; influence on Chinese life, 29-30; compared with Legalism, 103; compared with other schools, 10

Taoist religion: described, 26-29, 171; "Hsiang-erh" commentary in, 77; Ho-shang Kung commentary in, 81; and retribution, 228; sects of, 171; superstition in, 188, 207. *See also* Immortality, Immortals, Yoga

Taoist School, 4, 28. *See also* Taoism

Taoka Reiun, 111, 155

te (virtue). *See* Virtue, Waley

Tea drinking, 15

Three ministers, 210

Three treasures, 12

Ting Fu-pao, 99, 189

Tower: spring, 134; of nine stories, 214

Traces, 147

Tranquility: attaining, 132, 170, 201; effect of, 126; state of, 128, 129; strength of, 146, 180

Transformation, 110, 166. *See also* Self-transformation

Treasures, 103, 210, 214, 219, 224

Trinity, 124

Tso chuan, 38, 47, 67, 68

Tsuda Sōkichi, 53

Ts'ui Hao, 84

Ts'ui Shu: on Lao Tzu, 35, 42-44, 45, 82; on the *Lao Tzu*, 62, 63, 73

Tsung, 45, 48, 49

Tu Kuang-t'ing, 77, 189

Tu Tao-chien, 91

Tuan-kan, 37

Tuan-kan Mu, 50

Tuan-kan P'eng, 50

Tun-huang, 77, 155

Tun-huang text, 102, 118, 129, 152, 198, 229

Tung Chung-shu, 70

Tung Ssu-ching, 155

Twelve classics, 45

Two Modes, 144

tzu, meanings of, 40-41

tzu-jan (Nature). *See* Nature

Tzu-kung, 44

Uncarved block, 6, 13, 126, 149, 150, 171

Utensils, 149, 150, 238

Utility, 119, 180

Vacuity, 71, 103, 104, 105, 107, 128, 168, 221. *See also* Great Vacuity

Valley, 13, 15, 82, 126, 149

Valley, spirit of, 81, 110

Violence, 197. *See also* Force

Virtue: described, 11; eternal, 149; repaying evil with, 71, 212; great, 137, 167, 174, 195; profound, 116, 190, 216; and Tao, 137, 141, 190; emphasis of, in Taoism, 10, 205, 207

Vital force, 116

Void, 110, 119

Wai-Tao, 108, 220

Waley, Arthur: emendation of text, 102, 104, 135, 203; interpretations of terms, 100, 106, 108, 111, 115, 118, 127, 133, 138, 162, 200, 206, 220; on Lao Tzu, 53; on the *Lao Tzu*, 11, 63, 66; as translator, 83; on virtue as power, 12; on yoga in the *Lao Tzu*, 29, 111, 116, 206

Wang An-shih: commentary on the *Lao Tzu*, 81, 98; interpretation of text, 99

Wang Ch'ang, 125

Wang Chung: on Lao Tzu, 35, 41-42, 44, 45, 48, 49, 52; on the *Lao Tzu*, 62, 73

Wang Fu-chih, 82

Wang Nien-sun, 39, 155, 194

Wang Pi: commentary on *Book of Changes*, 128, 146; about his commentary on the *Lao Tzu*, 29, 75, 77, 78, 80-81, 83, 117, 135, 156, 160; his comments on passages, 98, 102, 117, 135, 151, 159, 168, 183, 204, 234, 240; interpretations of terms, 99, 100, 108, 110, 114, 117, 118, 145, 186, 189, 198, 221; on Lao Lai Tzu, 47; Neo-Taoism of, 23; punctuation of passage, 99; his text referred to, 74, 84, 87, 102, 104, 115, 117, 123, 127, 138, 146, 148, 152, 155, 162, 163, 171, 175, 181, 187, 198, 208, 217, 218, 226, 233

Wang Yang-ming, 107, 135, 184

Wang Yin-chih, 123

War, 152, 181, 221, 222, 233. *See also* Force, Military strategy, Military weapons

Water: as good, 113; strength of, 236; Tao as, 13, 110. *See also* Rivers

Way of Five Bushels of Rice, 27

Weakness, 13-15, 116, 152, 173, 178, 233. *See also* Meekness

Wealth, 115

Wei, 37, 48, 49

Wei Yüan, 108, 133, 146, 196

Welch, Holmes, 89, 108

Wen, Duke, 50

wen (ornament). *See* Ornament

Wen Tzu, 48

Western philosophy, 8

Wilhelm, Richard, 90, 108, 133

Wisdom, 132, 159. *See also* Knowledge

Words: and action, 210; beautiful, 240; in Buddhism, 101-2, 120; in Confucianism, 101-2; in Taoism, 101, 107, 130, 141, 178, 199

Worthy, exaltation of the, 68, 70, 103

wu (non-being). *See* Non-being

Wu Ch'eng: commentary on the *Lao Tzu*, 82, 213; interpretations of terms, 100, 111, 159; rearrangement of text, 76; his text referred to, 125, 130, 132

Wu Ching-yü, 127

Wu, John, 99, 133, 162, 200, 220

wu-ming (nameless). *See* Nameless, the

wu-wei (taking no action). *See* Taking no action

Yamamoto Doun, 111, 155, 238

Yang. *See* Yin and Yang

Yang Chu, 52, 73, 122, 196, 226

Yang Liu-ch'iao, 156, 166

Yang Tseng-hsin, 111, 136

Yao Fan, 49

Yao Nai: emendation of text, 135, 141, 153, 156; on Lao Tzu, 38, 39, 40, 45; on the *Lao Tzu*, 76

yeh (final interrogative particle), 66

Yeh Meng-te, 189

Yeh Shih, 35, 73

Yellow Emperor, 27

Yen Fu, 82, 100, 115, 160

Yen Hui, 116

Yen Jo-ch'ü, 43, 44

The Library of Liberal Arts

Below is a representative selection from The Library of Liberal Arts. This partial listing—taken from the more than 200 scholarly editions of the world's finest literature and philosophy—indicates the scope, nature, and concept of this distinguished series.